Philos

Barry Stocker

Philosophy of the Novel

palgrave
macmillan

Barry Stocker
Istanbul Technical University
Istanbul, Turkey

ISBN 978-3-030-40482-6   ISBN 978-3-319-65891-9   (eBook)
https://doi.org/10.1007/978-3-319-65891-9

Library of Congress Control Number: 2017951525

© The Editor(s) (if applicable) and The Author(s) 2018
This work is subject to copyright. All rights are solely and exclusively licensed by the Publisher, whether the whole or part of the material is concerned, specifically the rights of translation, reprinting, reuse of illustrations, recitation, broadcasting, reproduction on microfilms or in any other physical way, and transmission or information storage and retrieval, electronic adaptation, computer software, or by similar or dissimilar methodology now known or hereafter developed.
The use of general descriptive names, registered names, trademarks, service marks, etc. in this publication does not imply, even in the absence of a specific statement, that such names are exempt from the relevant protective laws and regulations and therefore free for general use.
The publisher, the authors and the editors are safe to assume that the advice and information in this book are believed to be true and accurate at the date of publication. Neither the publisher nor the authors or the editors give a warranty, express or implied, with respect to the material contained herein or for any errors or omissions that may have been made. The publisher remains neutral with regard to jurisdictional claims in published maps and institutional affiliations.

Cover credit: T Scott Carlisle

This Palgrave Macmillan imprint is published by the registered company Springer Nature Switzerland AG
The registered company address is: Gewerbestrasse 11, 6330 Cham, Switzerland

Contents

1

Introduction from Analysis to Form

Analytic and Continental European Approaches

One way of practicing the philosophy of the novel is to analyse aesthetics, literature, fiction, narrative and novel as concepts, with regard to necessary and sufficient conditions of usage. In this kind of practice, not much is said about the concept of the novel since this is not an approach suited to dealing with genre, or at least genre has not been dealt with much as part of this approach. The first way is Analytic aesthetics applied to the novel. The second way is Analytic ethics applied to literature, including the novel. A path is indicated from analysis to form, because these are approaches concentrating on Analytic clarity with regard to what a literary aesthetic object is and how a literary work may serve as an exploration of ethics. Considerations of the form of the novel, as part of the question of genres as different forms within general literary form, are not completely absent, but are secondary. The chapter moves through Analytic aesthetics and more ethically oriented philosophy of literature, before a conclusion which lays out the approach of the book as a whole.

© The Author(s) 2018
B. Stocker, *Philosophy of the Novel*,
https://doi.org/10.1007/978-3-319-65891-9_1

Another related approach is to look at novels, as well as other genres of literature, as ways of exploring ethics as part of life as imagined in the novel. Again the issues of genre are not so much explored, as what is important in literature becomes ethical situations rather than form, which emerges in its most basic ways in the distinctions between genres. This is dealt with below under the heading of 'Ethics, Poetics, Erotics', primarily in relation to the work of Martha Nussbaum. Peter Lamarque perhaps fits better with the paradigm of Analytic philosopher than Nussbaum, given that he is more concerned with concepts and boundaries distinguishing non-conceptual work from conceptual work. The distinction between Lamarque and Nussbaum does not undermine the idea of a distinctly Analytic approach though. There are more conceptual and more applied versions of Analytic philosophy, the concern with pure conceptual clarity which guides our understanding of non-conceptual reality is persistent. The following discussion of Lamarque and Nussbaum will establish the need for an approach to the philosophy of the novel more concerned with the interactions between philosophy and literary form, as well as more focused on history and culture. A discussion of Lamarque's approach to literary criticism is the basis of the section following this section, which sets up issues and outlines the Analytic contribution to literary aesthetics.

Distinguishing between Analytic and Continental European philosophy is notoriously difficult, as we can see just in the fact that one term refers to a way of doing philosophy and the other term refers to a geographical location. There is no neat geographical split between where the two modes exist and there is no neat split between modes of doing philosophy. However, just about everyone knows the difference when they see it, though not in the same way in all cases. A definitional distinction is offered here, with a very rough sketch of relevant philosophical development. No claim made that it will be satisfactory to most people working on the issue. Analytic philosophy is concerned with concepts abstracted from historical and cultural context with regard to logical consistency and clearness of meaning. Some argue that a distinction should be made between Analytic philosophy and Naturalistic philosophy though there are clear overlaps in who engages in these approaches and their historical roots. Philosophers in both of these groups tend to go back to the eighteenth century and look to David Hume (1975, 2000) as the chief precursor. Both groups are concerned with concepts. The 'pure' Analytics are concerned with what concepts are separate from their existence in consciousness. The Naturalists are concerned with concepts as they exist in consciousness and in the brain. In twentieth-century philosophy, both can look back to Willard Van Orman Quine, who discussed Analytic and synthetic aspects of concepts, in his essay 'Two dogmas of empiricism' (in Quine 1980). He questioned the sharpness of the distinction, but not in such a way as to eliminate the distinction. He was also concerned with the evolution of concepts as part of adaptation to the environment and as part of the study of the physiology of perception (Quine 1969). None of this leads him to think of concepts in terms of historical or cultural context, and certainly not the literary use of words. The interest in change and context in Quine is subordinated to the general referential unity of concepts, existing outside context even if contextual use varies. There is a choice of frameworks for organising the world, and the framework as a whole may condition understanding of objects, but language itself is not important to experience and to understanding the world (1960).

The Continental European approach can be traced back to the German thinkers who reacted to the philosophy of Immanuel Kant, starting with the writings in the 1780s of Friedrich Heinrich Jacobi and Johann Georg Hamann, continuing though the work of Johann Georg Fichte, Friedrich Wilhelm Joseph Schelling and Georg Wilhelm Friedrich Hegel from the 1790s to the 1840s. What these philosophers both reacted to and continued in Kant was an interest in concepts as produced in the mind, shaping reality. Kant himself, followed by Schelling and Hegel addressed philosophical aesthetics, while in Hamann and Jacobi, philosophy and literary writing interact. This is one major aspect of Continental European philosophy: aesthetic philosophy and literary writing as philosophy are major concerns. Kant's philosophical aesthetics (2000) is sufficiently concerned with aesthetic qualities, as belonging to objects and as what can be expressed as stable concepts to be taken up within the Analytic philosophy which emerged in the late nineteenth century. In the other German philosophers just mentioned, aesthetics has a historical contextual aspect in which discussion of genres and changes in form is central, with philosophy itself having an aesthetic aspect in its basic attempts to delineate reality.

The Continental European approach itself evolves through continued concern with variability, subjectivity and interpretation, in which philosophy is concerned with its own status and how to write in ways which bring out these aspects. In this approach, concepts are taken to be culturally and historically located, so only fully grasped with attention both to immediate context and the residue of earlier context which still attaches to concepts. There is a tension between: an Analytic search for clarity of meaning and delimitation of possible meanings within any text on one side; and on the other side, a literary theory combined with Continental European Philosophy range of approaches which tend to value extreme plurality of meaning, exploration of the limit of meaning and creative confusion about whether meaning is more an aesthetic experience or more part of philosophy. This is a simplified polarisation and there are philosophers who are difficult to categorise in this way, such as Edmund Husserl and Ludwig Wittgenstein, but the contrast has considerable value in distinguishing approaches to philosophy. Even in the cases of Husserl and Wittgenstein, it is mostly accepted that the former is 'Continental' and the latter is 'Analytic'.

There is a proportion of the more literary theory and Continental philosophy approaches which are rooted in work by writers concerned with these approaches to non-meaning. Maurice Blanchot and Georges Bataille both contributed to the literary and philosophical-theoretical sides of this interest, as will be discussed in Chap. 8. While the literary theory and Continental approaches are not so focused on limits of meaning, they are focused on historical, social, political and cultural context. This latter aspect is less the target of Analytic polemic than the limits of focus on meaning content, though the more contextual work still tends to be marginalised as sociological rather than philosophical by Analytic thinkers. Adding the contextualist interest in what is external to the text and its most direct meaning inherently tends to be in some tension with the Analytic approach.

The ethics and literature approach is explored as practiced by philosophers of broadly Analytic orientation. Jonathan Bennett's article 'The Moral Conscience of Huckleberry Finn' stands out as a widely cited text from within Analytic philosophy, though in many cases coming from people self-consciously at the limits of Analytic philosophy, e.g. Stanley Cavell in *The Claims of Reason* (1979), which is concerned with tragedy rather than the novel, but is suggestive for the reading of the novel, or those whose work has included history of philosophy, e.g. Martha Nussbaum, who is discussed in detail below. There is much more of this kind of material from literary critics, political and legal theorists and other disciplines distinct from philosophy, if overlapping with it. This tells a story in itself. Nussbaum's work is the most influential body of relevant work and this to a large degree comes out of a classics background, so a background covering philological and literary critical approaches to text.

The tendency with Analytic philosophers is to see literature as a way of dealing with moral problems and that tends to be reductive in relation to the complexity of the novelistic text. While reduction is inevitable in some form when dealing with theory and philosophy of literature, seeking an approach to a moral problem as the essential aspect of a narrative is a constitutively reductive situation and inevitably tends to direct attention to the moral problem, rather than all the interpretative possibilities of the novel in question.

There is some creative interaction with the other work Analytic philosophers do, which often brings very short narrative thought experiments into arguments about political philosophy, such as John Rawls on 'the veil of ignorance' in *A Theory of Justice* (1971); metaphysics, such as Saul Kripke on natural kinds and essences in *Naming and Necessity* (1972); semantics, such as Hilary Putnam in 'The Meaning of "Meaning"' (1975); epistemology, such as Edmund Gettier in 'Is Justified True Belief Knowledge?' (1963). These are, however, very far from novels and do not include any reflection on the nature of narrative fictional or the style and form of storytelling. Analytic writers on aesthetics are at least sometimes inclined to see narrative, including the novel, as not as inherently aesthetic as some other forms such as music and painting and this fits with the tendency for literature and ethics to be more about the ethics than the literature.

The Analytic approach in particular, is less open to the way that literary forms and concepts of literary understanding evolve over time in comparison with the more essayistic, literary, historical, subjective ways and ambiguous ways of writing philosophy. Though the topic of genre might seem suitable for conceptual analysis and narrative schema, literary genre in all cases and certainly in the case of the novel needs the qualities in philosophy, not so obvious in Analytic approaches.

Lamarque's Analytic Aesthetics

Peter Lamarque provides a significant example of Analytic philosophy dealing with a literary critical approach informed by Continental European philosophy. His general approach to literary narrative is to emphasise some fixity of meaning determined by context. He does deal with the possibility of an unbounded sense of writing in his earlier book *The Philosophy of Literature* (2009) drawing on his 1990 article 'The Death of the Author: An Analytical Autopsy', particularly with regard to '*écriture*' in Roland Barthes, concentrating on the essay 'The Death of the Author' (in Barthes 1977a), though Barthes discusses it in various longer texts (1968, 1974). Lamarque also excludes Jacques Derrida's understanding of '*écriture*' in *Writing and Difference* (1978), *Of Grammatology* (1997) and so on, which has been more influential and which offers an account that takes the issue of 'writing' into philosophy, social science and the humanities in general, as well as literary studies. Barthes' account is elegant but rather less philosophically extended. Lamarque recognises the value of an account of writing as unconstrained by authorial intentions and rigid determination of meaning, but argues that it is less successful as a way of thinking about literature than the contextualism he advocates. The contextualism offers constraints of interpretation which keep the text meaningful. That is because contextualism, with regard to the circumstance of writing and plausible references, suggests distinctive fixed interpretations of a text, or any aesthetic object, it prevents the text collapsing into a series of signs which are arbitrary in meaning and can be taken in any way in a subjective decisionistic way. This is perhaps something of a parody of Barthes, along with the work by Michel Foucault and Jacques Derrida, Lamarque associates with Barthes.

The culmination of Barthes' work on literary narrative is *S/Z* (1974), an exhaustive analysis of Honoré de Balzac's novella *Sarrassine*. This takes the writer most associated with literary Realism, with literary writing that apparently represents social reality, away from this kind of mimesis towards desire and death disrupting our grasp of reality. The centre of the story is a man, Sarrasine, who falls in love with a beautiful opera singer, in Italy, who he fails to understand is a castrato rather than a woman. Sarrasine is ultimately murdered on the orders of the castrato's 'protector', a cardinal. The story is a story within a story, appropriate to a sense of a world that is all fictions with no reality. The whole story reverberates with a sense of uncanny uneasiness with regard to desire, beauty, death, emasculation, art, sexual difference and the darkness at the centre of nineteenth-century progress. All of this is brought out by Barthes, who reduces reality to an effect of one code amongst five in literature, but who does nothing to undermine the sense of representation of a social world in Balzac. What Barthes emphasises is that here Balzac heightens uncertainty about reality and our basic distinctions to the point at which stability of meaning may be undermined, reaching even into the feminised name of the murdered man. That is 'Sarrasine' looks like the feminised version of 'Sarrazin'.

Whatever the limitations of Barthes' reading, it is rather literary in itself, turning a close reading into an exuberant encounter with the possibilities of literature and the unsettling crossing of boundaries that underly the excitement. It is not an unbounded interpretation likely to lead anyone to see a literary work as a mere series of symbols on paper (or a computer screen). Barthes' brings in his own context of interests in psychoanalysis and the kind of limits of mimesis explored before Barthes by French writers, discussed in Chap. 8 of this book. We could introduce an authorial biographical reading, Barthes who was a protean writer himself went on to write in an autobiographical vein, *Roland Barthes by Roland Barthes* (1977b) though not in a way such as to invite any belief in revelation of the author behind the text. Barthes adopted the most classical of French novelists as an object of analysis, and while he tilted away from some of the Realism so associated with Balzac, overall *S/Z* contributes to the traditional sense of Balzac as the writer of a world which is both apparently self-confident but unsure of its foundations, the world of late eighteenth- and nineteenth-century statecraft and capitalism presented as both heroic and morally horrifying. Lamarque's criticisms of Barthes is on this basis exaggerated and is perhaps more a reaction to the excesses of the literary theory scene of the 1980s and 1990s, along with a few of Barthes' more provocative remarks, than a careful account of Barthes' contribution, though he does refer to some positive aspects. We can see at least some continuities between the ethics, poetics and erotics of Barthes and the approach of Martha Nussbaum who is the main focus of the next section.

Ethics, Poetics, Erotics

Martha Nussbaum is an important point of reference for ethics and literature in relation to the novel, because though her considerations of ethics and literature do not include a book-length treatment of the novel, she does discuss novels and her other literary considerations give weight to philosophical work of a kind that feeds into the form of the novel, that is the dialogues of Plato. Martha's Nussbaum's work is discussed here with reference to *The Fragility of Goodness* (1986), *The Therapy of Desire* (1994) and *Love's Knowledge* (1990). *Love's Knowledge* is the major focus since the other two books focus on ancient tragedy, but do still provide important parts of Nussbaum's views. *The Fragility of Goodness* includes chapters on Plato's *Symposium* and *Phaedrus*, germane to the present book as Plato's dialogues are part of the pre-history of the novel. *Love's Knowledge* covers novels by Henry James, Marcel Proust, Charles Dickens and Samuel Beckett, along with some Plato dialogues.

Nussbaum presents a largely Aristotelian view of literature as an ethical endeavour with some gestures towards late Wittgenstein, in both cases out of a commitment to particularism and moral judgement based on detailed attention to the actions of others. Nussbaum does not have a philosophy of the novel, or any view of its status as a genre, but does implicitly give it the status of the major modern literary form from the point of view of moral judgement. This may be the product of Nussbaum's commitment to Rawls' principle of reflective equilibrium in morality (Nussbaum 1990, 174), which he puts forward in *A Theory of Justice* (1971) as a means to arrive at conclusions about political theory through balancing concerns. We are all faced with difficulties in reconciling basic principles with each other and with our judgements about particular situations. In reflective equilibrium, there is a work of integration, balancing and working out trade offs that suggests something like a novel, a philosophical novel, in terms of unifying a complex assembly of particularities, perspectives and judgements. There is something novelistic about some big works of recent philosophy including *A Theory of Justice* which provides its own justification in reflective equilibrium. There is an implicit principle in Rawls: large-scale works of political and moral theory are necessary to deal properly with the need for reflective equilibrium, though shorter texts on details are also necessary. There is a parallel implicit principle in Nussbaum: novels are necessary to deal properly with the need for reflective equilibrium, though short literary forms on moral details are also necessary. Rawls' own implicit principle explains Nussbaum's own large books.

Nussbaum differs from some Analytic writers on ethics and literature in taking an approach in which style is of some importance, the novel is not just a cover for some statement of moral dilemma. Seeking illustration for moral dilemmas in literature is comparatively likely amongst philosophers more interested in ethics than literature. Despite Nussbaum's relative interest in the literary text as literary text, she can be said to be rather didactic in what she expects from literature, that is she expects it to convey some very clear moral messages, or even messages about moral theory as when she refers approvingly to Dicken's criticisms of Utilitarian ethics in *Hard Times* (Nussbaum 1990, 76–77). She emphasises attention to detail the particulars of behaviour in which ethics operates. Moral education comes from practices sensitive to others and to particular occasions, learning from both. This applies to late nineteenth- and early twentieth-century novels, as it also applies to Plato's dialogues and Attic tragedy. The discussion of ethics in the novel gives a particular place to Henry James, a writer of carefully observed situations and inner reflection in such detail that the narrative can be hard to follow. Nevertheless, Nussbaum focuses on the process of learning in James' novels rather than what is learned of any philosophical significance, which for Nussbaum always seems anyway to be the need for a neo-Aristotelian approach.

Nussbaum's detailed comments on Plato's *Phaedrus* and *Symposium* are intriguing in relation to her later discussion of novels in that there is much more interaction between narrative development and specific moral development. A lot of it is embedded in speculative comments about Plato's life and the intentions behind the dialogues concerned. To some degree, Nussbaum creates a fiction of Plato's life to interact with his fictional dialogues. An abyss of fictionality is implicitly built up in which fictional dialogues are interpreted with regard to Nussbaum's fictional biography of Plato, itself drawing on the dialogues, and so on. This has some resemblance to Derrida's commentary on Nietzsche in *Spurs* (1979), which Nussbaum herself comments on critically if with some respect for Derrida's technique: '[....] one feels, at the end of all the urbanity, an empty longing amounting to a hunger, a longing for the sense of difficulty and risk and practical urgency that are insepa-rable from Zarathustra's dance' (Nussbaum 1990, 171). This refers to Derrida's arguments for denying determinacy of meaning to short pas-sage in Nietzsche's diary. There is a double strategy for Derrida which is to deny, in a playful way, that Nietzsche can be interpreted accord-ing to Martin Heidegger's use of 'Being', that is there is no moment of 'Being' in Nietzsche, and to deny that meaning can ever be determinate, can ever be free from variable context. The second argument confirms Derrida's first argument and is interwoven with it. The combined argu-ment is made, in part through a playful attitude to an entry in which Nietzsche says 'I have forgotten my umbrella', as if it could be taken as an expression of Heidegger's inquiries into the forgetting of Being. Nussbaum's own speculations on a circle of interpretation between Plato's supposed life and the meaning of the dialogues itself comes close to what Derrida mocks in *Spurs* and his own perspective. Nussbaum seeks certainty of interpretation, while also emphasising what she con-siders to be Plato's own inclinations towards accepting poetic-aesthet-ic-erotic attitudes to texts and life at some points.

Nussbaum argues for the ethics of literature, against a supposed Derridean detachment, even seeming at times to argue for a really ten-dentious attitude in literature at times, quoting approvingly from a conversation with the moral philosopher, R.M. Hare: 'What are novels anyway but universal prescriptions?' (Nussbaum 1990, 160). She concedes this is a strong way of expressing things, but nevertheless accedes to the central claim that literary work gives ethical prescriptions. The trouble with this is that the more we refer to clear ethical messages, the more we tend to refer to the most rhetorical aspects of the novel and the most literal reading of whatever appears to come from the voice of the author. We might conceive of literature as exploring ethically significant situations with regard to how these relate to ethical debates, how the novel presents many ethical positions, rather than the conveying of a message.

There is some difficulty for Nussbaum in arguing for the ethical nature of literature, while approaching literary-philosophical texts which claim to communicate truths of ethics, using an interpretative approach guided by Plato's supposed liberation from anti-poetry and anti-erotics at some point in his life, with very little in the way of verifiable information. Nussbaum creates a fiction herself and a fiction which suggests something non-ethical at least in the most systematic sense. The importance of the erotic in Nussbaum's reading of *Phaedrus* might be part of an ethics urging enjoyment of the sensual realm, but that is not what Nussbaum advocates in general. She has some moves in that direction in the context of the *Phaedrus*, but in general, she elaborates on ethical particularism, Aristotelianism and Rawls. That is, she builds on: discussion of the uniqueness of individual cases, plurality of goods as part of a happy life, reflective equilibrium between different ethical demands in theory and in cases.

Nussbaum makes a valuable contribution in that she leans towards a kind of philosophy-poetry fusion in the work of scholarship and in argument, and so narrows the difference between philosophy and dialogue or novel. This is both an impressive achievement and an incomplete achievement if we think what might come out of some of her readings, particularly concerning the *Symposium* and the *Phaedrus*. It is in these cases where she moves most strongly away from treating literature as the object of philosophical consideration and moves towards seeing interaction. Of course, she brings philosophical claims into her discussion of Attic tragedy, but it is for the very specific purpose of defining literature as the place where the rigidity of ethical concepts is challenged, so that literature is something living that turns the formal concepts of dead philosophy into something more organic and evolving.

It would be going beyond the scope of this book to say much about the readings of Attic tragedy in Nietzsche and Heidegger, particularly Heidegger since narrative fiction is not something he ever addresses. Nietzsche does at least discuss Homer and some novelists at times. It is worth suggesting a comparison of Nietzsche's *Birth of Tragedy* (in Nietzsche 2000) or Heidegger's *Introduction to Metaphysics* (2000) with Nussbaum's *Fragility of Goodness* just to see how they explore literature as philosophy, or even as the ground of philosophy, rather than as an example of consideration of philosophical issues. Nietzsche is someone Nussbaum does take into account, but Heidegger appears to off her range of worthy philosophical references. The significant difference for her presumably is that Nietzsche engages in literary and cultural history of a kind, while Heidegger deals in a kind of poetic pre-metaphysics and is ostentatiously non-historical in approach. This is not to belittle Nussbaum's considerable contributions to the study of philosophy and literature, or to suggest she should be more like Nietzsche or Heidegger, but to establish a frame in which we can see there are possibilities other than Nussbaum's approach to philosophy and literature, within which we can develop an account of the fusion of philosophy and literature as it may appear in the novel, or closely related forms.

In discussing Nussbaum's contribution, the aim has been to put her work in the context of Analytic philosophy and Continental European philosophy along with the issues of the interaction between philosophical text and literary text. Nussbaum's approach to the latter is particularly strong, with an emphasis on the erotics of literary texts and those philosophical texts which are most literary. Erotic in the sense that desire for truth and wisdom interact with the desire for beauty. What Nussbaum concentrates on in *The Fragility of Goodness* is the erotics and Plato's writing and how this might undercut some of his more ascetic suggestions about the relation of truth to the world of appearances. There are some related investigations of Stoicism in *The Therapy of Desire* and Nussbaum continues investigating these themes in *Love's Knowledge*, if in a less systematic way.

The mixture of Analytic philosophy, classical scholarship, a literary awareness of philosophical texts and some engagement with Continental European philosophy she brings to her approach produces some significant results, but stops short in important ways with regard to what happens when the relation between philosophy and literature is investigated in the strongest possible way. The strongest possible way is not limited to Nussbaum's own concerns with knowledge and emotions in literature, valuable though they are. She does not fully pick up on what can be found in Kierkegaard and Nietzsche, particularly though not only in the texts where philosophy becomes novelistic.

Conclusion: Approach to the Philosophy of the Novel

Despite her interests in Plato, Nussbaum gives limited attention in other contexts to how philosophy may be transformed by encounters with literary form and reveal something about itself. What is revealed includes the following aspects: the historically and temporally embedded objectivity of writing as objective; subjectivity and relativity in writing; subjectivity and absolute individuality in philosophical writing; temporally embedded writing as an exploration of style; writing as representation in a political context; desire and the limits of representation; and the absolute nature of writing as inclusive of all writing. These are the themes of the following chapters until we return to the relation of philosophy and novel as the theme of the last chapter.

The interceding chapters discuss the novel and its forerunners, including Platonic dialogue and Romance, but particularly the epic, with regard to the different forms of literary fictional narrative. As the discussion is with reference to the philosophical, or at least philosophically oriented texts, which discuss the novel and its forerunners, this will also be a discussion of the possibilities of philosophical writing. If philosophical writing is concerned with these themes in literary texts and the forms of literature, then that is always saying something about what philosophy is, what philosophy incorporates and how philosophy understands writing. In these respects, philosophy more or less betrays some desire to be literature even in the case of philosophers known for an austere style, for example Aristotle and maybe he is the main example. When we consider the main figures in the philosophy of the novel, we can see various ways in which their writing tries to incorporate some sense of the form of what is being discussed. Even Aristotle is deeply concerned with Homer, often quoting from him, so resting on this literary achievement and incorporating part of it. Even the more abstract writers in the philosophical tradition in practice bring style, time, representation, desire and politics into philosophical writing. The most austere philosophers have a style of writing and austerity is a style. The most abstract philosopher deals with time and its effects. All philosophers are trying to represent reality of some kind.

The novel is considered here very largely with regard to its European aspect. This is no doubt a limited approach, but an approach hard to avoid given that the European novel has been taken up as the global model. The ways in which the novel has developed differently outside Europe, and then back in Europe, through the different ways the different cultures have taken it up and have different precedents, are hard to cover in a single volume, particularly given that the relevant philosophers really are very largely European. Given these circumstances, it is very difficult to understand the pre-history and early history of the novel while having no knowledge of ancient and medieval European society, including areas closely associated with Europe through the integrating structure of the Roman Empire and before that the diffusion of Hellenistic culture, briefly turned into an integrated political structure by Alexander the Great. It would be difficult to understand the early history of the modern novel with no idea of political, intellectual and social conditions in Spain, France, Britain and Germany. The later history of the novel can hardly be isolated from such events as the Glorious Revolution of 1688 in Britain or the French Revolution of 1789. Some notion of developments in religion, literacy, state formation and political economy are just inevitable, even if just assumed in very vague ways, when assessing the development of the novel.

What follows does not enter much into the details of political and social history, but certainly links the pre-history of the novel with ancient and medieval history, while looking at the early modern novel in terms of the Europe of Renaissance humanism, religious Protestantism and Catholic counters to Protestantism along with the formation of strong centralised states. This is also the time of a growing commercial society as was increasingly noted in the seventeenth and eighteenth centuries. The nineteenth-century novel is embedded in the growth of democracy, nationalism and socialist movements, along with reactions to them. The novel reaches a limit of some kind in the early twentieth century in works which take the absolute, that is the unity of history, ideas, experience, subjectivity and transcendence, discussed in the late eighteenth century, as explored in Chap. 3, appear in various novels including those of James Joyce, Robert Musil, Virginia Woolf and Hermann Broch. Chapter 9 concentrates on Marcel Proust as the great figure in this moment.

What is significant about the historical context is that this is the time in which the liberalism, individualism, parliamentarianism, legalism and limited government ideas and institutions of the late eighteenth century, informing the idea of the absolute novel, reach some kind of limit in the growth the administrative state. That there was a historical moment of this kind has been recognised by a range of thinkers including Friedrich Hayek, James Dewey, Theodor Adorno and Carl Schmitt, that is from older liberal, 'new liberal', Marxist and conservative perspectives. After this moment of the novel, which takes exploration of complexity of the individual and of civil society relations to an extreme, along with the place of the state, perhaps most obviously present in Franz Kafka's novels, the novel lacks the grand ambitions of High Modernism. This has benefits for the study of the novel in that the collapse of grand transcending humanist unity is what informs work on desire and mimetic limits in Chap. 8. The discussion of Proust in Chap. 9 is subsequent to this because the work that cones from disintegration is necessary to the study of the great modernist masterpieces given that they are pushing at the limits of mimetic unity in their ambition.

Within the historical arc sketched above, Chap. 2 explores the epic as pre-novel, in Aristotle and Vico. Chapter 3 explores the first philosophical thought about the novel in Hegel and German Romanticism. Chapter 4 examines the more sustained discussion of the novel in Kierkegaard. Chapter 5 discusses the first major work which takes the novel as focus, in the writing of Georg Lukács along with his later considerations of the novel. Chapter 6 concentrates on Bakthin's understanding of the novel in terms of historical time and plurality of voices. Chapter 7 engages with thought on the novel as concerned with representation and a humanist view of history, particularly in Auerbach, the Marxist explorations of this in Benjamin and the Marxist sense that it is a lost ideal in Adorno. Chapter 8 looks at the erosion of mimesis as representation in Girard's understanding of rivalry, along with the place of desire, violence and death in Bataille, Blanchot, Foucault and Derrida. Chapter 9 draws on the preceding chapters to explore Proust's attempt at the absolute novel, followed by Chap. 10's return to the theme developed here and touched on across chapters of the fusion of philosophy and the novel.

References

Barthes, Roland. 1968. *Writing Degree Zero*, trans. Annette Lavers and Colin Smith. New York, NY: Hill and Wang.

Barthes, Roland. 1974. *S/Z*, trans. Richard Miller. Malden, MA and Oxford: Farrar, Straus and Giroux.

Barthes, Roland. 1977a. *Image Music Text*, trans. and ed. Stephen Heath. London: Fontana Press and Harper Collins.

Barthes, Roland. 1977b. *Roland Barthes by Roland Barthes*, trans. Richard Howard. Malden, MA and Oxford: Farrar, Straus and Giroux.

Cavell, Stanley. 1979. *The Claim of Reason: Wittgenstein, Scepticism, Morality, and Tragedy*. Oxford and London: Oxford University Press.

Derrida, Jacques. 1978. *Writing and Difference*, trans. Alan Bass. Chicago, IL: University of Chicago Press.

Derrida, Jacques. 1979. *Spurs: Nietzsche's Styles*, trans. Barbara Harlow. Chicago, IL: University of Chicago Press.

Derrida, Jacques. 1997. *Of Grammatology*, trans. Gayatri Chakravorty Spivak. Baltimore, MD: Johns Hopkins University Press.

Gettier, Edmund. 1963. Is Justified True Belief Knowledge? *Analysis* XXIII (6), 121–123.

Heidegger, Martin. 2000. *Introduction to Metaphysics*, trans. Gregory Fried and Richard Polt. New Haven, CT and London: Nota Bena and Yale University Press.

Hume, David. 1975. *Enquiries Concerning Human Understanding and Concerning the Principles of Morals*, ed. P.H. Nidditch. Oxford and New York, NY: Oxford University Press.

Hume, David. 2000. *A Treatise of Human Nature*, ed. David Fate Norton and Mary J. Norton. Oxford and New York, NY: Oxford University Press.

Kant, Immanuel. 2000. *Critique of the Power of Judgement*, ed. Paul Guyer, trans. Paul Guyer and Eric Matthews. Cambridge and New York, NY: Cambridge University Press.

Kripke, Saul A. 1972. *Naming and Necessity*. Cambridge, MA: Harvard University Press.

Nietzsche, Friedrich. 2000. *Basic Writings*, trans. and ed. Walter Kaufmann. New York, NY: Modern Library and Random House.

Nussbaum, Martha C. 1986. *The Fragility of Goodness: Luck and Ethics in Greek Tragedy and Philosophy*, 2nd ed. Cambridge and New York, NY: Cambridge University Press.

Nussbaum, Martha C. 1990. *Love's Knowledge: Essays on Philosophy and Literature*. New York, NY and Oxford: Oxford University Press.

Nussbaum, Martha C. 1994. *The Therapy of Desire: Theory and Practice in Hellenistic Ethics*. Princeton, NJ: Princeton University Press.

Putnam, Hilary. 1975. The Meaning of "Meaning". *Minnesota Studies in the Philosophy of Science* VII, 131–193.

Quine, Willard Van Orman. 1960. *Word and Object*. Cambridge, MA. Harvard University Press.

Quine, Willard Van Orman. 1969. *Ontological Relativity and Other Essays*. New York, NY: Columbia University Press.

Quine, Willard Van Orman. 1980. *From a Logical Point of View: Nine Logico-Philosophical Essays*. Cambridge, MA and London: Harvard University Press.

Rawls, John. 1971. *A Theory of Justice*. Cambridge, MA: Harvard University Press.

2

Epic in Aristotle and Vico

Introduction

This chapter proceeds in a distinct way, compared with other chapters. The philosophy of the epic, the necessary prelude to the philosophy of the novel and a lingering presence in the philosophy of the novel as the novel is always divided between a more epic side of ornate language with outstanding heroes and a more novelistic side of inclusive language with a common point of view, rather than the view of a semi-divine Hero. The philosophical texts on epic before a philosophy of the novel emerged are really limited to the writings of Aristotle and Vico, if we are limited to really thorough engagement. So a large part of this chapter will consist of detailed discussion of how Aristotle and Vico approach epic, largely Homer. This helps set up later chapters in all the ways they deal with narrative fiction in the ways it creates and presents the world. That is the world structured by unifying myths and filled with rhetorical language. This comes through most directly with regard to Joyce's use of Vico, discussed in the final chapter.

It also serves the purpose of showing how philosophy can be shaped by an encounter with a narrative genre while also taking that genre as

© The Author(s) 2018
B. Stocker, *Philosophy of the Novel*,
https://doi.org/10.1007/978-3-319-65891-9_2

an object of discussion. This is a clear example of the intertwining of literature and philosophy, which are both part of and a forerunner to the intertwining of philosophy and the novel. The terms for the philosophy of the novel can be found in Aristotle and Vico though neither mention the genre. There is no better preparation for reading the genre of the novel in a philosophical way than the reading of Aristotle's *Poetics* and *Rhetoric* (both in Aristotle 1984a) and then the *New Science* (1984) of Giambattista Vico, which is rooted in Aristotelian poetics and rhetoric.

The novel to some significant degree has roots in epic, but is not just the product of epic. Epic in this context largely means Homer, but may also mean Virgil and Dante. It could mean Apollonius Rhodius (author of the *Argonautica*), but very rarely does, which is a significant omission. It might sometimes refer to Ariosto, Tasso and John Milton, though in these cases the epic overlaps with romance and Christian apologetics. As Bakhtin suggests, Wolfram von Eschenbach's thirteenth-century romance, *Parzifal* (a romance overlapping with epic) might be an important precursor, though along with various earlier forms including the Greek or Sophistic novel. How far this is the case is a matter of debate to be discussed in Chap. 6: 'Bakhtin, Ethics and Time'.

Whatever view we may take on the sources of the novel, maybe giving it greater origin in ancient novels, ancient satire or medieval romance (which strongly overlaps with epic in any case), it is clear that before there was philosophy of the novel, there was the philosophy of the epic, with very little in the way of philosophy of other forerunners of the novel. Philosophy of the epic continues after the philosophy of the novel emerges, but at least in the most significant cases, it is tied to philosophy of the novel.

Examining philosophy of the epic as it existed before the emergence of philosophy of the novel in the late eighteenth century is one way of establishing a basis for philosophy of the novel, by looking at these thinkers for whom the epic was fundamental and the novel not worthy of notice. Two philosophers and two texts stand out here, Aristotle and Vico, the *Poetics* and the *New Science*. Just two texts separated by two millennia, from Classical Athens and Enlightenment Naples. This concentration on two texts is a consequence of the lack of discussion of literature in philosophy over this time, along with the small role of philosophical aesthetics. Vico himself was writing early in the process of the growth of philosophical aesthetics following on from Anthony Ashley Cooper (Third Earl of Shaftesbury and usually known as Shaftesbury, which is how he will be referred to from this point onwards), roughly contemporaneous with the aesthetic work of Frances Hutcheson, David Hume and Alexander Baumgarten, preceding the work of Edmund Burke and Immanuel Kant. Vico may have had direct knowledge of Shaftesbury's work and as Shaftesbury lived in Naples towards the end of his life, there may have been a personal connection. As with much else on Vico's influences and indeed his own influence, there is a lack of certainty, but there is at least reason to see them as following related ideas, particularly with regard to *sensus communis*, common sense as a community of sense or taste, rather than just widely accepted commonplaces (Shaftesbury 2000).

Aristotle follows on from the discussion of poetics and beauty in Plato. The contributions of Plato and Aristotle were not followed up at length in antiquity, or even until the time of Shaftesbury. After Aristotle, the main notable work of aesthetic philosophy is a section in the *Enneads* of Plotinus, followed by small parts of other philosophical works, but not enough to get any philosopher after Plotinus at all widely read now as an aesthetic theorist. The nearest thing to an exception before the time of Shaftesbury is Thomas Aquinas, and this is more to do with Aquinas' general influence than the centrality of Aquinas to work on aesthetics. It is always possible to argue that this or that short section a philosophical work is deserving of more attention or that works on poetics from a more exemplary setting out of rules perspective, as in Horace or Philip Sydney, deserves more attention, but as far as material that has much impact on philosophers working in aesthetics, and certainly as far as what makes it into university teaching or much in the way of relevant publications are concerned, the situation is as outlined above.

Rhetoric can be added, in a tradition starting with Aristotle's, but by far the most influential work, and certainly the one read most now is Aristotle's *Rhetoric*, so this does not expand the range of widely discussed writers on aesthetics before Shaftesbury. Rhetorical studies were part of the eighteenth-century growth of aesthetics, and Vico himself was a professor of rhetoric at the University of Naples. It must also be said that he was disappointed to not become a professor of law, which was several times better paid. However, apart from his work and Adam Smith's *Lectures on Rhetoric and Belles Lettres* (1983), there is very little within the field of rhetoric that has had lasting and major influence, outside specialists in the field, since antiquity. The field as such is important in the development of various kinds of writing and humanistic education, but not important in terms of producing texts that are now widely read.

The novel is a more subjective form of literature written in a more demotic way than epic. The elevated register of epic and its more universal reference fits with the ways in which rhetoric uses very recognisable deductions and tropes, which tell the prospective speaker in a law court, political assembly or public ceremony what is proper to such occasions, what attracts the support of the audience while signalling authority. Epic itself originates with singing in public performances, which applies particularly to Homer.

Philosophy starts to be written in the vernacular, in modern languages rather than in Latin, at about the same time as the novel becomes a major genre. Cervantes and Descartes overlap in time and in situations they imagine. In Descartes, we see the subjective mind placed at the centre of philosophy and this is fundamental to the development of aesthetics as a philosophical field, as it is concerned with how the subject has experienced.

Descartes not only contributes towards a subjective orientation in Renaissance and Early Modern culture, but also provides the terms for the emergence of modern aesthetic philosophy. His focus on ideas, types of ideas and combinations of ideas, as mental events which copy external objects and are the source of knowledge, develops through John Locke and Gottfried Wilhelm Leibniz. They both followed up elements of Cartesian philosophy on the nature of ideas in ways which have an influence on aesthetics. Locke provided a comprehensive account of the 'idea' (introducing the word into English) in terms of primary and secondary qualities, pain and pleasure, combination, abstraction and so on in *Essay Concerning Human Understanding*. Leibniz developed innatist (concepts in the mind from the beginning), intellectualist (rational relations), sensationalist (perception) and occasionalist (harmonisation of processes by a higher intelligence) aspects of Descartes to build up a philosophy of perception, separation of individuals, harmonisation of perceptions by individuals in one universe of compossible individuals, existence through unique description, predicates as necessary parts of subjects, and force as part of motion. Leibniz dealt with: uniqueness of existence, harmonisation of multiple perspectives, differences in perception from different perspectives, the necessary connections of qualities of things with the substance of things, force as necessary accompaniment to formal relations between things. All of these aspects of Locke and Leibniz are taken up by subsequent aesthetics theory. Shaftesbury was Locke's personal student and grandson of Locke's patron Anthony Ashley Cooper, 1st Earl of Shaftesbury. The path from Leibniz to Baumgarten is a bit less direct in terms of personal connection, but is clear enough in the development of philosophy in Germany after Leibniz in Christian Wolff and then Leibniz (Beiser 2009).

Aristotle: Metaphysics and Poetics

The above sketches out a development to be discussed further in the next chapter. What needs to be taken into account in the present chapter is the change in foundational philosophical concerns between Aristotle and Vico. Aristotle's view of art and poetics is defined by a metaphysics and physics of four causes (or four types of explanation), which he partly explains in the *Physics* with regard to an example of art, a statue. The four causes are material, formal, efficient and final, which can be expanded as: the matter in an object; the arrangement of the matter in the object; the immediate reason for the existence of the object; the purpose and final state of the object. This is not brought directly into the *Poetics*, but these categories perhaps exist in the discussion of tragedy in the diction, plot, fall, author, and production of the play. That we do not have Aristotle explaining literary texts in terms of the four causes might be an accident, since the *Poetics* is only a fragment and we can see him occasionally invoking literary texts in the *Metaphysics*, for example where Homeric epic is put forward as an example of identity, implicitly of the existence of an identity for an object, which is rather aggregative in nature rather than simple and immediately unified. There is one reason to suspect that the non-existence of an account of literature genres in terms of the four causes is not an accident of which manuscripts survived. Literature is in words as in philosophy and there are distinct difficulties in philosophy taking literature as an object. This is not to say complete barriers since Aristotle did write on literature as an object of philosophical discourse. However, he does make poetry closer to philosophy than history, implicitly recognising that writing about literature is philosophy writing about itself. There may always be an element of philosophy referring to itself even when philosophising about non-philosophical objects, but there is a particular issue when philosophy directs itself towards what can be a form of philosophising. The *Rhetoric* while clearly identifying rhetoric as less than a pure philosophical area does refer to enthymemes, that is deductions in rhetoric, using examples taken from literary texts.

Aristotle's literary categorisation and hierarchical ranking make tragedy higher than epic, but make epic the source of tragedy, which contains more than tragedy. In both cases, Aristotle is not concerned with the inner life of characters or their psychology. Characters have errors of judgement which lead to regret, but not as a matter of internal introspection. There is the psychology of some kind in Aristotle's philosophy, but not in the sense of a description or theory of consciousness. There is perception, appetite, will and reason, not inner reflection. There is very little sense of a sphere of consciousness within the human mind distinct from external actions. The greatest happiness is maybe that of a god contemplating and the philosopher who comes close that state, but this is the contemplation of universal truths and objective facts, not inner states of mind. There are inner thoughts in Aristotle's world, but directed by external goals and situations. The audience of tragedy experiences fear and pity in relation to the misfortunes of the hero, it does not feel aware of the inner life of the hero. The epic gathers incidents, not psychological insights. The idea of inner deliberation has a limited role in Aristotle's philosophy, certainly where it regards the self that is deliberating, and that informs how he sees literature.

There are good reasons for arguing that ancient Greek literature was not focused on a private inner life or any sense of inner worlds of imagination and thought distinct from the observable world. Muses apparently inspire Homer to sing, not inner motives or the bringing into words of the products of inner imagination. There is certainly no reference to an inner memory or the subjectivity of individual awareness. There is no doubt about the reality of what characters observe. Speech can sometimes be deceitful, and Odysseus is a master of this, but it is truthful in its basis. There is no doubt that speech is true when guided by honesty, there is no great difficulty in connecting words with the world. Odysseus might be making up the encounters with mythical forces, but not in a way in which reality is fragmented or swallowed by imagination. Odysseus might be an unreliable storyteller, but the *Odyssey* does not have an unreliable narrator and Odysseus' tales fit into a morally and physically structured world in which myths confirm shared values and systems of belief.

In Aristotle's definition of epic, which revolves around Homer, it is established that epic refers to a high kind of human being, better than we are (1448a/1984b, 2317 [standard Bekker numbers for Aristotle's works followed by page number of text in bibliography]), and that means a king or at least the member of a royal family. All the main characters in *The Iliad* and *The Odyssey*, with the addition of Olympian gods and minor deities, are of royal status those they encounter if not royal are often very close in status. This view from the highest level in society is something epic has in common with tragedy (1448a/1984b, 2317). Even though Aristotle ranks tragedy above epic, he makes Homer the highest poet of all, 'poet of poets' (1448b/1984b, 2318), so that the Homeric epics are culturally definitive. Epic is close to tragedy in the 'imitation of serious matters in metre' (1449b/1984b, 2319–2320), expanding on the thought about the higher kind of person, in that such a person is a serious thing to imitate. The differences between epic and tragedy are in the kind of verse, the use of narrative, length and fixity of time: 'It differs from it, however, in that is in one kind of verse and in narrative form; and also by its length—which is due to its action having no fixed limit of time' (1449b/1984b, 2319–2320).

Epic is potentially infinite, like number itself or the divisions of time and space. This is its inferiority to tragedy, the lack of closed form. However, Homer apparently rises above this in containing an admirable abundance of poetry to counteract any tendency to formlessness.

Despite the status of Homeric epic, tragedy is more encompassing than epic, containing more of epic than an epic contains of tragedy (1449b/1984b, 2320). This arises from the performance of drama, which brings elements song and spectacle into poetry. The high status of Homer may arise from the unity of action Aristotle perceives in *The Iliad* and *The Odyssey*: 'he took as the subject of the *Odyssey*, as also of the *Iliad*, an action with the unity of the kind we are describing' (1451a/1984b, 2322).

> In saying that there is less unity in epic, I mean an epic made up of a plurality of actions, in the same way as the *Iliad* and *Odyssey* have many such parts, each one of them in itself of some magnitude; yet the structure of the two Homeric poems is as perfect as can be, and the action in them is as nearly as possible one action. (2362b/1984b, 2340)

Homer has imperfect moments as in the use of divine intervention to explain plot twists, but this can arise in tragedies of the best kind as well, as in Euripides' *Medea*: 'the dénouement also should arise out of the plot itself, and not depend on a stage-like artifice, as in the *Medea* or in the story of the departure of the Greeks in *The Iliad*' (1454a-b/1984b, 2327). Apparently, Aristotle refers to an incident in *The Iliad*, Book II, lines 142–210, in which the gods intervene to prevent the departure of the Greek army from the coast near Troy. The looseness of plot and abruptness of shifts in the action are not unique to Homeric epic then, and Homer maintains a place equal with or maybe superior to the tragic authors.

> in epic poetry the narrative form makes it possible for one to describe a number of simultaneous incidents; and these, if germane to the subject, increase the body of the poem. This then is a gain to the epic; tending to give it grandeur, and also variety of interest and room for episodes of diverse kinds. (1459b/1984b, 2336)

Posterior Analytics, Book II, 93b. An account is a unity in two ways—either by connection, like the Iliad, or by making one thing clear of one thing non-accidentally (1984a, 155).

Poetics.

> His two poems are each examples of construction, the *Iliad* simple and a story of suffering, the *Odyssey* complex (there is discovery throughout it) and a story of character. And they are more than this, since in diction and thought too they surpass all other poems. (1459b, 1984a, 2336)

[H]e alone amongst epic poets is not unaware of the part to be played by the poet himself in the poem. The poet should say very little in his own character, as he is no imitator when doing that (1460a/1984b, 2336).

Homer is further honoured towards the end of the *Poetics* when Aristotle defends him against Protagoras, a persistent antagonist in the *Metaphysics*, where Aristotle is particularly eager to distinguish his own philosophy from that of the famous Sophist, already a target for Plato in *Protagoras* and *Theatetus*. The main issue for Aristotle is that Protagoras takes 'man as the measure' in his famous phrase, entirely inadequate from the perspective of a metaphysics, which defines reality with regard to necessity independent of human awareness. Aristotle's *Metaphysics* and *Physics* put forward a structure of the first mover, motion in three aspects, substances, essences and properties, four types of the cause, which are what humans measure, not the product of human measurement. Aristotle presents Protagoras as undermining the idea of a permanent substantive reality, in a similar way to that of Heraclitus and Cratylus, who only think of reality in terms of what changes in perception. Judging by his comment on Protagoras in relation to Homer, Aristotle also considered him to be something of a pedant obsessed with irrelevant distinctions and certainly unable to tell the difference between written and performance aspects of a literary work.

> As regards the diction, one subject for inquiry under this head is the turns given to the language when spoken; e.g. the difference between command

and prayer, simple statement and threat, question and answer, and so forth. The theory of such matters, however, belongs to acting and the professors of that art. Whether the poet knows these things or not, his art as a poet is never seriously criticised on that account. What fault can we see one see in Homer's 'sing of the wrath, Goddess'?—which Protagoras has criticised as being a command where a prayer was meant, since to bid one do or not do, he tells us is a command. (1456b/1984b, 2331)

The line in question is the opening of the *Iliad*, where Homer refers to the wrath of the Greek hero and king of the Myrmidons, Achilles as it arises in a conflict with the leader of the Greek kings, Agamemnon of Argos, but also Achilles' general character, which is highly warlike and quick to anger. For Aristotle, Protagoras was wrong to challenge Homer for using a command instead of a prayer, as if he was being insolent to the gods. The difference between command and prayer becomes apparent in performance, in the singing or declamation of Homer's poetry. Oral performance in general rather than stage acting is what Aristotle is referring to here. This reminds us that Homeric epic was not written down because people were reading Homer as the main form of encountering him, but as an accompaniment to the performance tradition.

The role of the singing of Homeric epic in Greek communities, as part of what made them communities, is in Vico's *New Science*. One problem in making epic part of the history of the novel is that epics were written to be sung, coming out of a tradition of oral performance, while novels were written to be read, certainly in the case of the modern novel. Musicality is maybe present in the modern novel as style, but this is an issue for later. We do not have to leave Aristotle's rejoinder to Protagoras as a distinction between writing and performance, it could be taken as an issue of possible multiple interpretations, though that is certainly not Aristotle's approach, which maybe refers to the sacred aspect of the performance of poetry linked with prayer.

Whatever the relation of Homeric poetry to the sacred, Aristotle deals with something excluded from the philosophy of epic in Aristotle and Vico, and which even after Vico tends to be regarded as not so much of an issue for epics: multiple possibilities of meaning and interpretation. Within the epic, Aristotle finds an element of what might be later on be defined as novelistic: a use of interpretative ambiguity and awareness of secondary meanings, even the loss of hierarchies of meaning, which are all evident issues in *Don Quixote*. Aristotle finds the necessity and deep structure of nature in poetics, with epic as the most comprehensive form in its version of the unity of action. As we see in his reaction to Protagoras, this kind of metaphysical visions was not universal in antiquity, what maybe closer to a universal point of view is the assumption of clarity of meaning. The criticism of Homer that Aristotle reports in Protagoras is one which takes Homer to task for not using words properly; it is certainly not Protagoras' aim to deny that clarity and stability of meaning are possible. According to Aristotle, Cratylus became silent in the face of the constant movement of the world, but there is no suggestion that Cratylus was troubled by the instability of meaning. Ancient sceptical texts, particularly those of Sextus Empricus, suggest some interest in differences of moral standards between societies and between the perceptions of individuals, according to the state of their body, but there is no suggestion of difficulty in grasping the meaning. Aristotle himself refers in the *Poetics* to the disturbance generated in poetry by too much mixing of foreign words, suggesting he sees the confusion of meaning as something foreign to a well constructed literary work, and that he does not see poetry as defined by an ambiguity of meaning. Aristotle is then sensitive to ambiguities of meaning, but does not think of meaning as itself prone to ambiguity in any literary context, or any context, presuming that the language used is not too full of oddities.

Aristotle: Poetics and Rhetoric

To fully comprehend Aristotle's contribution to literary aesthetics, it is necessary to examine the *Rhetoric* as well as the *Poetics*, which enables us to see how literary works connect with the language of the political assembly and the law court. That is we can see that there can only be a poetics where there is also an account of public persuasion. Current work on the novel, and since the late eighteenth century, has not always directly addressed legal and political language, but increasingly the novel, like other literary genres, has been discussed in relation to communication as a whole. The rhetoric of the legal and political centres does not have the dominating role in a modern nation it has in an ancient city state, which is why we do not have the equivalent of Aristotle's *Rhetoric*. The ways in which the language of the novel, like languages of specialist knowledge, is part of many different uses of language receives a major modern account in Michel Foucault's *Archaeology of Knowledge*. Aristotle himself thought in terms according to which rhetoric is inferior to deductive reasoning and is characteristic of the institutions of Athenian democracy. The Athenian democracy was a political regime Aristotle found less than ideal, but acceptable as a legitimate regime. What he writes in the *Rhetoric* suggests that literary language is formed by and forms public speech. The idea that this is important to the Athenian polity was a major point in Hannah Arendt's discussion of the origin of politics. Aristotle's understanding of Homeric epic is shaped by the ways in which Homeric language is taken up in rhetoric as we will see by looking at a number of examples.

In Book I, Chap. 3, Aristotle defines three kinds of rhetoric: Deliberative, Forensic and Epideictic. Epideictic rhetoric is rhetoric which praises of criticises someone and is concerned with the present, how that person can be seen now. An example of epideictic rhetoric is speeches in praise of Achilles. It is normal to praise Achilles for choosing to avenge the death of his friend Patroclus, in which he chose death for himself. What is referred to here is the end of the Trojan War which is the setting of *The Iliad*, referring to a conflict between Greeks and the Aegean Anatolian city of Troy. The Trojan prince, Hector, kills Achilles' friend and follower Patroclus in battle. The gods give Achilles the chance to live a normal full-length life if he leaves the Trojan War. Achilles chooses an early death in battle and glory in later memory that follows, so that he can kill Hector in revenge for the death of Patroclus.

In Chap. 6, Aristotle also introduces an idea that what is good is what is desired and is therefore something for which people compete. He mentions honour as a basic good, which is something that requires being placed above other people and therefore leads to conflict about who is highest or at least competition, though this is more by implication than direct statement. He does go onto note that having a good can mean excluding an enemy from it and brings in some lines from Homer's *Iliad*, a text about jealousy and competition leading to war and the prolongation of that war. The jealousy and conflict begin when

Prince Paris of Troy steals Queen Helen of Sparta from her husband Menelaus, leading to an army lead by a league of Greek kings attacking Troy. *The Iliad* shows the Greek leaders as jealous and violent towards each other. Aristotle also notes that the best goods are those which belong only to one individual, again suggesting competition and even conflict as behind the happy life. These conflicts are why rhetoric is necessary, though Aristotle does not note this directly, as legal and political struggles come from jealousy, envy and violent conflict.

In Chap. 7, Aristotle goes on to build up the idea that the greatest good is what belongs to me alone by quoting Homer's *Odyssey*. The line is 'I have learnt from none but myself'. This is a singer poet who is a servant to enemies of King Odyssey asking to be spared from the death he is giving to his enemies. The point the poet-bard makes here is that his capacity is unique, though he gives credit to the gods rather than himself only. Aristotle's point is that the greatest good is the one deep inside me and that belongs to me alone, possibly ultimately as a gift of the gods, which would be the good luck Aristotle referred to earlier that inspires the kind of envy behind legal and political conflicts discussed by Aristotle and the wars at the centre of Homer's poems.

Aristotle moves into a further discussion of what is pleasant, what gives pleasure in Chap. 11. This is repeatedly explained with examples from literature.

It can be pleasant to remember pain, but not to expect pain as Aristotle suggests with reference to *The Odyssey* XV, line 400. This refers to the swineherd Eumaeus who tells of his painful fall from the happy life he had as the son of a king in the beautiful carefree island. Aristotle also quotes *The Iliad* on the pleasure of anger. This is from Book XVIII, line 109. The Greek hero Achilles speaks to his mother Thetis on the pleasure of anger with enemies, though the context is that he wished the world was not full of strife. Aristotle links anger as a pleasure with the expectation of being able to take revenge. Where we do expect to be able to take revenge, we do not feel anger with the gods. Aristotle goes on to quote Homer's *Iliad* XXXIII, line 108 where Achilles mourns his friend Patroclus at his great funeral but the mourners also feel pleasure at remembering the good things about Patroclus because Achilles has been able to take revenge on the Trojan hero Hector.

In Book II, Chap. 2, Aristotle starts with the emotion of anger, which as before he defines as an emotion directed towards someone against whom we believe we can inflict revenge. Aristotle expands on the earlier discussion to define anger as a desire for revenge, which is accompanied by anger. As in the earlier discussion of anger, he quotes Book XIII, line 109 from the *Iliad*, where Homer discusses the pleasure of anger.

Aristotle continues the discussion of anger with reference to further quotations from Homer. He quotes Achilles again, as he speaks in the *Iliad*, Book I, line 356 of dishonour that he suffers because someone took his prize away. This refers to King Agamemnon, the head of the league of Greek kings in the Trojan War, who takes a favourite slave girl away from Achilles. This incident is at the centre of the *Iliad*, as Achilles the greatest warrior of the Greeks now refuses to fight and the Trojans nearly win the war. It is only near the end of the *Iliad* that Achilles is willing to fight again. For Aristotle, this illustrates the anger which comes from the insolence of someone more powerful insulting someone.

Aristotle goes on to another quotation from the *Iliad*. Book II, line 196, which refers to the anger of kings descended from Zeus (the chief Greek god). It is Odysseus, King of Ithaca, who tries to get the Greek kings to back their chief king Agamemnon, who claims descent from Zeus. It is a bad moment in the war and many of the Greeks are willing to return home, so Odysseus refers to the great anger that will come from Agamemnon. Aristotle gives this as an example of someone who is angry because that person does not believe that person's authority is respected.

In Chap. 3, Aristotle quotes *The Odyssey* IX, line 504 in order to make a point about the importance of knowing who has done something bad to us in order to be angry with them and of the person who did something bad to someone making sure the person they damaged will be angry with them. This is also the condition for Odysseus to be angry with the person he has damaged since according to Aristotle, we are only angry with the person who knows we harmed that person. Presumably, this is because we fear their revenge and seek further damage against them. What he quotes from Homer is Odysseus telling the Cyclops Polyphemus who he is while sailing away from Polyphemus Island.

The Cyclops is one-eyed monster, sons of the sea God Poseidon. Odysseus blinded Polyphemus when Polyphemus trapped King Odysseus and his men in his cave and started eating them. This is an early part of King Odysseus' long journey back from the Trojan War to his home kingdom of Ithaca, an Island off western Greece. The shouting his name at Polyphemus is important to the story, because Polyphemus tells his father the sea god Poseidon, who delays Odysseus' journey for twenty years during which time all his men die.

Aristotle now moves onto a quotation from *The Odyssey*, Book XXIV, line 54. The god Apollo speaks to the other gods of the anger of the Greek hero Achilles. Achilles has killed the Trojan hero Hector and is dragging his body through the dust. This is revenge on Hector for killing Achilles' friend and follower Patroclus (who is sometimes seen as Achilles' lover). The dragging of a corpse through the dust is obviously very insulting and went against the extreme important ancient Greeks gave to correct burial of the dead, including honourable burial for soldiers who die in war. The belief that death in battle is very acceptable if followed by honourable burial is a constantly repeated idea in *The Iliad* and has some importance in *The Odyssey*, because it is important for Odysseus to not die at sea during his ten-year voyage home, as there is no honour in disappearing into the sea. Apollo is condemning the impiety (lack of respect for the gods and eternal laws) of Achilles' behaviour and demanding that the gods condemn him. Aristotle's main point here is that anger against those who are dead and therefore cannot harm us or are the objects of any further revenge that they will be aware of, is excessive and that normal behaviour is for anger to become calmed when the object of our anger dies.

In Chap. 9, Aristotle discusses indignation with reference to Homer. He appears to have remembered a line of Homer incorrectly or misquoted it, since the lines quoted refer to an incident which was different from what appears in Aristotle's transformed quotation of Homer, *Iliad*, Book XI, line 542. What happens in Homer is that Hector, the main Trojan hero, does not attack Ajax (one of the Greek heroes) at that moment. Then, Ajax retreats from the Trojans under the influence of the god Zeus, because Zeus is controlling what happens and does not want the Greeks to win at this point. What Aristotle suggests is that

someone refused to fight Ajax because Ajax was above them in greatness and they feared angering Zeus by attacking someone of higher
status. However, at this point, it is Hector who avoids attacking Ajax,
and Hector is the second greatest of all the heroes Greek or Trojan, after
Achilles. He is greater than Ajax. Anyway, the misquotation refers to a
reality of Homer's world and Aristotle's world centuries later, that everyone must stay in their proper place in the social hierarchy and not challenge people above them in the hierarchy or behave as their equal. We
have correct indignation, according to Aristotle against those who try to
behave as if of higher social standing. Aristotle also says we feel indignation at those who commit the worst crimes, murder, particularly the
murder of a father. We enjoy their suffering in punishment. The idea
it is right to enjoy the punishment of others and that is part of being
a good person is not going to seem to the right way of thinking to all
modern readers of course, but is taken as uncontroversial by Aristotle.

In Chap. 21, Aristotle describes the use of maxims alone as an inferior form of argument, most associated with uneducated country people and is most appropriate for speakers using maxim for subjects where
they have genuine experience. Aristotle takes examples from *The Iliad*,
XII, line 243: 'one omen of all is best, that we fight for our father-
land'. The Trojan hero, Hector is persuading his soldiers to ignore a bad
omen, which as is normal in ancient Greek omens relates to seeing a
bird. Aristotle gives another example from *The Iliad* XVIII, 30: 'The
war-God shows no favour' (*Iliad*, Book). Here, Hector is speaking to
persuade his men that they can defeat Achilles, the greatest Greek hero.
In Chap. 22, Aristotle goes on to emphasise the importance of basing
arguments on facts and collecting many facts to use in speeches. Achilles
appears as the example of someone who could be the object of a speech
of praise and eulogy.

So what we have in Aristotle's account of Homer is not just the place of
Homeric epic in literature, but the role of Homeric epic in showing the
world of ethics, psychology and informal practical judgement. Aristotle
attributes a kind of psychological and social realism to Homer although
the poetry was written down more than 300 years before Aristotle's own
philosophical career, and carrying traces of Mycenaean Greece from
at least 800 years before Aristotle. So for Aristotle, the Homeric poetry

delineates the world of judgements and expected structures of behaviour, which are permanent and still condition his own society.

We see some indication in Aristotle of the Viconian program of using Homer to open up the world of the 'Heroic' Age (corresponding with Bronze Age Mycenaean Greece), though for Aristotle, Homer seems to belong to some continuous time of unchanging human actions and institutions. It seems hard to believe that Aristotle made no distinction between the world of Homeric heroes and the city life of Athens, particularly as his teacher Plato was a critic of Homer's influence. We can take it that Aristotle had some kind of historical consciousness and awareness that his ethics were not exactly those of characters in epic fiction, but not one that was fully articulated. We do not get a sense from Herodotus or Thucydides, the 'founders' of history not long before Aristotle's career, of the shifts that had taken place in the Greek world, with regard to its ethics and political structure, from the heroes and kings of Homer to the city states of their time. It is Giambattista Vico, as much as anyone, who marks the shift into what we would regard as a fully historical consciousness, in the sense of changes over history. Arendt suggested that Vico's writing is the point at which the shift took place just as she had suggested that the Greek polis saw itself in Homeric terms.

Introduction to Vico

Vico also pioneered the idea that literature should be at the centre of the study of human history, the nature of human institutions, structures of human societies and philosophical reflection on these topics, and therefore that literature itself should be studied with reference to all these aspects of communal human life. Aristotle came as close as anyone in anticipating Vico through the accumulated weight of his *Poetics*, the *Rhetoric* and more sporadic literary references across his philosophy.

Vico uses a frontispiece to introduce the *New Science*, in which he establishes his view of the beginnings of human society and its foundational institutions. Explaining the frontispiece would go beyond the scope of this book, but one detail should be picked out.

There is a ray from God reflected from a jewel worn by metaphysics, which goes down to a statue of Homer. Homer is there is because for Vico, 'Homer' is the source of information about the mental, moral and civil world of early human communities. Homer is 'Homer' because unlike Aristotle, Vico does address the issue of the authorship of Homer. In Aristotle's time, the Homeric epics had existed in written form for 400 years. There was no information about who Homer was, or the source of these poems either in earlier poetry or in the Bronze Age Mycenaean Greek war at the centre of them. Despite this, Aristotle and apparently other ancient Greeks did not concern themselves with the history of Homer the person, the history of the Homeric poetry or the history referred to in Homer. There was anyway little they could use and they followed the tradition of Homer the great Wiseman composing poems with some historical basis. Vico first raised the possibility that 'Homer' was a stand in name for many Greek singer poets who had composed the epics collectively over time, reflecting the Greek society of their time.

In Vico's view, *The Iliad* and *The Odyssey* were composed at different times in different parts of Greece. He thought the long progress of composition could be seen in reference to different stages of antique history compressed in the poem, where hero warriors descended from the gods, imagined in a pre-commercial age live at the same time as traders and aristocrats living with traded luxury goods. Vico anticipated influential work by Friedrich August Wolff at the end of the eighteenth century arguing for the collective oral authorship over time before the writing down. The question of authorship of the Homeric epics is still open and nothing is advocated here about which answer is to be preferred. What is relevant here is that at a time when a more subjective and ambiguous form of long fictional narrative had appeared, the novel, Vico emphasises the distance from Homeric epic by turning it into the collective product of a society.

Vico's philosophy replaces Aristotelian metaphysics of nature with a philosophy of human consciousness, examining human institutions created by human consciousness as distinct from the philosophy of nature. Vico sees this as a non-Cartesian project because Descartes was concerned with nature, not history. Vico takes Francis Bacon as his model, though he does not say much about how this works. The more revealing indications of intellectual tradition are those referring to six-teenth- and seventeenth-century writes on laws, politics and state insti-tutions: Niccoló Machiavelli, Jean Bodin, John Selden, Hugo Grotius, Thomas Hobbes, Samuel Pufendorf. Vico has criticisms of these think-ers, particularly with regard to what he regards as a tendency to confuse the civil law resulting from history with the natural law of the earliest humans. For Vico, the Cyclops monster in *The Odyssey* is evidence that the earliest human communities were hostile to outsiders and were based on the power of kings claiming divinity. This form of sovereignty was based on force and religious sanction rather than law and the gen-eral interests of the community. It followed natural law in the sense of recognising the rights to self-defence of the lower non-divine, and even animal-like, lower classes and nothing else, so it was natural law in the sense of recognising the natural unavoidability of every individual resist-ing death and coercion, but not in the sense of a whole set of laws, cus-toms and principles encouraging humans to live according to natural purposes happiness and justice. Bacon fits in, maybe, with regard to his enthusiasm for both strong monarchy and law, which Vico regards as prerequisites for the most human kind of society.

Machiavelli, Bodin, Selden, Grotius, Hobbes and Pufendorf pro-vide overlapping examples of how law and political institutions develop historically. In this thought, jurisprudence and civil institutions vary between eras and have non-ideal origins, tending towards the most just outcome over time, but not with any certainty. Their thought is histor-ical and contingent, in contrast to ancient writers who think more of a perpetual present than of historical change. Machiavelli and Grotius thought of laws as something that had been developed in the past leav-ing them with the possibility of reflection which had not existed before.

They are writing at the time of the emergence of the modern novel. Machivalli died (1527) a few years before François Rabelais published the first part of *Gargantua and Pantagruel* (1532) and just a few decades before the anonymous Spanish novella *Lazarillo de Tormes*. Pufendorf died shortly after the novel moves into a post-Cervantes phases with the publication of: *Simplicius Simplicissimus* (1668) by Hans Jakob Christoffel von Grimmelshausen in Germany; *The Princess of Cleves*

(1678) by Marie-Madeleine Pioche de la Vergne, comtesse de Lafayette (better know as Madame de Lafayette) in France; the novelistic religious narrative *The Pilgrims Progress* (1678) by John Bunynan in England; the novella *Oronooko* (1688) by Aphra Behn in England. Large numbers of novels appear in Britain and France in the eighteenth century, and these works connect Rabelais and Cervantes with the marked growth of the genre two centuries later.

These novels and proto-novels raise the issues of war, social disintegration, amorous passions in a courtly society, religious faith, colonialism and slavery, attempting to make sense of them or at least order seeming incoherence, through narrative. The appearance of political and legal investigations into war, natural, human passions, contracts at the social foundation, conquest, slavery, the place of religion in society is a related phenomenon. The novels and the treatises are the two ways of presenting and investigating the same phenomena of interest, in ways concerned with complexity, integration and dynamism.

The late seventeenth-century novels are less grand in scale and integration than *Gargantua and Pantagruel* and *Don Quixote*, but develop ways of writing less reliant on the fantastic than Rabelais and less reliant on the imagination of the fantastic than Cervantes. There is some similarity in the development of political theory and jurisprudential texts. In the eighteenth century, Adam Smith's *An Inquiry into the Nature and Causes of the Wealth of Nations* and Montesquieu's *The Spirit of the Laws* are exercises in integration across history and between ideas, at how whole complex social systems work, beyond their sixteenth- and seventeenth-century predecessors, even compared with Grotius' very lengthy *The Rights of War and Peace*, which lacks the sense of dynamic integration of the later books. Montesquieu and Smith are preceded in this kind of exercise by Vico in the *New Science*.

Vico's Philosophy of Literature

Vico does not address literary developments since the sixteenth century, so it is not possible to construct any ways in which novels influenced the composition of the *New Science*. In the case of Machiavelli, political discourses are written in a distinguished literary style, especially in *The Prince* where storytelling and allegory, most famously the ruler as a centaur, then as lion and fox in Chapter XVIII is at the centre of political thought. In any case, the whole development of ways of writing in fiction and in discursive essays is behind the *New Science* whatever may arise in tracing how direct any influence is. The *New Science* puts epic at the centre of its literary discussion but belongs to a period where intellectual construction is already conditioned by the novel, along with related forms of writing. The *New Science* addressed the epic from the point of view of a culture conditioned by the novel. Vico cannot articulate this directly, because he is himself caught up in the classical approaches to art in which prose cannot be at the same level as poetry. Italian literature means Dante, Tasso and Ariosto. European literature largely means the Italian writers, though he does give an important role to the French medieval epic, *The Song of Roland*. Vico's view of ancient literature is that it has a pre-conceptual imaginative peak in Homer, carried on into the Attic drama, but leading into Aesop's *Fables*, so prose allegories to demonstrate a simple maxim. The role of Virgil may disrupt this to some degree, but Vico takes the *Aeneid* as a prolongation of the poetic imaginative world view of Homer, rather than as something new and different.

Vico assumes that history is cyclical, with two great cycles: from pre-agricultural times in Greece up to the end of the Roman Empire (in the west); the repetition of the first cycle from the new barbarism following the fall of Rome in the west to the age of human monarchies in Vico's own time, which he regards as repeating the Rome of Augustus and the subsequent emperors. Given this framework, in which *The Song of Roland* and *The Divine Comedy* repeat Homer and Virgil, with Tasso and Ariosto as a prolongation, we would not expect Vico to pay any direct attention to the novel. Indeed, he does not and the same applies to the short story cycles of Giovanni Boccaccio or Marguerite de Navarre, which had a major influence on narrative fiction and novel writing, particularly where stories within stories are present, for example *Don Quixote*. His silence regarding Rabelais and Cervantes is very noticeable. This is an apparent blind spot in Vico's thought, though not in any way detracting from his importance for philosophy of literature, along with figures standing between philosophy and literature. Michel de Montaigne, Blaise Pascal, Jean de la Bruyère and François de La Rochefoucauld are also notably absent from the *New Science*. Machiavelli stands out as a thinker at least briefly acknowledged by Vico who was a major literary writer.

Despite all these omissions, Vico can only be understood as a thinker conditioned by prose literary and philosophical literary culture going back to the fourteenth century, in the case of Boccaccio. The imagination he brings to the *New Science* is a product of novelistic, historical, political and jurisprudential writing in which ways of writing fit with other aspects of a society, including its laws, religion, language, property forms, morality and knowledge. The view he has of Homeric epic as full of imaginative universals, and a poetic directness impossible where abstract thought has developed, is a product of the literary and literary-philosophical background of late Medieval, Renaissance and early modern Europe. machiavelli advocates a political life based on active passion and mythology in *The Prince*. Montaigne refers to people without abstract philosophy in his account of cannibals and a legendary place in France without laws. Madame de Lafayette gives the reader characters driven by passion. Pascal suggests an inherent impossibility of successful reason. Hobbes argues for the unreasoning imagination and fear of peoples without a state. The importance of fear in Hobbes has equivalents in Vico with regard to the origin of language and religion, along with the whole move to agriculture and cities, in the fear barbaric men have of the thunder and lightening they take to be supernatural in origin. Vico wrote a philosophy of the epic and a not a philosophy of the novel, but it is not a literary philosophy which could have been written without the emerging modern novel and allied forms of writing, along with the political and jurisprudential texts, which show affinities with novelistic writing and which are directly highlighted by Vico.

Vico sets forward some methodological points about the union of philosophy and philology, partly contained in the 'axioms' of the 'Elements' section in *New Science*, Book I. An important is in axiom ten: 'Philosophy contemplates reason, whence comes knowledge of the true; philology observes that of which human choice is author, whence comes consciousness of the certain' (1984, 63). Philosophy is concerned with truths known by reason that is from pure thought, not observation. Philology observes what comes from human choice, where we become conscious of certainty. Philology includes all study of language, literature, history, laws, customs, institutions, and trade. Philosophy and philology belong together and have been weaker separate from each other than they will be unified in Vico's science.

Axiom sixteen: 'Vulgar traditions must have had public grounds of truth, by virtue of which they came into being and were preserved by entire peoples over long periods of time' (1984, 64). Uneducated traditions of belief come out of public truths of history preserved over time. Vico's Science is to uncover the grounds of truth, which have become covered in falsity due to changes in languages and customs over time. So the study of language and of national customs is part of the Science, which must be extended to the study of myth and heroic poetry.

The age of Saturn refers to the Golden Age before the universal flood, so presumably, Vico means that these laws came from the earliest time in Roman history, the foundation of the city, centuries after the universal flood. Axiom twenty: 'If the poems of Homer are civil histories of ancient Greek customs, they will be two great treasure houses of natural law of the Gentes of Greece' (1984, 65). The epic poems of Homer, *The Iliad* and *The Odyssey*, are histories of the ancient Greeks, so histories of the institutions of law, and so inform us about natural law as understood by the ancient Greeks.

> Axiom twenty-one: The Greek philosophers hastened the natural course which their nation was to take, for when they appeared the Greeks were still in a crude state of barbarism, from which they advanced immediately to one of the highest refinement while at the same time preserving intact their fables both of gods and of heroes. (1984, 65–66)

So Vico takes the period from the foundation of the city by Romulus to the political rights of the plebeians as the period of heroic-aristocratic rule. The popular stories recollecting that period (presumably as known to us via the first-century BCE Roman historian Livy) are the equivalent of the myths of the Greek heroes (presumably referring to Homer). Vico compares the abrupt movement of the Greeks from aristocratic-heroic barbarism to philosophy, with France in the twelfth century. Vico believed that history is a cycle of repetitions of an eternal plan, in which Europe after the fall of the (western) Roman Empire goes back to barbarism.

In twelfth-century Paris, the stories from the eighth century of Bishop Turpin of barbaric paladins and knights were still current representing the heroic mythology of France, while the philosopher Peter Lombard was lecturing on what became his philosophical–theological classic *Four Books of Sentences*. Vico seems a bit confused about Bishop Turpin who was associated with Rheims, not Paris as he suggests. There are a number of slips like this, suggesting that Vico was often thinking more of the flow of argument that the exact facts.

In Vico's view of humans at the beginning of historical development, in which they move towards poetic epic before philosophy, the earliest humans lack knowledge and reasoning power. Poetic imagination fills the gaps and is very strong therefore in early humans in relation to science and rational thought. The poetic imagination results in fables and poems, like those of Homer, which have a metaphysical-poetic truth rather than a physical truth. That is generalisations are created in poetry which are true as generalisations, though not in particular facts. The earliest humans had an energy which meant language was singing rather than speech and that combines with poetic imagination to give us the tradition of poetry composed for singing and transmitted by a tradition of singing, rather than writing.

In 'Establishment of Principles', Section IV Method, Vico refers to the need to investigate the earliest humans with regard to their appearances in ancient literature, as in Virgil's epic poem the *Aeneid*, the cyclops (one eyed monster) in Homer's *Odysseus* and various myths. We can also look at the references to the early cooking of frogs in Epicurus, references to wild men and big footed men in two great early modern thinkers in law and politics, Hugo Grotius and Samuel Pufendorf and references to Homer in Plato.

The New Science uses a metaphysical art of criticism on the early writers based on the common sense of humanity in the harmony of institutions that is looks at early texts as part of the common pattern of repetition in history. The person who creates something narrates it. Just as geometry explores the world it creates, the New Science is concerned with what comes from the human mind, and which is more real in the institutes than the shapes of geometry. Mythologies agree with institutions. They are the civil history of early peoples in poetry. Etymology shows us the history of the institutions named. Philology gives us truth through the mental vocabulary of institutions, vulgar (popular) traditions and the fragments of antiquity (its literature). The philological proofs coincide with philosophy unifying reason and authority. The basic institutions of religion, marriage and burial are widely agreed upon and are the limits of human reason, so that breaking them is to break the basis of humanity.

Vico continues these considerations on philology and philosophy, poetry and philosophy in Book II of the *New Science*, Poetic Wisdom. Vico refers to a definition of the muse in Homer with regard to 'knowledge of good and evil'. However, the passage mentioned from *The Odyssey*, inserted by Bergin and Fisch, the editors and translators of the edition used here, begins on line 63 of *The Odyssey VIII*, refers to the infliction of good and evil on the poet/reciter of poems rather than knowledge of poems. According to Vico, knowledge of good and evil (he appears to mean in the poetic inspired sense) becomes divination. Divination is forbidden to humans in ancient Judaism, and then in Christianity, as beyond what humans can naturally know. The muse was first the practice of divining by auspices. In antiquity, this included observing the flights of birds, and the results of cutting up sacrificed birds. The practice of divination gives its name to divinity in the sense of God as divine being. This wisdom was used by the theological poets, and the idea of wisdom was then seen in various wise man and good rulers.

Wisdom then became the metaphysics used in the knowledge of God as a source of truth, a regulator of good, which has the function of the humanity of preserving belief in a provident divinity, which is necessary to the preservation of humanity. Vico refers to the roots of such ideas amongst Jews and Christians. He also mentions Tuscans, presumably the writers and scholars of Tuscany from the thirteenth to fifteenth centuries, including Dante Alighierei, whose *Divine Comedy* features as an equivalent to Homer for the medieval Italians, in Vico's thinking.

This reference to the sacred poetry of the Middle Ages connects with the divine origins of poetry according to Vico. Frightened individuals believe what they hear, and that is how poetry originates, using perturbation, a fear inducing disturbance of the mind (*New Science*, Book II 'Poetic Metaphysics'). In the time of the great flood, some human giants on mountain tops became aware of lightening and therefore the sky. They imagined the sky to be full of something like themselves, so a great moving body called Jove, the origin of the chief god of all the gentes. The giants thought Jove spoke to them through thunder. They regarded him as a saviour because he did not destroy everything and as establisher for ending the savage wanderings of the giants. Jove was born naturally in poetry as a divine character or imaginative universal. He is an imaginative universal because Jove stands for power and strength as a personification rather than appearing as a properly transcendent monotheistic god. Ignorance increases imaginative power, which is why Homer's poetry is so sublime and is the greatest poetry as well as the earliest according to Vico.

In Section 2, 'Poetic Logic' of *New Science* Book II, Vico argues that metaphysics is what contemplates things in all the forms of their being. Metaphysics is logic where it is concerned with things with regard to all the forms with which they may be signified. The metaphysics of the poetry of the theological poets (principally Homer) imagines most bodies to be divine substances, and there is a poetic logic in that poetry, which signifies those substances. In Vico's philology, the word 'logic' comes from the Greek 'logos', which in its origin means 'fabula' or fable (story). That becomes 'favella' in Italian which means speech. However, 'mythos', myth, also means fable in Greek.

The first language spoken by the theological poets was not like the language God taught Adam. In the Garden of Eden, which must have been divine onomathesia, that is giving names to things according to the nature of each thing. The language of the theological poets was a fantastic speech making use of physical substances given life and mostly imagined to be divine. The theological poets thought of the gods as substances of earth, sky and sea. Since the theological poets could not paint or use understanding for spiritual things. Therefore, the poets attribute senses and passion to bodies like the earth, sky and sea.

As abstraction took over from imagination Personification became minute signs. Metonymy (substitution of an associate idea for the original idea) introduced a later appearance of scholarship into the ignorance, so that Jupiter flies on an eagle and so on. Myths are the language of fables and contain the allegories corresponding to fables. Allegory brings in qualities common to individuals as when the hero Achilles is used to stand for the courage of all strong men, Odysseus is used the stand for the prudence common to the wise. The allegories contain the etymologies of words in poetic languages. Allegories in vulgar languages are more analogical, more concerned with comparisons.

In *New Science*, Book II, Section 3, Poetic Morals Vico argues that logic (presumably reasoning about metaphysical questions like God, rather than deductive logic in the strictest sense) enables the mind to use clear and distinct ideas. The references to clear and distinct ideas lead us to Descartes, a philosopher of whom Vico is often very critical. Poetic morality begins with the fear of God, while atheism is arrogance against God and arrogance in general. Vico explains this with a quotation from Horace who was living during the time the Emperor system was formed in Rome and is much further removed from the barbaric-heroic age than Homer. Vico also seeks support from Homer, with reference to the story in *The Odyssey* of Polyphemus, the one eyed giant, who respects the god Poseidon, who also happens to be his father. Vico emphasises that augurs (priests interpreting the will of the gods) lived amongst the Cyclops (a race of one-eyed giant), which would not be possible for atheists.

In Section 5 of Book II 'Poetic Politics', Vico uses mythology to illustrate his view of the status of plebeians as non-citizens, even strangers, in the cities governed by the heroes. He refers to ancient stories in which a male hero abandons a woman who has offered him assistance and hospitality in a time of need and is willing to become his wife. He refers to such a story in *The Odyssey* where Odysseus is washed ashore towards the end of his adventures and is cared for by a local princess, Nausicaa, who falls in love with him. Odysseus, however, leaves to return to his queen and wife, Penelope. There is a parallel story in Virgil's sequel to the *Iliad*, *Aeneid*. Vico brings in a third story from Homer, a story in the *Iliad* of the Greek hero Achilles refusing offers of wives from King Agamemnon, which again stands for contempt for the plebian-'stranger' population of the 'heroic' cities who are standardly represented as a woman who can be rejected and betrayed.

In a corollary 'It is Divine Providence that Instituted Commonwealths and at the Same Time The Natural Law of the Gentes' (1984, 234), Vico argues that the first commonwealths were based on a division between the heroes and plebeians regarded as 'the other people', as Telemachus, the son of *Odysseus* suggests in *The Odyssey*, referring to the plebeians. They were based on a lack of interest in other people so were about protecting self-interest rather than the public good. The aristocratic form of the first governments was a product of self-interest, solitariness and the need for institutions separating humans from an animal existence in the forests.

In 'Heroic Politics Resumed' (1984, 237–249), Vico refers to the violence, robbery and inhospitality towards strangers of the early heroes. In general, early stages of human history and government are characterised by violence. Contests of the song in early poetry and myth refer to heroic contests over the auspices (aristocratic struggle over the control of religious ceremonies), which marks an early stage in the appearance of civil institutions. The relevant stories include the sirens described in Homer's *Odyssey* who lure sailors to their death with their song and then kill them; the witch Circe who turns Odysseus' men into pigs in the *Odyssey*. Those defeated and killed are sailors, wonderers, travellers who represent plebeians.

Vico looks at other ancient stories and myths as showing conflicts between heroes, which lead them into an exile that may end with the return of the kings as in the return of the Greek kings after the Trojan War. Others show the struggles between heroes and plebeians, which refer to a rising power of the plebeians. Vico interprets the conflict between Odysseus when he returns home to Ithaca, and the 'Suitors' who have been abusing the hospitality of his family and trying to marry his wife, as such a conflict.

In 'Epitomes of Poetic History' (Vico 1984, 257–259), the story of Cadmus gives us the divine and heroic history as presented by the theological poets (particularly Homer). Cadmus was a Phoenician prince who appears in various myths and in the *Histories* of Herodotus, as the founder of Thebes and the inventor of the Greek alphabet. Vico refers to him as the divine age hero who killed the great serpent, which refers to the clearing of forests. The serpent can also be regarded as a dragon and Vico thinks the existence of dragon myths across cultures refers to some common early human experience in clearing dangerous snakes. Cadmus then sows the teeth of the serpent dragon in the ground, which Vico takes as a metaphor for the implements used in ploughing the land for agriculture. Armed men spring up from the dragon's teeth, which Vico takes as standing for the Heroes-Aristocrats. They fight the plebeians by forming orders or ranks, which are indicated by the furrows in which the dragon's teeth are sown, and which give stability to the first cities. Cadmus turns into a dragon himself at the will of the gods, which Vico claims stand for the aristocratic senates of the early cities, and the laws of Draco (that is the legendary seventh-century Athenian lawmaker famous for the harshness of his laws), and presumably, all the laws created by aristocratic rulers. Vico claims that the standard interpretation of this story as referring to the invention of letters is mistaken, as it a story of how laws hidden from the plebeians are created.

Vico suggests that Homer gives us the equivalent of the real meaning of the Cadmus myth in *The Iliad II*. In a passage finishing about line 100, Homer describes the divine origin of the royal sceptre carried by King Agamemnon, the symbol of his power. Vico then moves onto Achilles' shield, which is described by Homer at the end of the *Iliad* 18, in a passage starting about line 420. It is a long passage describing how the mother of the great Greek hero Achilles asks the god Vulcan to forge a protective shield for Achilles. The shield is cored with intricate pictures of wars and different aspects of life. Vico interprets the images described on the shield in line with his own theory of history, starting with cities where heroes are married, but in fact, there are two cities, which Vico interprets as the heroic-aristocratic/plebeian distinction. The images of the two cities portray the conflict between them and the heroic-aristocratic creation of religion and laws. Vico interprets other images on the shield as showing the growth of human arts through agriculture, urban architecture and dance.

In the 'Poetic Physics' section of *New Science*, Book II, Vico gives an example from Homer of how he thinks poetic metaphysics refers to the way that early humans saw nature. That is Proteus who appears in *The Odyssey* IV, from about line 555, and who is a shape-shifting humanoid. Vico thinks he is an expression of the early human experience of looking in water and seeing their own shifting reflection.

In a 'Corollary on Heroic Sentences', Vico argues that Greek and Roman poetry shows traces of the ways that in the age of theological poets every sensation cancels out the previous sensation, and all sentences are singular. Abstract, reflective, discursive and plural sentences belong to the age of philosophy at the end of the heroic-aristocratic age. In a 'Corollary on Heroic Descriptions', Vico argues that in the theological poets of the heroic-aristocratic age, primarily Homer, the senses are understood as grasping things, so that vision is a reaching out to grasp things, and so on. The Latin word for wisdom, sapienta, has a concrete origin in the senses, the tasting and savouring of something. The senses were most strong in the earliest age, something that divine providence gives to protect us, though it also appears to come from the weakness of intellect. Vico thinks there is clarity and grandeur of theological poetry, which comes from the greater strength of the senses and the weakness of reflection, related to the idea that poetry is more powerful when based on ignorance. Achilles has no later reaction or emotion after his extreme outburst on first losing his favourite slave girl, Briseis who had been a princess, to King Agamemnon. Menelaus shows no jealousy at the thought of Paris having intimate relations with his wife Helen, though Paris seducing Helen and eloping to Troy with her was the cause of the war between Greeks and Trojans.

According to Vico, in the Poetic Cosmography, the theological poets were building a map of the earth, heaven and hell, which becomes the basis for later reflection. A lot of what Vico says here refers to Virgil's *Aeneid* unfinished on Virgil's death in 19 BCE, which complicates his position since it comes from centuries after the heroic era. Virgil lived during the reign of the first Roman Emperor, Augustus, so Rome has passed through the first phase of the human world, in Vico's definition, which is a democratic republic that emerges from struggles between lower class plebeians and aristocratic patricians. It has passed into the second phase of the human world, which is a form of monarchy that represents the whole people and not just the aristocracy.

The places where the dead are buried are replaced as a focus by a sense that the afterlife is connected with the furrows made in the ground by ploughing. There is an account of a descent to the land of the dead is in the *Aeneid.* Vico refers to a sacrifice of Misenus. The Trojan Misenus had died sometime before Aeneas descended into Hades. Aeneas mourns the death of Misenus according to proper rituals before he can make the journey. Perhaps, Vico regards this as a poetic way of referring to the role of sacrifice in the earliest religions. Virgil descends after observing the correct rituals and is able to visit his father and learn about the future. Vico refers to Aeneas as a military and then political hero, his descent to the underworld seems to be connected with a transition between the two. His political mission is to go to Italy and prepare the way for the foundation of Rome, though Vico does not directly mention that.

Vico associates the cosmography of the underworld in Virgil with the boundaries established for Roman territory, so appears to regard Virgil as the creator of metaphors for the definition of the Roman state as an incorporator of peoples into its fixed, but growing boundaries. The clearly bounded world underground is the analogue of the political power of Rome over its clearly defined territory, suggesting the two go together. Vico briefly mentions journeys of Hercules and Theseus not the underworld presumably to establish the role of such journeys in the myths of Greece, but has little to say about a journey of Odysseus in Homer.

In the 'Poetic Geography' section of Book II, Vico constructs a history of ancient geography from his reading of sources. His chronology suggests that the ocean beyond the Straits of Gibraltar was not known to Homer, so the journey of Odysseus must be understood as taking place strictly within the Mediterranean. He particularly argues that the Lotus-Eaters episode in Homer's *Odyssey* took place within the Mediterranean.

It is in Book III, Discovery of the True Homer, that Vico is most obviously focused on a Homeric epic, though as we have seen Homer pervades the whole of the *New Science.* Poetic wisdom was the popular wisdom of Greece, first in theological and then heroic poets, in Vico's account. It is not very clear how Vico distinguishes between divine and heroic poets since he sometimes refers to Homer, his major source on the heroic age as divine. The best way to make sense of this maybe that Homeric epic contains many traces of the divine age, but that the divine poets proper are represented by Orpheus, a legendary maybe mythical figure, from early Greek history.

According to Vico, Homer conformed to popular feelings and customs of the time. Part of this is that the gods are shown to be godly through their physical strength, rather than a more spiritual understanding of divinity. For this reason, the human warrior Diomedes can harm the gods, Aphrodite and Ares, as shown in *The Iliad* V. The greatest Greek hero of the *Iliad*, Achilles and King Agamemnon, the chief of the Greek league insult each other, Achilles calling Agamemnon a dog in Book I. As Vico points out, *The Iliad* shows that Achilles, himself inclined to ethically very poor behaviour much of the time, has to pressure Agamemnon to behave well, with regard to releasing a female prisoner Chryseis in response to the diseases her father the priest Chryses inflicts on the Greeks. This is on the opening pages of the *Iliad* where Agamemnon behaves in an insulting and arrogant way towards Chryses despite his priestly power and associated link with the god Apollo. Even when Agamemnon gives up Chryseis, he demands the prisoner Briseis from Achilles, prolonging the crisis for the Greeks.

Odysseus is shown getting drunk, in *The Odyssey* VIII which is typical of how Homer shows warrior using alcohol consumption as a solution for a troubled mind, something that Vico says is unworthy of a wise man who should be using philosophy as a consolation. Homer's poetic comparisons use animals and 'other savage things', which may have been necessary for his poetry to be understood by the savage, nevertheless it is not the poetry of someone civilised by poetry. The same thought applies to the descriptions of violence in war. The instability of character of the gods and heroes also suggests a lack of philosophical civilisation. Homer's heroes switch suddenly between distress and calm, anger and tears in *The Iliad* XXIV.

Vico goes onto compare Dante with Homer, calling him 'the Tuscan Homer' bringing out Vico's interest in repetition as an aspect of literary history as well as general history.

Referring to Cola di Rienzo, a popular Roman leader in the Middle Ages. Vico describes him as sharing the unstable emotionalism of Homeric heroes, and therefore as a repetition of barbaric customs, though also transitional figures in the movement towards a human-democratic world, as opposed to the divine-heroic world of aristocratic barbarism. Evidence of the instability of character of the Homeric heroes is now offered by Vico with regard to an episode of the *Odyssey* in which Odysseus switches from troubled mood to laughter at a feast.

The story takes up a large part of *The Odyssey* VIII, where Odysseus has been released by the goddess Calypso and is seeking the help of a king on whose territory Odysseus arrived by sea. He is trying to complete his journey home after a period detained by the demi-goddess Calypso who is in love with him. More evidence of the barbaric instability of the Homeric heroes comes from an incident towards the ends of *The Iliad*, where King Priam of Troy visits the tent of Achilles, to ask for the body of his son Hector. Achilles receives him with respect and kindness, but suddenly becomes angry in *The Iliad* XXIV. Vico goes on to argue that the many stories Odysseus makes up in the *Odyssey* makes him unworthy of the attention of a philosopher. All of this suggests that Homer did not possess 'esoteric wisdom', knowledge of hidden and secret things, so should be regarded as poetic rather than philosophical, though containing knowledge which was later taken up by philosophers.

Vico notes that most cities of Ancient Greece claimed to be the birthplace of Homer, and claims were made of Greek colonies in Italy. There is no writer older than Homer Vico claims, referring to the first-century CE Jewish-Roman historian Josephus. This is certainly not true, but anyway enables Vico to develop the idea of Homer as a father of the Greek nation, which is true in the sense that Greek culture, language, religion and identity were very tied up with Homeric poetry. Vico now takes a radical leap and claims that there must have been different authors of the *Iliad* and the *Odyssey*.

The argument for different authors is based on the claim that in the *Odyssey*, that the farthest known land is referred to as territory close to Troy, though Troy is not mentioned at that point. Vico appears to be arguing that the two poems display different assumptions about places, peoples and territories. He also refers to Roman debates, via the philosopher and dramatist Lucius Annaeus Seneca, about whether the poems had the same author. The different cities of the ancient Greek world, which included colonies in western Anatolia and Southern Italy, claimed Homer, because they could all see idiom and dialect words of their own in the poems.

Vico assembles evidence from the poems of when they are written on the grounds of what time in Greek history certain kinds of things appeared. Games commanded by Achilles from the funeral of his friend Patroclus come from the Olympics past the barbaric age. Vico claims that the food of the Homeric characters, including the use of spit roasting and fishing, belongs to a later age than that of heroic barbarism. He also argues that the Homeric poems must have been written centuries after the Trojan War, because bans on marrying foreigners and on non-legitimate sons succeeding to kingdoms have ended. There are references to Egypt, Libya, Phoenicia, Italy and Sicily, which Vico argues can only refer to a time centuries after the Trojan War. The mixture of references to the world over centuries after heroic barbarism ended shows the poems were written by many people over these centuries.

Despite claiming, there was no one Homer, Vico continues to use phrases which sound as if they refer to a unique Homer, now arguing that he came from the people. Vico develops an argument about Homer's historical place, with reference to the Poetics. What Vico concludes is that the invention of new characters was very difficult after Homer, and the Homeric poems in the version, we know must have incorporated wisdom from the poets of a much later age than the barbarism represented by Homeric heroes. In these arguments, Vico to some degree picked up on an emerging folkish nationalism in which the antiquity of the nation is associated with a poetry supposed to come from the people of antiquity. He did so at a very early stage, since this kind of enthusiasm did not become widespread until much later in the eighteenth century. The same applies to the idea of a collective composition of Homeric poetry, which was put forward by Friedrich August Wolf in his 1795 *Prolegomena to Homer* (1985). No one now doubts that Homeric epic emerges from a long collective development, though many still think that there was a Homer figure revising and writing down the tradition.

In Vico's account, Homeric epic includes imaginative universals, poetic presentation of typical characteristics of different human types, which are necessary to appeal to the uneducated mind and then become firmly embedded in a culture so that everyone knows them. So Homer's portrait of Achilles dominates Greek ideas of heroic courage, with his quick temper, strictness, anger, single mindedness, violence and assumption that might is right. Odysseus is given all the feelings and customs of heroic wisdom.

Humans naturally preserve the memories of the laws and institutions, which bind them to the societies in which they live. History is a simple statement of truth so must have come before poetry, which is an imitation. However, the first poets must have come before the vulgar historians that is the historians living in the human age after aristocratic hero-barbarism. The first poems were true narratives. However, they seemed so crude that the original meanings were later changed so that they came to seem fantastic. It is this that Homer used as the starting point for his poetry.

Vico supports his argument with regard to Aristotle's *Rhetoric* (II.21, 1395b, 1–1) 'Educated men lay down broad general principles; uneducated men argue from common knowledge and draw obvious conclusions. We must not, therefore, start from any and every accepted opinion, but only from those we have defined—those accepted by our judges or by those whose authority they recognise' (Aristotle 1984b, 2224). This is why Homeric poetry contains the imaginative universals like the characters of Achilles and Odysseus. Vico does not base his analyses on an explication of Aristotle's *Rhetoric*, but at a few points, like this, we can see the importance of it for Vico coming into the open.

For Vico, that limited thinking that uses imagination, but is restricted to the senses makes it necessary to represent the divine as large, which we can see in the Christian art of the 'returned barbarian times' (that is the early Middle Ages). We can see it in the poetry of Dante, which is analogous to that of poetry, as it mixes divine themes with the representations of crowds of people, and in the whole transition in France and Italy from the repeated barbarism to the repeated human age, which includes philosophical reflection. The barbarian period, and the ways it lasts into the human period, must use imagination, which is rooted in the body and is the same as memory.

Memory has been known as the mother of the muses (poetic wisdom), because it has three parts: remembering things, imagination in altering or imitating those things and invention when it gives those things a new turn or puts them into proper order. Poetry forms the first history of nations, but can only refer to the particulars and the senses, as opposed to metaphysics-philosophy, which is concerned with universals and abstraction. The heroic-barbaric language was based on similes, images and comparisons, because humans did not have the idea of species grouping individuals and genera grouping species. All early humans speak in heroic verse, because of the lack of abstractions.

All ancient secular histories begin in fables like those of Homer. All barbarous peoples record the history of their beginning in verse; the examples given by Vico are those of ancient Germans and American Indians. Vico thinks of the heroic verse as musical as well as literary and refers to a passage from *the Odyssey* XI as confirmation.

In Vico's interpretation, Homer is the Greek people, in his youth 'he' (the Greek people) composed a poem devoted to rage (*the Iliad*) and in his maturity, he composed a poem devoted to prudence (*the Odyssey*). Philosophical wisdom was placed into it by the time it was written as we know it in the seventh-century BCE. In general, philosophical wisdom emerges from reflection on poetic wisdom, a process which is compressed in the late modifications of Homer. The settings of the two Homeric poems show a movement from north-eastern to south-western Greece. He stands for all the wondering singing poets of Greece.

In Book V, The Course of Nations, Vico sets up the pattern of history followed by all nations with reference to the main themes of the preceding books: Book I, principles of the science of the history of nations; Book II, origins of religious (divine) and political (human) institutions; Book III, the Homeric epics contain the natural law of the peoples of Greece, and the Twelve Tables of Roman Law contain the natural law of the peoples of Latin speaking Italy. This course of history depends on a pattern of divine followed by heroic followed by human being which can be found in all the basic institutions of civil communities.

There are three kinds of written character in human history. The first were hieroglyphs, which were imaginative universals (Granatella 2015) following from the tendency of the mind to take pleasure in uniformity. In the absence of logical abstraction, uniformity was achieved by logical abstraction. The universals were reduced to standing for that universal, so that Jove stood for the auspices and so on. The second kind of characters were heroic characters who stood in for universals, so that Achilles stood for all deeds of warriors, and Odysseus stood for all the tricks of clever people. These were imaginative genera that became intelligible genera as the human mind learned to think of abstract forms and properties separate from individuals. The intelligible genera allowed for the emergence of philosophy.

There are three kinds of jurisprudence, like the three kinds of characters corresponding to the three main stages of human history. The first kind of jurisprudence is mystic theology, which is the understanding of the auspices, of the ways of inferring the will of the gods. That was the origin of the art of interpretation. The second kind of jurisprudence was the heroic jurisprudence, which was care in the use of words. Odysseus was the example of a hero who could play with the careful and apparently correct use of words that is he was a subtle liar.

In the barbarian heroic periods of history, duels are a part of the divine judgement. Vico also suggests a comparison between ancient barbarism and medieval Europe in which armed combat was regarded as one way of settling legal disputes. Aristocrats continued to fight duels to settle private disputes in Vico's time and later. Vico refers to duels setting private wrongs and not covered by civil laws in the early commonwealths. Vico says we can see traces of the early use of duels in accounts of war that started with personal conflict. One example he gives is of Menelaus and Paris fighting in an early passage of *The Iliad*. The second example is from early Roman history, with regard to war between Romans and Albans, settled by combat between three brother heroes from each side, Horatii and Curiatii. These ideas linger on in the assumption that war is a form of judgement between nations, which comes from the innate concept of providence, that is God's will operating in an indirect way. This suggests Vico believed duelling could bring justice, at least between nations, or he was making an oblique criticism of the idea of wars as bringing justice by equating it with barbarian beliefs, or most likely he contrasted ideas of justice from barbarian times with the ideas of the more human world. The basic properties of the aristocratic commonwealth are the guarding of the confines and the guarding of the institutions. The guarding of the confines refers to boundaries' first set-up to prevent animal like promiscuity between the sexes, and so were established between family homes. These became the starting point for boundaries between tribes, peoples and nations. Vico suggests that the political boundaries between states have their origin in the early boundaries between families. Homer refers to this in *The Odyssey* IX, in the story of the Cyclops giants. That is the one-eyed giant Polyphemus who tries to eat Odysseus and his companions. They were on the margins of savagery and lived in their caves with their wives and children in isolation from each other, killing any visitors.

Children by slaves, former slaves and foreigners were excluded as far as possible from inheritance rights, along with all female relatives and relatives by female connection, compared with sons by legitimate marriage, or the relatives closest to such a status; so presumably sons by a brother were preferred to sons by a sister and so on. This retained the powers of the Cyclops, the near savages in Homer, over their families a major point in the various ways that Vico uses Homer as a key to history, while also reflecting on the poetic nature of history itself as memory and imagination are always at play.

Conclusion

The present chapter elaborates on the following themes in Aristotle and Vico which are necessary to a philosophical grasp of the novel: episodic nature of the novel, comprehensiveness, use of tropes, use of informal deductive reasoning, relation to public rhetoric, tension between heroic-divine and plebeian-worldly, competing linguistic registers, competing notions of law and morality, historical embedding, universals as imaginative and universals as abstract, character conflict, archetype and psychology, national particularism and universalism, narrative prose and imaginative poetry. What overshadows all of this is the tensions between mythical archetype in literature and the language of the modern city or nation in its linguistic variety and human activity. The Viconian analysis of Homeric epic (Haddock 1979) places these tensions within *The Iliad* and *The Odyssey*, so finding what is novelistic within them, building on the ways that Aristotle takes up Homer in the *Poetics* and the *Rhetoric*. The *New Science* together with the *Poetics* and the *Rhetoric* are the essential foundations of the philosophy of the novel. The discussion of examples from Aristotle and Vico shows how thye put literature at the centre of their philosophy, literature of an epic kind anticipating the novel. Vico's more elaborate commentary on Homer indicates that he belongs to a world where the novel had already appeared as a growing genre bringing imaginative instability into the heart of long narrative.

References

Aristotle. 1984a. *The Complete Works of Aristotle, Volume I*, ed. Jonathan Barnes. Princeton, NJ: Princeton University Press.

Aristotle. 1984b. *The Complete Works of Aristotle, Volume II*, ed. Jonathan Barnes. Princeton, NJ: Princeton University Press.

Beiser, Frederick C. 2009. *Diotima's Children: German Aesthetic Rationalism from Leibniz to Lessing*. Oxford: Oxford University Press.

Granatella, Mariagrazia. 2015. Imaginative Universals and Human Cognition in the *New Science* of Giambattista Vico. *Culture and Psychology* XXI (2): 185–206.

Haddock, B.A. 1979. Vico's "Discovery of the True Homer": A Case-Study in Historical Reconstruction. *Journal of the History of Ideas* XXXX (4); 583–602.

Shaftesbury, Earl of, Anthony Ashley Cooper. 2000. *Characteristics of Men, Manners, Opinions, Times*, ed. Lawrence E. Klein. Cambridge: Cambridge University Press.

Smith, Adam. 1983. *Lectures on Rhetoric and Belles Lettres*, ed. J.C. Bryce. Oxford: Oxford University Press.

Vico, Giambattista. 1984. *The New Science*, trans. Thomas Goddard Bergin and Max Harold Fisch. Ithaca, NY: Cornell University Press.

Wolf, Friedrich August. 1985. *Prolegomena to Homer, 1795*, trans. Anthony Grafton. Princeton, NJ: Princeton University Press.

3

Idealism and Romanticism

Eighteenth-Century Literary Aesthetics

There is not much philosophy of the novel before the very end of the eighteenth century, certainly none in terms of major philosophical texts with any kind of discussion of the novel as a genre or even with regard to individual examples. There is a rich history of aesthetic philosophy and related work on the arts in the eighteenth century, but the phenomenon of the 'rise of the novel', as it is referred to in Ian Watt's book (1972), is absent until the end of the century. We saw this in the last chapter with regard to Giambattista Vico. Going back to his predecessor (as well as possible influence and possible acquaintance) Shaftesbury (Anthony Ashley Cooper, Third Earl of Shaftesbury), his 1711 *Characteristics of Men, Manners, Opinions, Times*, contains no more than one reference to *Don Quixote*, referred to in these dismissive terms:

> Had I been a Spanish Cervantes and, with success equal to that comic author, had destroyed the reigning tastes of Gothic or Moorish chivalry, I could afterwards contentedly have seen my burlesque work itself despised and set aside, when it had wrought its intended effect and

© The Author(s) 2018
B. Stocker, *Philosophy of the Novel*,
https://doi.org/10.1007/978-3-319-65891-9_3

destroyed those giants and monsters of the brain against which it was originally designed. (Shaftesbury 1999, 445)

Shaftesbury was certainly not suggesting that *Don Quixote* was a particularly bad novel, and he hardly expresses a view of the genre at all. It just seems obvious to him that the great foundational novel of the European and western tradition (or at the very least, a major contribution to these traditions) was characterised by the supposed emptiness and lowness of the chivalric literature parodied which covered some lasting contributions to literature, at least in the cases of Wolfram von Eschenbach, Chrétien de Troyes, the Pearl Poet, Thomas Malory, Torquato Tasso, Ludovico Ariosto and Edmund Spenser. All of this is classified as Gothic and Moorish literature, so two branches of medieval crudity taken as self-evidently inferior to the Graeco-Roman classics.

Shaftesbury is not in general concerned with a systematic approach to literary genres or indeed a very systematic kind of philosophy in any way. His mixture of impressions and a general orientation towards Platonic idealism (as in believing there are pure forms of things existing separate from the perceptible things) received a damning response from Adam Smith in Lecture 11 of his *Lectures on Rhetoric and **Belles Lettres*** (1983, 56–59). For Smith, Shaftesbury stands as an example of lack of clarity in style and weak grasp of abstract ideas, so that he only follows subjective preferences. Smith was a persistent follower of system, combining systems of ideas with a systematic understanding of the history within which they appear. This can be seen for political economy in *Wealth of Nations*, ethics in *The Theory of Moral Sentiments*, law in *Lectures on Jurisprudence* and literature in *Lectures on Rhetoric*. From Smith's point of view, Shaftesbury may have seemed like a dilettante writing in a conversational way, dwelling on occasions and not integrated into a system. However, his writing both contains significant ideas about aesthetics and presents taste developed through a conversational style. The writing connects with the emergence of the novel, as a form less rule governed than epic and less unified in a single voice. The development of conversational style in a philosophical treatise is itself part of the emergence of the novel or is at less part of a broad process covering the novel and the philosophical treatise.

The understanding of the novel is also prepared by Smith's own understanding of the complexity of human communication in societies taken as dynamic wholes. The possibilities of commerce in *Wealth of Nations*, ethical feeling in *Theory of Moral Sentiments* and of common justice in *Lectures on Jurisprudence* as well as common literary tastes in *Lectures on Rhetoric* prepare the way for appreciation of the novel. Though Smith pays some appreciative attention to Jonathan Swift's *Gulliver's Travels*, so to the merits of prose narrative as a literary form, the evidence from the Scottish Enlightenment and elsewhere is that the novel was not a genre regarded as the equal of those containing the great classic works of literature.

Despite the efforts of Shaftesbury, Frances Hutcheson, Edmund Burke, David Hume and Smith in developing thought on literary topics in eighteenth-century Britain, no work emerged that put the novel at the centre as a form. Though the concepts of idea, impression, pleasure, pain, sympathy, passion, history, literary history, history of style, national variations in style, social cooperation, social self-organisation and civility all supply elements that can be taken up in the philosophy of the novel, in accounting for its integration of extreme diversity in a language close to everyday life, there is no major advance on Shaftesbury in discussing the novel as a genre. It looks like German Idealism was necessary for full philosophy of the novel to appear. If it was not necessary, it is still a matter of fact that German Idealism did lead to the first major philosophical work on the novel as a focus. German Idealism drew on the empiricism of the British thinkers just mentioned, along with the products of French thought on history, society and consciousness, with the addition eighteenth-century German writing on philosophy and aesthetics. Against this background, Immanuel Kant made the first major contribution to German Idealism with the first edition of the *Critique of Pure Reason* in 1781. The other obvious peaks of early German Idealism are Kant's 1788 *Critique of Practical Reason* and Fichte's 1794 *Science of Knowledge*. Kant's 1790 *Critique of the Power of Judgement* had a less obvious influence on early philosophy of the novel, though the first half is Kant's main contribution to aesthetics. Going back a bit further, G.W.F. Lessing's *Laocoon* of 1766 is a major part of the background to the aesthetics of the novel, of a less purely philosophical kind as are Friedrich Schiller's 1794 *Letters on the Aesthetic Education of Man*. The more strictly philosophical work goes back to Alexander Baumgarten's *Reflections on Poetry* of 1735 and the *Aesthetica* of 1750. This line can be taken back to G.W.F. Leibniz through Christian Wolff. Leibniz was of course a major critic of Locke, but from the point of view of a shared interest in combining diversity and privacy of perception with an integrated universe working according to natural laws. The German Romantics, who were concerned with using Idealist philosophy to discuss the form of the novel, were admirers of Laurence Sterne's 1759 novel *The Life and Opinions of Tristram Shandy, Gentleman*, which engages with some aspects of Locke's theory of ideas. Shaftesbury's aesthetic cannot recognise the kind of unity and diversity that constitutes the novel as a fully developed genre, which can be taken as the novel since *Don Quixote*. The unity of different levels of discourse and different levels of reality, taken up through frequently reflection on the reality of what is written exceeds a sensationalist perceptual approach to the aesthetic object. Shaftesbury can only think of form as a container rather than as part of the energy of an aesthetic object concerned with its own representational status and its own unity as prime themes. The Baumgarten approach cannot get beyond another kind of thin form, though it allows for metaphysics as part of the form of objects. The unity of diverse perceptions that Baumgarten is concerned with does not allow for the ways in literature might combine endless diverse perception in a form that both create narrative unity and fragmentation as the unity and reality of the literary form becomes an issue within literary form. Having completed a circle of some kind, or filled out a web of connecting influences, between German Romanticism and English Empiricism, it is time to enter into a discussion the Romantic philosophy of the novel.

Romantic Philosophy of the Novel

Work in the Romantic philosophy of the novel comes from a very limited period in the late 1790s, particularly associated with 1798 and 1799 when a group of philosophers and writers in Jena collaborated on the production of the journal *Athenäum*. We can go back to Friedrich Schlegel's *Critical Fragments* of 1797, where we can see the central claims of Romantic philosophy of the novel emerging. These fragments can be found in their entirety in *Philosophical Fragments* (Schlegel 1991) along with 'Athenäum Fragments' and excerpted along with 'On Comprehensibility', 'Athenäum Fragments', 'On Incomprehensibility', 'On Goethe's *Miester*', 'Ideas' and 'Letter about the Novel' in Wheeler's anthology, *German Aesthetic and Literary Criticism: The Romantic Ironists and Goethe* (Wheeler 1984). Paraphrase is used here to communicate Schlegel's philosophy, since his aphoristic and fragmentary writing style, across a number of texts, does not lend itself to quotation or straightforward summary. The novel is a secularisation of the search for heaven on earth and is the contemporary equivalent of Socratic dialogue in which sense escapes from empty formalism. Philosophy should be in a dialogue, not a system, as dialogue it is the home of irony. Rhetoric contains bits of irony but poetry is on the same level as philosophy, that is it is completely ironic. Irony is transcendental buffoonery, the mood which is infinite, rising above all limitations, including its own art. Irony is the form of paradox.

Plato's Eros (in the *Symposium*) is the stage of negative feeling, that is the love of what is not possessed, the wanting of what can never be had. The best novels are often encyclopaedias or compendia of the spiritual life of a brilliant individual, great literature can be novelistic in this sense even if it does not belong to the genre of the novel. Every cultivated person contains a novel. Socratic irony is involuntary and deliberate concealment; it unifies the playful and serious, the hidden and the open, life and science, instinct and consciousness. In Socratic irony, there is the unavoidable conflict of the absolute and the relative, the impossibility and necessity of absolute communication, self-transcending freedom and the laws of necessity. It is continuous self-parody. The individual idea becomes whole through concentration on a single point. Poetry and philosophy should be one, so that poetry can be criticism of poetry, as real philosophical criticism must be poetry.

The 'Athenäum Fragments' (1798) from fragment 260 to fragment 451 are particularly significant in developing a philosophy of the novel. Schlegel refers to self-cultivation as both becoming human and becoming God, expressing the Idealist-Romantic conception of self-perfection, the infinite growth of the individual, and humanity as more than just a collection of individual humans. Poetry expresses a human tendency towards the higher and the mystic. Knowledge is infinite which means that the more we know the more we realise we are ignorant since we can never have infinite knowledge. Schlegel prefers the philosophy of Spinoza to the philosophy of Leibniz, because while Leibniz thought of the universe as composed of an infinity of different points of perception; Spinoza thought of the universe as essentially one. Breaking into the paraphrase of Schlegel, though Lebniz is more obviously important as the source of German Idealism and Romanticism, Baruch Spinoza's unification of perceptions in a world of one substance exercised its own influence as a model for unifying the diversity within consciousness, nature and literary work. Friedrich Heinrich Jacobi's letters to Moses Mendelssohn during the 1780s, addressing Spinoza had a considerable influence on Idealist and Romantic thinking.

Returning to the paraphrase of Schlegel, he suggests that writers should write for themselves and hope that they can create their own audience. Philosophy is the union of two conflicting forces: poetry and practice. Where philosophy disintegrates the result is mythology (poetry without practice) or life (practice without poetry). The naïve plays with the contradictions between theory and practice. The grotesque plays with different combinations of form and matter; it loves the illusion of the random and the strange in a flirtation with infinite arbitrariness. Humour refers to being and nonbeing; the essence of humour is reflection. The spirit of an object is in its essential individuality not in what it has in common with other objects. Ancient art created artistic forms guided by mythology. Ancient art conceived of its forms in the highest and noblest sense and joined the highest degree of beauty possible that did not destroy the form.

The ideal of a work should have the same life as a real person. The work should be an interaction of characters in which none is just a means for the others. We have talents, but we can only be a genius, not have genius. Genius is a system of talents. An idea is the interchange of two conflicting thoughts. In an idea, the concept is perfected as irony in the absolute synthesis of absolute. The ideal is both fact and idea. A mind containing fullness and maturity contains a plurality of minds and a system of persons, so that it can move arbitrarily between spheres, forgetting parts of one's being in giving one's soul to another part. Man has an incomprehensible spiritual duality, expressed in the ancient distinction between men and their gods. Plato combines all the types of Greek prose, with the mimetic type as the basis of the rest. The mimesis often appears next to the dithyrambic (what Nietzsche later calls the Apolline and the Dionysian).

Wit is the principle of universal philosophy. Philosophy is the spirit of universality, the science of all uniting and dividing sciences: a logical chemistry. Scientific discoveries are witticisms, because their origin is contingent, there is unifying force in their thought, their expression is baroque (systematic but incomplete). This material wit has infinite value. In content, they are more than poetic wit which is unsatisfied. Philosophy has brilliant ideas but does not have the steady progress which relies on correct method. There is no unifying art and science so far, only dialects of philosophy. Philosophy lacks a general syntax. The highest value is the communal education of humanity as a whole. Transcendental poetry which has an essence between the ideal and the real. It includes satire, elegy and idyll. Like transcendental philosophy, it should refer to the conditions of its own production as well as what is produced. Such poetry should describe itself. So that it is both poetry and the poetry of poetry. For the classical point of view, aesthetics is the struggle between art and raw beauty, absolute opposites, resolved in the harmony of artistic and natural poetry.

A philosophy of poetry (romantic) would start with the proposition 'I = I' (referring to Fichte's *Science of Knowledge*) and show that beauty is distinct from truth and morality and has equal rights. It would consider the parts of poetry and the distinction between poetry and philosophy in order to reach the unity of poetry and the unity of poetry with philosophy. It would rest on a philosophy of the novel, beginning with Plato's political theory. Philosophy brings nothing new to experience, but through philosophy, experience becomes knowledge and takes on a new form. Individuality, variety, universality, system, parody of the letter and irony of the spirit all unite in Shakespeare. Fragments are the real form of universal philosophy, a resistance to spiritual slowness and a stimulation to knowledge. Fichte's philosophy is the philosophy of philosophy, the philosophy of Kant's philosophy, philosophy reflecting on its own production. A cultivated work has limits but is limitless within its limits; it is consistent but is raised above itself. There is intellectual intuition in friendship, where we are aware of what is most holy in the other's heart. This is the conviviality and sociality which belongs to society and poetry.

In the 'Athenäum Fragments', Schlegel develops a philosophical way of looking at literature. He refers to the genres which literature is divided into, the need to be precise and have many genres, and the tendency of genres to mix. He suggests looking at Bible just as a book rather than as a religious text, which suggests that the highest activity for Schlegel is literature itself. Philosophy is presented as what should always be a philosophy of itself, a form of self-reflection, which is when philosophy becomes poetry. Schlegel refers to Ancient Literature, particularly Homer's epics as 'naïve' or 'classical'. It is naïve because it is more natural and instinctive than modern literature. However, it can never be purely naïve, natural or instinctive. There is always reflection and irony in literature. There is no literature which is just the product of the use of language with no intentions behind it. Though what Schlegel suggests for 'naïve' literature in Homer is that the intention may be of nature itself rather than in the author of the literature. Schlegel emphasises contradictions in literature and philosophy. The mind must have both a system and a non-system, therefore philosophy is always caught in the contradiction between a system which forces everything into a framework that is still a non-system in which nothing is organised or explained. Schlegel emphasises 'wit' which he regards as the combination of opposing ideas as an essential part of literature and philosophy, which come tighter in the coincide of philosophical reflection and poetry. Criticism of literature and of philosophy is not just a reaction to literature and philosophy; it is part of philosophy and literature. This is because both philosophy and literature exist in the possibility of their own self-reflection and self-criticism. They both come from the mind's capacity for self-reflection and self-criticism. Romantic poetry is modern poetry, and it is the opposite of classical or naïve poetry. Romantic poetry is the fusion and mixture of all genres of writing: philosophy and poetry rhetoric; inspiration and criticism; poetry and prose; and nature and society. This is part of sociability and communication between individuals in the dialogue which is social communication, poetry and philosophy.

Like Friedrich Schlegel, Novalis (the pen name of Friedrich von Hardenberg) was deeply interested in the philosophy of Immanuel Kant and J.G. Fichte. He was not so much concerned with the novel as a form, but given he was a novelist himself and the overlap between his ideas and those of Schlegel, he deserves to receive some attention in the context of the philosophy of the novel. Fichte's philosophy is particularly relevant with the role that Fichte gave to absolute subjectivity in the 1790s (Fichte 1982), though not in his later philosophical development. Fichte's philosophy developed from an absolute 'I' as the subject of all possible knowledge and of the world that we know. All experience and all thought for Fichte refer to the subjective ego experiencing itself and its own negation of itself. Novalis took this in the direction of artistic and poetic creativity, which he saw as interconnected with the creativity of philosophy. Novalis thought that both philosophical and poetic creativity contain unlimited reflection self-reflection, as expounded in 'Miscellaneous Observations', 'Logological Fragments I', 'Logological Fragments II', 'Monologue' and 'On Goethe' (in Novalis 1997), along with 'Dialogues' and 'Studies in the Visual Arts' (in Wheeler 1984).

In Novalis' account, for Fichte words are an unreliable means for communicating spirit. He thought it is necessary to decode a symbolism in language, which begins with hieroglyphics before the emergence of alphabetic language. The symbolism is symbolism of a spirit world. Perception of the material world is illusory. We live in the world as the world grasped by our mind, which must be the world of spirit as mind is spirit.

For Schlegel, the mind is always active and always creating. Literature and other arts only appear to be mimesis of reality. In reality, they are always the free creation of the mind and show the deep reality of the world as spirit. In painting, the painter does not copy something as a painting. The painting comes from the activity of the mind in creating images. Novalis has a theory of 'aesthetic autonomy'. That is, aesthetics has a value and meaning of its own which does not refer to values and meanings outside art. Art is not absolutely autonomous for Novalis, since it is rooted in the activity of the mind. Aesthetics gives examples of the reflective autonomy of the mind.

Novalis aims for a synthesis of the intuitive/dynamic and the discursive/atomistic. The intuitive refers to perception, and the dynamic refers to inner life. The discursive refers to concepts, and the atomistic refers to the materiality of the world. Here Novalis is taking and developing ideas from Kant. Kant thought judgements of the mind unify the intuitions of perception and the concepts of understanding. This was a way of unifying the world of the ideal (ethics and free will) with the material world. Novalis thinks this is the essence of poetry and philosophy. Primitive philosophy comes from the material mechanical discursive world; primitive poetry comes from the intuitive dynamic world. At first, they are both crude and are crudely opposed to each other. The opposites are unified by the poet who realises that the division is a division of being within the individual self.

In some poetic works, we experience a conversation inspired by a higher being, a pure form of communication. This is the communication of the self with itself. The self experiences itself normally through the not-self (as Fichte suggests). The not-self is where the self negates itself in experiencing things other than itself. The necessity of the not-self gives rise to the illusion of a material world outside the ideal world of the subjective self. The higher kind of poetry has a necessity in it in which we become aware of the self as self before the not-self.

Philosophy is the poem of the understanding. Novalis here refers to Kant's idea of the understanding which is of a power for applying general concepts. Kant thinks that experience and knowledge come from combining understanding with imagination. In Kant, 'imagination' refers to the power to produce intuitions of perception. This is why Novalis refers to philosophy as the poetry which joins understanding with imagination. Poetry requires philosophy to be complete, and thinking requires poetry to be complete.

The naïve according to Schiller's distinction between naïve and sentimental, taken up by Friedrich Schlegel and other Jena Romantic Ironists, shows the role played by eighteenth-century literary aesthetics in developing ideas necessary for the appreciation of the novel, which come out of classicism at the same time as Idealism and Romanticism are formed (Sweet 1999). For Schlegel et al., the naïve classical epic is contrasted with the sentimental modern novel. That novel is traced back to the Platonic dialogue. The structure of the novel is treated as irony, taking Cervantes' *Don Quixote* as a model, and is traced back to Socratic irony. The elevation of the novel in the Jena Romantics (and Schelling) was criticised by Hegel, who condemned the Romantic Ironists in general. However, in Hegel, the work of the Romantic Ironists and the way he responded to that work are a central issue for his literary aesthetics.

Critical Fragments 85: 'Every honest author writes for nobody or everybody' (Schlegel 1991: 10; Wheeler 1984: 42). Schlegel's comments on Homer anticipate a Hegelian line of argument about the impossibility of a purely natural consciousness, following on himself from Fichte's argument in *The Science of Knowledge* (Fichte 1982), about negation, the absolute and circularity as conditions for all positing. Nietzsche follows in the wake of this Idealist and Romantic philosophy, without acknowledging it, just as Hegel failed to acknowledge what he owned to Fichte and the Jena Romantics.

The Jena Romantics referred themselves to the Fichtean reading of Kant's philosophy, establishing a Kantian aesthetics distinct from the aesthetic Kant established in the *Critique of the Power of Judgement* (Kant 2000). The Jena Romantic movement itself did not last long, largely associated as it is with their contributions to the *Athenäum* between 1798 and 1800. Its tendency in critical writing and in their own novels towards a restless multiplication of relative forms in the search for the absolute was quickly criticised by Hegel as a 'bad infinite'. Kierkegaard added to this in his *Concept of Irony* (Kierkegaard 1989), and even in the twentieth century, Carl Schmitt had an important critical examination at the political aspects in *Political Romanticism* (Schmitt 1986). The result of this examination is to observe that Romantic Irony tends to evolve into an interest in an eternal order in literature taking priority over ironic subjectivity, while the political side moves from individualistic republicanism to traditionalist conservatism. That Hegel, Kierkegaard and Schmitt thought it necessary and important to make critical examinations also shows that Romantic Irony was itself part of the constitution of their own thought, and they were therefore obliged to find a way of distinguishing their work from it. The Jena Romantics found it necessary to resort to religious and political conservatism over time in order to escape from the self-undermining play of Irony.

Hegel's Critique of Romantic Philosophy of the Novel

For Hegel, the novel is a decadent form of the epic. Even in Cervantes, the novel is a mere play of subjective points of view, theorised in the Romantic Irony of Friedrich Schlegel and other Jena Romantics. The novel is not discussed in any kind of sustained way. Cervantes, Sterne and Goethe feature briefly in a negative comparison with epic. Epic itself exists in its most pure form in antiquity, particularly Greek antiquity. Hegel's aesthetics, and philosophy of history, which permeates his philosophy as a whole, assumes a Greek world in which there is no distinction between human, divine and natural law. Law is accepted as what is given by all three sources, with no sense of conflict between inner self and external law. The presumption is that in Greek antiquity, no distinction was felt or articulated between individual conscience and external law. The harmony of conscience and law is exemplified in Homeric epic. Greek antiquity has a history in which individuals come to question given law. This is more from the position of conflict between different levels of law rather than an emergence of distinctively individual conscience.

Tragedy deals with conflict, and for Hegel, it is the tragic awareness of conflict between different codes which exemplifies this movement. He selects *Antigone* as the dissolving moment of Greek simplicity. The conflict between a sister's desire to follow divine law and bury her brother and a king's desire to impose civic law and forbid his burial marks the transition from Greek to Roman antiquity according to Hegel. Roman antiquity is marked by law: law and legal concepts have an autonomy in the Roman world, they did not have in the Greek world. The Roman world produced a great epic, Virgil's *Aeneid*, but the pure epic form of Homer has already been shaken. In the Roman era, the Christian world emerges. That is marked by an aesthetic transformation from Classical to Romantic.

For Hegel, Romantic refers to a separation between the world of the senses and the ideal world. Christianity establishes that there is another world and a single transcendent God. Therefore in the Christian era, art cannot show the world of the natural senses as beautiful in itself. The origin of beauty in spirit, rising above natural materiality, is made explicit. Art is Romantic because it now refers to a beauty in the absolute, so that the artwork itself contains the tension between immediacy and the absolute. It is the reconciliation of those opposites which is beauty. That was always the case implicitly: it can only become explicit in Christian Romanticism. Dante's *Divine Comedy* is a Romantic epic. It is epic because Dante presents a coherent objective world in which everything is presented through the naturals senses. It is Romantic because the beautiful and the ideal are shown to be in another world, although presented with the immediacy of Homeric epic. Dante's epic cannot show an immediate union of the ideal and the natural, and that is impossible in the Romantic era. It does, however, show a mediated unity in which the natural, human and divine worlds belong to a common absolute and objective structure. That is a peak from which narrative declines.

Don Quixote, taken as the starting point of the novel as a form, uses an irony which refers to the absence of the ideal from the immediate world. There is no absolute structure in the world of Cervantes, just a play of subjective points of view. The history of the novel is a disintegration of Romanticism into Irony. Hegel is particularly targeting Friedrich Schegel, Novalis and the rest of the Jena Romantics. He takes Schlegel as the leading representative. For Hegel, aesthetic Irony is advocating a bad infinite. In Hegel, the bad infinite is the infinite which only negates the finite. Infinity, as the good or positive infinite, must refer to the absolute and the negation of the finite as the making explicit of the infinite within the finite, the absolute within the particular. The bad infinite in philosophy and religion leads us into mystification and irrational subjectivity, which both require an abandonment of the proper philosophical and religious concept of the absolute or God. The incapacity of the novel to deal with the absolute and present an objective structure is a sign of the decline of the aesthetic in relation to philosophy and religion. The essential work of the aesthetic in presenting the absolute through sensory beauty has come to an end as religious and philosophical concepts of the absolute are developed after Kant, and particularly in Hegel's own philosophy.

Hegel's all encompassing *Aesthetics: Lectures on Fine Art* (Hegel 1975), in its all comprehending scope has a notable gap. The novel is mentioned but is not the object of a sustained constitution of its object, as is the case for all the other branches of literature/poetry, and of fine art in general. What makes this all the more strange is that Hegel was both preceded and followed, by work on the philosophy of the novel, in terms similar to those of his own philosophy. Friedrich Schlegel, and other Jena Romantics, during the 1790s in which they were writing interconnected work, had drawn on Kant and Fichte in order to establish a philosophical poetics, including a significant role for the novel. Just under a century later, Lukács was able to construct a philosophy of the novel in terms which are Hegelian and which are rooted in the *Aesthetics*, in *The Theory of the Novel* (Lukács 1971b). Although this is not made explicit in the main body of the text, Lukács discusses the relations in the 1962 Preface (Lukács 1971b, 15–19). Hegel mentions various novels. However, this does not build up into a philosophy of the novel. There is a philosophical exposition of the concept of the epic, but only scattered remarks on examples of novels. The novel appears as a limit term, where the aesthetic is dissolving as it gives way to something higher or returns to the indeterminacy from which it came. Schlegel and the other Jena Romantics appear with regard to their literary and critical works, but only in order to expose and attack the concept of Irony to which they are referring. 'Irony' is often used to label them as Romantic Ironists, and their view of irony is essential to their conception of the novel.

Friedrich Schlegel is taken by Hegel as the most significant representative of the Romantic Ironists and of what is worst about them. The marginalisation of the novel and the criticisms of Irony emerge in a distancing from Schlegel which is fundamental to Hegel's aesthetics and his whole philosophy, particularly with regard to the infinite.

The Difference Between Schlegel and Hegel

There is much here that is close to Hegel's philosophy, which makes it particularly necessary to distinguish what is 'Hegelian' and what is 'non-Hegelian'. The closeness to Hegel evidently stimulated his condemnation in the need to achieve separation and maybe to cover up philosophical debts. Before examining Hegel's more specific comments on Schlegel, irony and the novel, an examination of the program set out in the Introduction to the *Aesthetics* (1975), explained through paraphrase, will help show why Hegel had to be philosophically distanced from his near name sake.

Art is often suspected of being frivolous, of being removed from the serious goals of life in duty and morality, so that it may even weaken character in this view by indulging pleasure as a goal in itself. Even if art is considered an object of philosophical reflection, it is regarded as not worthy of scientific treatment because it seems to only belong to the senses and imagination. It seems impossible to bring art under science, because it seems inexhaustible in its invention of products and unconstrained by law. Science is concerned with necessity, so that while art can make pure concepts more entertaining if we look at art from a pure scientific point of view, what is specific to art will disappear. Art refers to what is beyond the immediacy of feeling and external objects. It is only substance with being in and for itself that is real actuality. That is what lies behind the chaos and arbitrariness of appearances. Art shows a higher spiritual reality. This also lifts art above history, which refers to accidental and arbitrary events. Art is not as high as philosophical thinking, religious and moral principles, but it is more able to take us to these truths than nature. The universal and absolute need for art comes from man's character as thinking consciousness who duplicates himself. Man is double because in his thoughts he represents himself to himself. There are two ways in which man is for himself: theoretically and in practical activity. Theoretically, man is the inward representation of his essence in consciousness. In practical activity, man produces himself in what is externally present in order to produce himself and recognise himself in that production, impressing his inner being on things by changing them. The practical activity can be recognised throughout life as man reduces the foreignness of the external world by acting on it, so that he can see it as an actualisation of himself. Man brings the inner and outer worlds into spiritual consciousness, making what is within him explicit to himself and giving outward form to the explicit self, so that what is in him can be perceived and known by himself and others. This is also true of moral and political action, religious portrayal and scientific knowledge. We must show how the work overcomes the opposition of the particular and the universal in the truth of spirit where the universal and particular are unified.

Like Schlegel, Hegel emphasises art as a place of unity of opposites. The natural and the spiritual are united, and the diversity of human consciousness or spirit in general is revealed and unified. The sensual and the abstract, the particular and the formal are mediated. Art, particularly poetics, contains the spiritual aspect of humanity. What distinguishes Hegel's position, making it necessary for him to reject Schlegel and the whole philosophy of the novel, arises from the separation from mere chaos and freedom of desire. Poetics must be what is guided by science and expresses the practical side of humanity. Hegel's concern is always to rise above a consciousness turned into itself in subjective self-reflection. As is made clear in the *Phenomenology* (Hegel 1977) in the passage at the end of 'Spirit: Morality' on 'Conscience. The "beautiful soul", evil and its forgiveness' (1977, 400), it is a consciousness which becomes evil because of its negation of everything outside itself, because it sees what is outside itself as evil. There is a related discussion in the *Philosophy of Right* (1991)§§ 139–140. This is overcome through action, and the immanence of spirit, which allows the proper realisation of morality and the move to religion. But in the structure of the *Phenomenology*, art appears as religion *after* morality and the beautiful soul, while the *Aesthetics* establishes art as what precedes religion and which already contains the beautiful soul. This can be partly resolved by remembering that the earlier stages of religion rise no higher than art, nevertheless some complications in Hegel's attempt to impose an overarching narrative on the development of spirit, to create a novel of spirit emerge. Hegel seems to be doing what Schlegel suggested, to create a philosophical novel of the highest dialogue by fitting all of knowledge, history, culture and religion into a narrative of spirit in the *Phenomenology* and even a narrative of logic in the *Science of Logic* (Hegel 1999). Various commentators have noted that Hegel's Phenomenology, in particular, has a novelistic structure. This idea is the source of Franco Moretti's *The Way of the World* (2000). The problem for Hegel is that the novel cannot cohere in either Schlegel's reading of the novel or Hegel's own reading. From Hegel's point of view, Schlegel's irony–poetry–dialogue–novel–philosophy is disintegrating between its parts. It is a play of oppositions which cannot overcome the paradoxes of opposite and leaves itself outside any science or laws, apart from those of pure self-introspection.

In the *Aesthetics*, the beautiful soul is situated in the evolution from Fichte's *Science of Knowledge* (Fichte 1982), where the ego is the source of creation and destruction, to Romantic Irony (1975, 64–69). The beautiful soul of Fichte's Ego and Romantic Irony is only apparently beautiful; it is a morbid soul which desires but cannot achieve the absolute. A truly beautiful soul acts and can therefore be actual and substantial, in being part of a community (1975, 66–67).

Resistance to the philosophical novel is accompanied by an admiration for the Homeric epic, which seems to anticipate philosophical system though Hegel does not say so directly.

> The earliest existence of this picture-thinking, *language*, is the earliest language, the Epic as such, which contains the universal content of the world, universal at least in the sense of *completeness*, though not indeed as the universality of *thought*. The Minstrel is the individual and actual Spirit from whom, as a subject of this world, it is produced and by whom it is borne. (Hegel 1977, § 729: 440–441)

The Minstrel is actual, so presumably is the good counterpart to the empty beautiful soul, though in other respects he is like the Poet–Philosopher of Romantic Irony. The whole discussion of 'Epic Poetry' in *Aesthetics* Vol. II (1975, 1040–1110) is relevant here. If we return to the passage in the *Aesthetics* which expounds and criticises the emergence of Romantic Irony, we see that the problem is that of the negation is complete unlike the limited negation of comedy. The Ironist destroys all character, not just bad character (1975, 67).

However, the structure of heroic Homeric epic is that of a lawlessness and free will which threatens to decline into chaotic violence and irrationality (1975, 186, 188). The modern age has lost this lawlessness and has therefore also lost its poetry (1975, 976–977). The law governed world which does not individual will at its centre is prosaic and lacking in the ideal. A novel is invoked, Cervantes' *Don Quixote*, a novel which has a claim to inaugurate the genre of the novel, and even modernity itself. It is what refers to the nobility of the Homeric world in its only possible modern form, as a parody of chivalric illusions (1975, 194, 196). However, this is not the opportunity for Hegel to offer a philosophy of the novel. He quickly moves into an extremely abstract discussion clash of different views, determinacy, differentiation and situation, leading back to the emergence of the earliest art. A slide takes place from historical exposition of the aesthetic, to its conceptual exposition and back to the historical in a way which avoids the question of the novel (1975, 196–201).

Almost immediately (1975, 203) Goethe's *Sorrows of Young Werther* appears, but only as an aspect—a *pièce d'occasion*—of lyric poetry. Another Goethe novel, *Elective Affinities*, is invoked later (1975, 297–298), but only to emphasise that '[t]he genuine originality of the artist, as of the work of art, lies solely in his being animated by the rationality of the inherently true content of the subject-matter' (1975, 298), which the playfulness of this novel does not achieve. One of the works which attracted the interests of the Romantic Ironists is also alluded to, Sterne's *Tristram Shandy*, but only to emphasise, 'an entirely naïve, light, unostentatious jogging along which in its triviality affords precisely the supreme idea of depth' (1975, 602). Hegel comes close to the themes of the Romantic Ironists, the depth which emerges from the play of differing ideas and perspectives. However, Hegel is contemplating the novel as something too light to do more than gesture at a science and spirit it lacks. Hegel's philosophy requires that it not be turned into a novel and therefore requires that the novel will be marginalised and trivialised, because it can only be discussed in the Ironic terms which will destroy the substance of Hegel's philosophy.

Art and Nature in Romanticism

Looking at the German Idealists from Kant, and the brief flowering of Ironic-Romantic philosophy in Germany in the last few years of the eighteenth century, art, science and nature are taken as coming together. It can be seen in Kant's *Critique of the Power of Judgement*, the first part of which refers to the beautiful and the sublime, and the second part of which refers to nature. Kant's articulation, a division between beauty and nature within a common account of judgement, establishes a pattern also found in Goethe, Schlegel, Schelling, Hegel and Schopenauer, that is a pattern in which questions of beauty, or art, and nature, are taken as different aspects of the same thing.

The World as Will and Representation, § 51

> Just as the chemist obtains solid precipitates by combining perfectly clear and transparent fluids, so does the poet know how to precipitate, as it were, the concrete, the individual, the representation of perception, out of the abstract, transparent universality of the concepts by the way in which he combines them. (Schopenhauer 1969, 243)

We can see that for Schopenhauer, art and nature as examined by science have parallel structures. The idea of parallel, or even shared structure between chemical processes and the creative processes of the poet, is important here. That comparison is not itself a scientific statement, but it puts science at the centre as a source of ideas about aesthetic processes and suggests that the best way to understand art is to compare its emergence with natural chemical processes. The attention to chemistry is significant as we do not see it in Kant, which is not surprising since chemistry was emerging as something like the science we known in the 1770s. There are maybe other reasons why Kant puts a strong focus on physics as the model science, as have other philosophers together with social scientists particularly economists, even since modern developments in chemistry and biology in the eighteenth and nineteenth centuries, because of its apparent certainty and determinism. The development of chemistry had proceeded just enough to have a major impact on aesthetic and philosophical thinking in the 1790s, as can be seen in the passages below from Novalis.

Novalis

General Draft (1798-9)

2. *Facture* is opposed to *nature*. The spirit is the artist. Facture and nature mixed—separated—united. When they are mixed they deal with transcendental physics and poetics—when united with higher physics and poetics.

The higher *philosophy* deals with the *marriage of nature and spirit*.

Chemical and mechanical psychology. Transcendental *poetics*. Practical poetics. Nature produces, the spirit makes. (Novalis 1997, 122)

The chemical enters here as opposed to mechanical psychology and is allied with higher physics and poetics. The higher and more transcendental poetics, the more its mixes with nature as physics which transcendental in its higher state. The Kantian language of transcendental physics and poetics suggests they are creations of the universal structure of the self, and 'chemical psychology' looks like a reference to the most productive aspects of the self in Kant. We should resist the temptation to define this as 'Romantic Metaphysics', since Kant is not usually labelled in that way, and Novalis is working up ideas from Kant, via Fichte, on the relation between laws of nature and the way the mind is structured. 'Romantic Metaphysics' is a phrase usually used to suggest a metaphysics which imposes subjective categories in a rather indeterminate way, but Novalis and Schegel are building on the transcendental thought which comes out of Kant. If we use the phrase 'Romantic Metaphysics', it should be understood as the continuation of Kantian, transcendentalism not a leap from Kant into arbitrary subjectivity and an anti-scientific conception.

As we have seen, Friedrich Schlegel offers a 'Romantic Ironic' view, similar to Novalis, in which he sees science and art converging, an activity which he links with philology. Philology is one way art and science link, which was examined at length in Chap. 2 with regard to Vico.

Schlegel's statement seems prophetic of his own later activity as a specialist in Indian philology, and Nietzsche's move from classical philology to philosophy and aesthetics.

Schlegel, *Athenäum Fragments* (1798)

(255)

The more poetry becomes science, the more it also becomes art. If poetry is to become art, if the artist is to have a thorough understanding and knowledge of his ends and means, his difficulties and his subjects, then the poet will have to philosophise about his art. If he is to be more than a mere contriver and artisan, if he is to be an expert in his field and understand his fellow citizens in the kingdom of art, then he will have to become a philologist as well. (Schlegel 1991, 54)

The status of the 'Romantic' conception of the unity of art and science, and its continuity with Kantian transcendentalism, is confirmed by a reading of Schelling, or at least that version of Schelling's thought present in the *System of Transcendental Idealism* of 1800, and probably in at least some of the other versions of his thought in other years. Schelling's vision of art and nature unifying, so unifying the inside and outside of the world seems far removed from scientific method. But if we compare the passage below with the passages from Novalis and Schlegel, we can see the relation with the idea of chemistry as movement, and combination in science is important. Schelling's conception of art and nature looks complete, but could be taken as an invitation to the use of imagination in science and to thinking about the place of knowledge of nature in poetry. Whether or not that is Schelling's conception, the work of German Idealist and Romantic thinkers from about 1798 to 1800 is very suggestive for thinking about how and science might be related.

Schelling, *System of Transcendental Idealism* (1800)

Part Six

§ 3: 2

If aesthetic intuition is merely transcendental intuition become objective, it is self-evident that art is at once the only true and eternal organ and document of philosophy, which ever and again continues to speak to us of of that philosophy cannot depict in external form, namely the unconscious element in acting and producing, and its original identity with the conscious. Art is paramount to the philosopher, precisely because it opens to him, as it were, the holy of holies, where burns in eternal and original unity, as if in a single flame, that which in nature and history is rent asunder, and in life and action, no less than in thought, must forever fly apart. The view of nature, which the philosopher frames artificially, is for art the original and natural one. What we speak of as nature is a poem lying lying pent in a mysterious and wonderful script. Yet the riddle could reveal itself, were we to recognise in it the odyssey of the spirit, which marvellously deluded, seeks itself, and in seeking flies from itself; for through the world of sense there glimmers, as if through words the meaning, as if through dissolving mists the land of fantasy, of which we are in search. Each splendid painting owes, as it were, its genesis to a removal of the invisible barrier dividing the real from the ideal world, and is no more than the gateway, through which come forth completely the shapes and scenes of that world of fantasy which gleams but imperfectly through the real. Nature, to the artist, is nothing more than it is to the philosopher, being simply the ideal world appearing under permanent restrictions, or merely the imperfect reflection of a world existing, not outside him, but within. (Schelling 1978, 231–232)

Art in Schelling's description is an unveiling of nature to find its most ideal existence, could be taken as an aesthetic metaphysics, again suggesting that Romantic aesthetics reaches a point of idealised eternal structure which cannot accommodate the novel. A thought confirmed by Schelling's brief treatment of the novel in *Philosophy of Art*, which hardly recognises the novel as existing outside *Don Quixote* and essentially treats that novel as a reaction to failed Romance literature.

Schelling, we can see, has some thoughts about chemistry related to Novalis and Schopenhauer. The understanding of chemistry as possessing a dynamism, holism and interactive aspect lacking in physics, understood as mechanical, reductive and focused on external influence, is part of an evolution of thought which incorporates a literary aesthetics that is dynamic, holistic and interactive, that allows, or should allow, for the novel as an elevated genre. There are other aspects of the chemical and even biological thought of Kant and Hegel, which space does not allow for, confirming this suggestion. A really significant piece of evidence is Goethe's novel *Elective Affinities*, the title of which certainly reflects the aesthetic interests in chemistry discussed above, as may the interactions between the characters, though this is of course a more difficult issue.

There is an enormous weight of interaction between chemistry and aesthetic thought, itself maybe demonstrating the power of the interactive chemical way of thinking, which is enormously suggestive, but only leads to consideration of the novel in an indirect way in Schlegel. It is a perhaps puzzling part of the relationship between science, philosophy of nature and philosophy of art, that an interest in a new scientific model for thinking about the material universe and about literary production, did not catch up with the novel as central literary genre. One reason is perhaps that the interest in the universality of chemistry as part of the laws of nature may have been in tension with the sense that the novel was something more subjective, relativistic, vulgar, formally unstable and linguistically varied compared with epic. It just did not seem possible to look at the formation of the novel as at all connected with the deep laws of nature. In any case, this chemical model as part of 'Romantic' or 'Idealist Metaphysics' of art and nature deserves to be considered part of the deep history of the philosophy of the novel.

The sense that the novel was too trivial to be seen in the light of the philosophy of chemistry may itself interact with a political issue. As noted above, Schlegel's adherence to 'republicanism', that is an interest in individual rights and liberal constitutionalism, collapsed. Schlegel became a Baron of the Austrian Empire, and a devotee of the arch traditionalist Austrian minister Klemens von Mettternich. Metternich was the intellectual leader and strategist of political reaction across Europe after the final defeat of Napoleon Bonaparte in 1815 right up to the Spring Time of the Peoples in 1848, the culmination of twenty-three years of royalist struggle against republican and then Bonapartist France. Schlegel wrote on literary history at an uninspired level compared with the work addressed above. British Romantic authors and thinkers like William Wordsworth and Samuel Taylor Coleridge followed a similar path. The existence of the novel was not a threat in itself to the European order of 1815. There is no clean break between early Romantic republicanism and late Romantic conservatism. Novalis' 1799 speech 'Christendom or Europe' (in Wheeler 1984) already looks like a utopian version of the 1815 order. It is nevertheless of some interest that the genre of the novel was given limited respect until the middle of the nineteenth century and was not the object of much philosophical attention until the twentieth century, except in Kierkegaard. The overcoming of the epic legacy is part of that, but maybe cannot be separated from general political and social anxieties about the elevation of a more demotic form of literature, which allows for, even demands, articulation of competing or conflicting points of view.

Schopenhauer certainly made art a privileged way of experiencing universal will. However, there is a naturalistic element in Schopenhauer's position, as indicated in the quotation from '*The World as Will and Representation*', § 55 above.

There are other ways in which we can find naturalistic ways of thinking in Schopenhauer, such as chapters ILII–ILIV in *The World as Will and Representation*, which anticipated Darwin in the discussions of 'Life of the Species', 'The Hereditary Nature of Qualities' and 'The Metaphysics of Sexual Love'.

The attention to chemistry in Schopenhauer is significant as we do not see it in Kant, who Schopenhauer claimed to be following, at least with regard to the first edition of the *Critique of Pure Reason*. Kant's oversight with regard to chemistry may be because chemistry was emerging as something like the science we known in the 1770s. There are maybe other reasons why Kant puts a strong focus on physics as the model science, as can be seen in the *Critique of Pure Reason* (1998), and which continues on into the *Opus postumum* (Kant 1993), that is, because of its apparent certainty and determinism. This interest in physics as the model of science continued for a long time afterwards. What is notable about the 'Romantic Idealist' writings after Kant, who is in some respects a Romantic Idealist particularly if we think of the *Critique of the Power of Judgment*.

As noted above chemistry had developed in such a way to influence philosophical and aesthetic thinking by time of the German Idealists as can be seen in the passages quoted from Novalis' *General Draft*.

The chemical here in a way that follows the Kantian language of transcendental physics and poetics and that suggests they are creations of the universal structure of the self; the 'chemical psychology' looks like a reference to the most productive aspects of the self in Kant. Novalis is working up ideas from Kant, via Fichte, on the relation between laws of nature and the way the mind is structured. 'Romantic Metaphysics' is a phrase usually used to suggest a metaphysics, which imposes subjective categories in a rather indeterminate way, but Novalis and Schegel are building on the transcendental thought which comes out of Kant. If we use the phrase 'Romantic Metaphysics', it should be understood as the continuation of Kantian, transcendentalism not a leap from Kant into arbitrary subjectivity and an anti-scientific conception. Friedrich Schlegel offers a 'Romantic Ironic' view, similar to Novalis, in which he sees science and art converging, an activity which he links with philology as seen above in the quotation from *Athenäum Fragments* 255.

What we have seen of Schelling might be taken as a pure example of 'Romantic Metaphysics', but it is a lot less metaphysical than Kant in the sense that it does not suggest an a priori construction of the laws of nature. There is a suggestion of the homology of the structure of mind and of nature, on the same grounds as Kant argues: we can only know nature through the structure of our mind. Even in this most apparently 'Romantic Metaphysical' moment, Schelling is concerned with natural science, directly in his reference to the unity of nature and history, and less directly in the use of language associated with chemistry.

If we compare the passage below with the passages from Novalis and Schlegel, we can see the relation with the idea of chemistry as movement, and combination in science is important. Schelling's conception of art and nature looks complete, but could be taken as an invitation to the use of imagination in science and to thinking about the place of knowledge of nature in poetry. Whether or not that is Schelling's conception, the work of German Idealist and Romantic thinkers from about 1798 to 1800 is very suggestive for thinking about how and science might be related.

Schelling's description of art and nature could be taken as an aesthetic metaphysics, anticipating Schopenhauer and Nietzsche, though Schopenhauer was very dismissive of German Idealism after Kant. This takes us away from Schlegel on the philosophy of the novel, which confirms the issue raised above with regard to Schlegel. Is his Romantic philosophy of the novel capable of accounting for the structural and objective nature of the novel, on the basis of very subjectivist and changeable 'chemical' conception? Does it tend to become divided between a very subjectivist understanding of the novel where myth collapses into poetic spontaneity, or does the 'myth' and 'chemistry' become solidified as very unchangeable notions of aesthetic tradition rooted in national tradition, where the subjectivity has disappeared under solidified myth. German Idealism and Romanticism moves away from the Lockean and Leibnizian models of the 'idea', even though they rely on this work. The Lockean understanding of 'ideas' inhering either in an object, as is the case for primary qualities, or consciousness as is the case for secondary qualities, has an empiricist aspect which is not adequate to Idealist thought about the productivity of art and imagination. The Leibnizian understanding of ideas, or perceptions, as arranged by metaphysical order, leaves a gap between ideas and form that does not match Romantic understanding of the flux of art. Locke provides a basis for the aesthetics of Shaftesbury as Leibniz provides a basis for the aesthetics of Baumgarten, but these aesthetic philosophies cannot account for the dynamic unity and diversity of literary work as understood through Idealism and Romanticism. The next chapter, on Kierkegaard, will continue the discussion of this tension within Romantic literary philosophy.

References

Fichte, J.G. 1982. *The Science of Knowledge*, trans. and ed. Peter Heath and John Lachs. Cambridge and New York, NY: Cambridge University Press.

Hegel, G.W.F. 1975. *Aesthetics: Lectures on Fine Art [2 vols]*, trans. T.M. Knox. Oxford: Clarendon Press.

Hegel, G.W.F. 1977. *Phenomenology of Spirit*, trans. A.V. Miller. Oxford: Oxford University Press.

Hegel, G.W.F. 1991. *Elements of the Philosophy of Right*, trans. H.B. Nisbet. Cambridge: Cambridge University Press.

Hegel, G.W.F. 1999. *Hegel's Science of Logic*, trans. A.V. Miller. New York , NY: Humanity Books.

Kant, Immanuel. 1993. *Opus Postumum*, trans. Eckhart Förster and Michael Rosen. Cambridge: Cambridge University Press.

Kant, Immanuel. 2000. *Critique of the Power of Judgement*, trans. Paul Guyer and Eric Matthews, ed. Paul Guyer. Cambridge and New York, NY: Cambridge University Press.

Kierkegaard, Søren A. 1989. *The Concept of Irony With Continual Reference to Socrates/Notes of Schelling's Berlin Lectures*. Kierkegaard's Writings, II, trans. Howard V. Hong. and Edna H. Hong. Princeton, NJ: Princeton University Press.

Lukács, Georg. 1971a. *History and Class Consciousness: Studies in Marxist Dialectic*, trans. Rodney Livingstone. London: Merlin Press.

Lukács, Georg. 1971b. *The Theory of the Novel: A Historico-Philosophical Essay on the Forms of Great Epic Literature*, trans. Anna Bostock. London: Merlin Press.

Moretti, Franco. 2000. *The Way of the World: The Bildungsroman in European Culture*, trans. Albert Sbragia. London and New York, NY: Verso.

Schlegel, Friedrich. 1991. *Philosophical Fragments*, trans. Peter Firchow. Minneapolis: University of Minnesota Press.

Schmitt, Carl. 1986. *Political Romanticism*, trans. Guy Oakes. Cambridge, MA: Massachusetts Institute of Technology Press.

Schopenhauer, Arthur. 1969. *The World as Will and Representation, Volume I*, trans. E.F.J. Payne. New York, NY: Dover Publications.

Shaftesbury, Earl of, Anthony Ashley Cooper. 1999. *Characteristic of Men, Manners, Opinion, Time*, ed. Lawrence E. Klein. Cambridge and New York, NY: Cambridge University Press.

Smith, Adam. 1983. *Lectures on Rhetoric and Belles Lettres*, ed. J.C. Bryce. Oxford and New York, NY: Oxford University Press.

Sweet, Dennis. 1999. The Birth of The Birth of Tragedy. *Journal of the History of Ideas* 60 (2): 345–359.

Watt, Ian. 1972. *The Rise of the Novel: Studies in Defoe, Richardson and Fielding*. London: Penguin Books.

Wheeler, Kathleen (ed.). 1984. *German Aesthetic and Literary Criticism: The Romantic Ironists and Goethe*. Cambridge: Cambridge University Press.

4

Kierkegaard, Irony and Subjectivity

Introduction

Kierkegaard did not present an explicit philosophy of the novel, but the ways he deals with the novel and idea connected with the idea of this genre in some texts does add up to a major body of work on the philosophy of the novel, the most important contribution between Hegel's lectures on aesthetics in the 1820s and Georg Lukács' work on *The Theory of the Novel* during World War One. Kierkegaard's contribution is also discussed in Chap. 10 'The Philosophical Novel', so the complete vision of his idea of the novel will not emerge until the final chapter. The discussion in the last chapter will be a general overview of texts which are both novels and contributions to philosophy so that though Kierkegaard's texts of that kind will get particular attention, it is the present chapter which will deal with Kierkegaard in a more expansive way, and in so doing will set up the later discussion, while also setting up themes which will come up in the discussion of Lukács, who had a significant interest in Kierkegaard and who will be the topic of the next chapter.

© The Author(s) 2018
B. Stocker, *Philosophy of the Novel*,
https://doi.org/10.1007/978-3-319-65891-9_4

What is discussed from Kierkegaard in this chapter is four texts in which there is some discussions of literary aesthetics, partly where is appears as part of a discussion of what is largely musical aesthetics in the third text. The first text covered will be *From the Papers of One Still Living* (in Kierkegaard 1990), published in 1838, which discusses the novels of Hans Christian Anderson, a good deal less well known to English readers than his fairy tales of course, and in a more marginal way the work of the novelist Thomasine Gyllenberg, which gives some build up to the more extensive discussion of Gyllenberg in the fourth text This short early text precedes the texts that really made Kierkegaard's name in philosophy, literature and theology in 1843, that is *Either/Or I* (1987), *Fear and Trembling* (in 1983), *Repetition* (1983) and *Two Upbuilding Discourses* (in 2009), but does already engage with their themes and arguments.

The second text is Kierkegaard's master's thesis of 1841, *The Concept of Irony with Continual Reference to Socrates* (1989), which is the equivalent of a doctorate now. It refers back to the idea of Socrates and Plato in Friedrich Schleiermacher, who had contacts with the Jena Romantics discussed in the last chapter, and German Romantic philosophy, along with Romantic views of irony and the novel, as well as Hegel's views on these matters, while in a more indirect way establishing a way of thinking about the novel and the essential aspects of its forms which goes beyond these earlier views.

Either/Or: A Fragment of Life, the third text under consideration here, was the first of the 1843 books and contains a lengthy discussion of aesthetics in an essay in Part 1, 'The Immediate Erotic Stages Or the Musical-Erotic' and the following essay on tragedy. As the title indicates, it is more concerned with music than literature, but the music considered is largely that of Mozart's opera, *Don Giovanni*, so that language does enter into the aesthetic discussion. Kierkegaard's comments on earlier versions of the Don Juan legend along with brief but important comments on Cervantes and on general aesthetics, means that this essay does contribute to the understanding of the novel with regard to the importance of sound and even musicality in words, the place of the erotic and passion in general in a large complex aesthetic object, the place of subjectivity and desire, and the use of old forms of storytelling in a modern context. Kierkegaard's subsequent comments on tragedy in *Either/Or* complete an aesthetic discussion important to Kierkegaard's understanding of the novel, and the discussion will start with that essay.

The fourth and final text by Kierkegaard to be considered here is *Two Ages: The Age of Revolution and The Present Age, A Literary Review*, published in 1846. Here Kierkegaard is again concerned with the novels of Gyllenberg, who published anonymously so that Kierkegaard did not know who she was and assumed she was a man. In this long review, which becomes a work of literary aesthetics and philosophy in itself, Kierkegaard develops earlier ideas about the aesthetics of the novel and places them in a political and social context.

Political and social themes are important in Kierkegaard, and it is important not to be distracted by the image of Kierkegaard as isolated apolitical individual in assessing his work in this respect. The idea of the individual, or single individual, both of which are employed to translate his use of the Danish word '*den enkelte*' ('*Enkelte*' in Kierkegaard's time when Danish nouns still had an upper case first letter, German style), is important, but does not at all exclude issues of the individual's relation to the community and the nature of community. Kierkegaard's ways of engaging with political and social issues sometimes appear most clearly in his literary discussions, as can be seen in his discussions of individuality and revolution in *A Literary Review*, indicating that Kierkegaard is important in constructing ways of thinking about the 'realist' functions of the novel as well as the issues of self-constitution, with which he is associated. 'Realism' here means the idea of literature as mimetic established by Aristotle, as applied to social reality and political reactions to it, which has become one way of characterising the dominant features of the nineteenth-century novel, and which also appears in the ways that some philosophers of the novel and critics think about what the novel should be, including Lukács and Auerbach, who will be discussed in the next chapter and in Chap. 7. While it is not argued here that Kierkegaard belongs in any 'realist' camp, it is argued that he was concerned with those issues and foreshadowed some of the 'realist' or mimetic approaches.

Kierkegaard's emphasis on the limitations of the aesthetic itself leads him into an analysis which has some realist aspects simply in that he is writing about the novel as the product of a society in which the aesthetic, and the associated term the reflective, dominate literature. As is made most clear in his discussion of tragedy the aesthetic reflective attitude is a product of the isolation of the individual in a world where ethical relations are placed above aesthetic immediacy, though there is a lack of strong ethical substance to the society. That lack of substance is a product of the individualism of Christianity and is what produces a consciousness of ethical thought as well as very aestheticised literature. From this point of view though literature can also serve as a critique of the aesthetic perspective, in exploring its limits.

From the Papers of One Still Living

From the Papers of One Still Living consists almost entirely of the essay 'Andersen as a Novelist' begins in a way that is familiar from later Kierkegaard texts, and the comparative obscurity of this early text means that most readers will have some previous acquaintance with Kierkegaard's most widely read texts. Here Kierkegaard adds above his name and below the title 'published against his will' (Kierkegaard 2009, 53). The introduction of uncertainty in the relation between signature and text, the questioning of the relation between what is written and the intentions of the person supposed to have written is a frequent issue in Kierkegaard, most obviously through the use of pseudonyms instead of his own name, though the pseudonyms more draw attention to a way of interpreting the text than they serve as a disguise. It does put Kierkegaard immediately into an ironic literary register. The playful irony of the title page epigram is continued in the Preface, which is attributed to the Publisher, but in fact suggests that the author and Publisher might be one person:

> We are, therefore, so far from being able to rejoice as friends in the unity for which poets and orators in their repeated immortalisations have only a single expression—that it was as if one soul resided in two bodies—that with respect to us it must rather seem as if two souls resided in one body. (1990, 55)

The play on, and inversion of, Aristotle's definition of friendship in the *Nicomachean Ethics* and Michel de Montaigne's account of his friendship with Étienne de La Boétie in the essay 'On Friendship', sets up an idea of multiple identities, which Kierkegaard takes up further in *The Concept of Irony* with regard to the status of the self in Fichte's philosophy and the irony of the Romantics, but also across his subsequent writing with regard to the different possibilities of the self, and self-relation. These concerns with the self and with selves are oriented overall by an absolute relation of the self with the absolute, which is the prerequisite for faith in God and is tied up with a sense of the self as enduring.

The idea that the novel might be a superficial product of the age, which Kierkegaard here and later endorses, but not in a way that philosophically diminishes the novel as genre as much as Hegel does, comes up in the Preface when the 'Publisher' explains the author's reservations about writing:

> "You know very well", said he, "that I consider writing books to be the most ridiculous thing a person can do. One surrenders oneself entirely to the power of fate and circumstance, and how can one escape all the prejudices people bring with them to to the reading of a book, which work no less disturbingly than the preconceived ideas most bring with them when they make someone's acquaintance, with the result that very few people really know what others look like? What hope can one entertain that one will fall into the hands of reader *ex improviso?* Besides, I feel tied by the fixed form the essay has finally acquired and in order to feel free again, will take it back into the womb once more, let it once again sink into the twilight from which it came […]". (57)

The book is said to be a way in which the writer becomes dependent on fate and circumstance, raising the issue of the novel as somehow lacking fixity, as only being reflective, which concerns Kierkegaard in all his thoughts on the genre. Though the remark applies to write in general, and in particular to a review essay rather than a novel, it fits with the way that Kierkegaard characterises the novel, which summons up all anxiety about weakness and failure in communication. Kierkegaard's comparison in this passage of the circulation of a book amongst readers

with people meeting each other refers backs to Romantic understandings of the relation between the novel and forms of sociability, and
beyond that the connections between aesthetics and civil society in
eighteenth-century philosophy. The main text begins with a 'Postscript'
(60) which invites the reader to skip the Preface and the essay, so again
invoking the kind of positive playfulness suggested by the Romantics
and Hegel's reservations about ironic self-negation and the substance
lacking reflective existence of the novel.

The opening of the essay on Anderson *From the Papers of One Still
Living* makes the interest in Hegel clear, mocking remarks about Hegelian
philosophy getting the world from nothing (61), which Kierkegaard suggests applies to the politics (63) and the literature (64) of the era.

> But precisely because Anderson thus cannot separate the poetic from
> himself, because, so to speak, he cannot get rid of it, but as soon as a
> poetic mood has acquired freedom to act, this is immediately over-
> whelmed, with or without his will, by the prosaic—precisely therefore it
> is impossible to obtain a total impression from Andersen's short novels.
> Precisely therefore it is possible that readers are put into the most singu-
> lar mood, very different from the one intended by Andersen, because as
> his fiction weighs one down like actuality because the whole collection
> of details, narrated as actuality, can surely have their interest, since one
> must presuppose the fundamental thought in the narrating individu-
> al's own consciousness going through all these, explaining everything,
> but this fundamental thought is first and foremost what the poet must
> make come alive. And his own actuality, his own person, volatilises
> itself into fiction, so that sometimes one is actually tempted to believe
> that Andersen is a character who has run away from an as yet unfinished
> group composed by a poet. And certainly it is undeniable that Andersen
> could become a very poetic person in a poem, in which case all his poetry
> would be understood in its fragmentary truth. Naturally the impression
> repeats itself if one lets reflection assist as a perpetual *Momento* that it
> is the other way round, and with an unshakable obstinacy, like that of
> Cartesian dolls, it emerges victorious from every battle with reflection.

What we have developed here will afford the requisite inner supple-
mentary thought of the correctness of our statement, a statement as
much about Andersen's misrelation to an epic development as about

his indeclinability also demonstrates the misrelation in its shallowness. In the same way, when one reads through one or several of Andersen's novels, what we have developed here, kept *in mente* as a provisional abstract result, will split up into such a quantity of isolated remarks with appurtenant *dicta probantia* that we must resist as much as possible by not letting these flutter round about as such, but reminding ourselves of the Latinists' significant *revocare ad lege artis*, by letting them advance in closer formation so that the reader, even when the most isolated remarks are most dispersed, may still at times seem to hear the "call to assemble," as it were calling them back. (75–76)

The passage above shows how Kierkegaard thinks of the novel as a form as caught between poetry and epic, inner experience and substantial world, volatility of life and narrative actuality. Kierkegaard uses this structure of thought in an account that on the face of it is directed specifically to the personality and literary output of Andersen, rather than an exposition of literary form as such. Nevertheless, he does use a language of general aesthetic terms, even appealing to the laws of art '*lege artis*', while making what might be taken as purely occasional remarks about Andersen's novels. Kierkegaard picks out particular aspects of Andersen's work, it is particularly prone to collapse into fragments, but even this is very suggestive of the German Romantic approach to what a novel is when it is most purely a novel. The specific qualities Kierkegaard attributes to Andersen's novels are themselves part of a general set of terms for discussing literature in which Andersen's novel is exemplary in formal terms, if not the best according to ranks of aesthetic value. The novel as a form is divided between the poetic aspect of words used in very precise ways to suggest inner individuality and the epic aspect of action in the world. The 'epic' here becomes a pole to which 'narrative' and 'fiction' are attached as opposed to the pole of 'poetry' to which 'person' and 'fragment' are attached. It is 'reflection' that enables the reader to see Andersen as poetic behind the 'epic' pole of fiction. Reflection itself is understood through figurative language, in Kierkegaard's rather muddled reference to Cartesian dolls, which themselves struggle against reflection to maintain the poetic personality. Reflection is then ambiguous, both suggestive and undermining of what it suggests, necessary to thought but inherently other than the substance of existence, in accordance with Hegel's account.

For the rest of the essay, Kierkegaard develops these thoughts on Andersen along with some directed to the work of Thomasine Gyllembourg, but as he does not refer to her novels, she will be left until the discussion of *A Literary Review*. Kierkegaard continues the essay on these lines until arriving at a final paragraph that brings us back to the initial suggestions of a link between the novel and politics, even though expressed as a desire to separate them.

> Not that at any moment it has been anything but a joy for me to be able to give him what is his due and what, especially in our time, anyone who who still has a little feeling for poetry in the *ecclesia pressa* in which we live must almost be tempted to give more warmly than the truth perhaps could demand. Not that such an utterance could not be brought into harmony with my whole earlier expressed view of Andersen, because in spite of all his tossing about, all his bending before every poetic breeze, it still always gives me joy that as yet he has not come under the all-embracing-devil-may-care trade wind of politics. —I wished to say this to Andersen rather than write it because such an utterance is on the whole very exposed to misunderstanding, something, however, I hope that I shall be able to put up with if only Andersen, in order to avoid it, will hold what I have written with sympathetic ink up to that light which alone makes the writing readable and the meaning clear. (102)

Kierkegaard sets up his concluding conciliatory words addressed to Andersen with the suggestion that a feeling for poetry is lacking in the present age, an age where the church is oppressed as Kierkegaard conveys through a Latin tag. This does carry the implication that both Christianity and poetry are lacking in the present age, with the further implication that the novel as a form is for a world without Christianity or poetry. *Either/Or*, as we shall see, strongly suggests that Christianity itself tends to undermine the unity of individual, community and sacral in which antique literary forms are embedded, though evidently the novel was growing in Kierkegaard's time while Christianity was losing some of its intellectual and cultural influence, many centuries after the appearance of Christianity. The phrase *ecclesia press* is ironic in that

Kierkegaard regarded the power of the state church as detracting from Christian spirituality, so it is the National Danish Church which in some sense oppresses the true church.

Kierkegaard continues with the argument that Andersen' novels are fragmented between points of view, but concedes that Andersen has not come under the influence of the political point of view. The trouble with politics is though the same as that of writing books as suggested in the Preface, the submission to fate as random chance. Kierkegaard reinforces that idea of politics with the idea that it is like a boat subject to the trade winds [*Passat*, which does not translate directly as trade winds, but does refer to those winds which have always been associated with oceanic trade], suggesting anxiety about both natural and commercial forces as undermining our self-command, any hope of separation from external forces. Earlier in the essay (76–77), Kierkegaard refers to Stoicism as 'unshakeable certainty in oneself' (76), which both anticipates and conceals the kind of self-relation necessary to Christianity. There is a link between the decline of Stoicism and the growth of philosophies of aesthetic experience in the eighteenth century, which are also associated with philosophies of moral feeling and commercial society. We can take this decline back to the *Maxims* of François de La Rochefoucauld in the seventeenth century, which cast doubt on the capacity of the human mind to restrain the passions in manner required by Stoicism. It could even go back to Montaigne's questioning of Stoic self-control in his *Essays* of the sixteenth century. The important point is that the idea of reason existing as detached from the passions and controlling them is questioned as the novel establishes itself as a major genre. It is appropriate then that Kierkegaard associates a substantial deep kind of poetry, preceding the novel, and presumably including the epic aspect as well as the lyric aspect, as in tension with a world of chance, commerce and growing liberal politics, that is the world of the novel.

The Concept of Irony

The themes for a philosophy of the novel that Kierkegaard develops in the very particular context of Andersen and Gyllembourg receive a more general philosophical exposition in *The Concept of Irony*, which looks at

Socratic and Romantic irony. What gives Romantic irony a high role in *The Concept of Irony* is its place in understanding subjectivity; what limits Romantic irony in *The Concept of Irony* is the need for subjectivity to reflect on what is outside itself and not just on the contents of itself. Only a small part though is devoted to discussing the novel as a general category, or with reference to any examples. There is just a short section discussing Friedrich Schlegel's novel *Lucinde*, which was not as influential as the roughly contemporaneous novels of Goethe and has never matches them as widely read classics. *Lucinde* suited Kierkegaard's purpose of assessing the philosophical significance of the novel as a genre.

The discussion of *Lucinde* is small part of the discussion of irony which begins with a full account of Socrates, largely but not only with reference to his appearance in the dialogues of Plato, already suggesting an encounter with the discussions of irony in the German Romantics and Hegel, comprising F. Schlegel, Ludwig Tieck and Karl Solger on the Romantic side. Kierkegaard also covers the background to Romantic irony in Fichte's account of the 'I' in the first two editions of the *The Science of Knowledge*. Kierkegaard builds up an account of subjectivity in this discussion of Fichte, which includes criticism of a tendency to shapeless limitlessness, but does not abandon the Fichtean idea of the infinitised 'I' which is produced and producing. The main criticism he establishes is that the Romantics applied Fichte's view of the 'I' in the wrong way, ignoring Fichte's goal of constructing the world, with a systematic construction. As Kangas (2007) points out, there is no deep engagement with Fichte here and Kierkegaard's overall philosophical development may have taken more inspiration from *The Vocation of Man* or even *Outline of the Distinctive Character of the Wissenschaftslehre* (Kangas 2007, 75), than from *The Science of Knowledge* (*Wissenschaftslehre*) itself. Despite these qualifications, the general discussion of the ego in *The Science of Knowledge* does inform Kierkegaard's discussion in *The Concept of Irony* and is in general the Fichte text most connected with Kierkegaard's thoughts about aesthetic subjectivity.

> [T]his externality, this Ding an sich [thing in itself], constituted the weakness in Kant's system. Indeed, it became a question whether the I itself is not a Ding an sich. This question was raised and answered by Fichte. He removed the difficulty with this an sich by placing it within

thought; he infinitised the I in I-I. The producing I as the produced I. I-I is the abstract identity. By so doing he infinitely liberated thought. (Fichte 1982, 273)

The main point Kierkegaard establishes in the succeeding paragraphs is that the Romantic ironists applied Fichte's view of the 'I' in the wrong way: 'Fichte wanted to construct the world, but he had in mind a systematic construction. Schlegel and Tieck wanted to obtain a world' (1989, 275). On Kierkegaard's reading, Fichte was concerned with the construction of our view of the world in consciousness and philosophy, while the Romantic Ironists over extended the infinitised 'I' to the world.

There is a strong complicity between the Fichtean and Romantic positions on negation, in Kierkegaard's exposition, which emerges in remarks on Fichte that demonstrate how Romantic aestheticism arises from Kant's transcendental ego (Part II, Introduction):

...we are referred to the development in modern philosophy attained in Kant and that is completed in Fichte, and more specifically again to the positions that after Fichte sought to affirm subjectivity in its second potency. Actuality bears out that this hangs together properly, for here again we meet irony. But since this position is an intensified subjective consciousness, it quite naturally is clearly and definitely conscious of irony and declares irony as its position. This was indeed the case with Friedrich Schlegel, who sought to bring it to bear in relation to actuality; with Tieck, who sought to bring it to bear in poetry; and with Solger, who became aesthetically and philosophically conscious of it. Finally, here irony also met its master in Hegel. (1989, 242)

Following Hegel, though not agreeing with him in every respect, Kierkegaard regards dialectic as abstract thinking at its highest, aware of the conditions, negations and limits of ideas in thought. Jon Stewart (2007, 103–127) strongly emphasises the positive aspects of Kierkegaard's references to Hegel in *The Concept of Irony*, and the use he makes of Hegel's version of the issues under discussion, but in doing so misses the extent to which *The Concept of Irony* gives more value to irony, including the irony or the Romantics than Hegel does, and in that way creates a stronger basis for the philosophy of the novel, even if Kierkegaard does not give an elevated status to the form here. Kierkegaard establishes a criticism of Hegel with the suggestion that he had too negative response to Fichtean subjectivism and Romantic irony: 'But on the other hand, it must be said that by his one-sided attack on the post-Fichtean irony he has overlooked the truth of irony, and by his identifying all irony with this, he has done irony an injustice' (1989, 265).

The Romantic position on irony to some degree informs Kierkegaard's understanding of Socratic irony and are both are informed by Kierkegaard's understanding of Friedrich Schleiermacher's account of the character of Socrates and the different forms of communication in Plato's dialogues, which is certainly distinct from Hegel's view. As Schleiermacher contributed to the *Athenaeum*, overall there is a complex interaction between all these areas of interpretation. Crouter sums up Schleiermacher's influence on Kierkegaard in a way particularly appropriate to *The Concept of Irony*, 'two Schleiermachers—the Plato scholar, interpreter, and translator, as well as the theologian whose dogmatics wrestles with the doctrines of sin, grace, and redemption—compete for attention' (Crouter 2007, 210).

Everything becomes a mood for the Romantic Ironist, so that life breaks down into a series of unconnected moods (Kierkegaard 1989, 285). Kierkegaard sees *Lucinde* as an example of all these negative aspects, so at this point gives the novel a low status, and overall across his work he never gives any novel other than *Don Quixote* any importance as art at the highest level, nevertheless what he says gives a philosophical account of what the novel is and lays the groundwork for later more admiring philosophical accounts of the novel, and even of the tendency of later novels towards prose poetic stylistic perfection combined with deep themes and integrated plots. The Romantic ironic position is based on an elevation of the poetic, but leads to poetic failure. Where the poetic is polarised between the actual and the ideal, which is the Romantic Ironic position, there is a failure of poetry. Poetry requires unity to be successful poetry and that unity must come from reference to the truth which is more than dialectic.

'If anyone desires an excellent picture of an ironist who by the very duality of his existence, lacked existence, I will call attention to Asa-Loki' (285). This sentence in itself encapsulates the conflict Kierkegaard elaborates in *The Concept of Irony* between the self at the source of irony and the irony that negates that self. Asa-Loki, as referred to in *The*

Concept of Irony is Kierkegaard's view of the human individual, if one lacking in the highest insights into the possibility of a relation between self and the absolute. The Asa-Loki reference says something about the universal definition of human subjectivity in this life.

The reference to the world of myth, which Asa-Loki belongs to, leads us to an earlier section in Part 1, I, named 'The Mythical in the Earlier Platonic Dialogues as a Token of a More Copious Speculation' (96–119): which includes this comment on the status of myth, 'if we ask what the mythical is basically, one may presumably reply that it is the idea in a state of alienation, the idea's externality—i.e., its immediate temporality and spatiality as such' (101). A few sentences later after remarks on myth in Plato's dialogue, Kierkegaard adds this about myth: 'The dialectical clears the terrain of everything irrelevant and then attempts to clamber up to the idea, but since this fails, the imagination reacts. Weary of the dialectical work, the imagination begins to dream, and from this comes the mythical' (101). After a few remarks on Hegel's view of myth, Kierkegaard limits myth in this way: 'It has validity in the moment of contact and is not brought into relation with any reflection' (101–102). In this passage, Kierkegaard builds up the role of myth while delimiting it, partly by putting forwards a view of Hegel's which he endorses to some degree and also strongly qualifies. Myth is less than dialectic and reflection, but there is no escape from myth since the dialectic can never reach the idea. However, much dialectic clears myth and imagination away, they keep coming back as a way of referring to an idea outside dialectic. The reference to Asa-Loki has a positive function of indicating something about human existence and is also the sign of a failure, the failure to give a dialectical account of the ironist lacking existence in the duality of his existence, and also an indication that myth must accompany philosophical reason, dialectic.

This section on myth links myth with irony as both resting on the same conditions, negation, abstract thinking and dialectic. Following Hegel, Kierkegaard regards dialectic as abstract thinking at its highest, aware of the conditions, negations and limits of ideas in thought. In this case, negation is part of thought and all thoughts are negated, which leads us to the Socratic and the Romantic Ironic position. Kierkegaard makes some distinction between Socratic-Platonic Irony and the Romantic Ironic position, though the elaboration of the difference between Socrates and Plato, the possible interpretations of Socrates, and the differences between Plato's own positions in different dialogues, makes the Romantic Ironic position less one that is simply opposed to Socratic Irony.

> The particular expressions of irony here are of course not in the service of the idea, are not its messengers who collect the scattered parts into a whole; they do not collect but scatter, and each new beginning is not an unfolding of what went before, is not an approach to the idea, but is devoid of deeper connection with the foregoing and devoid of any relation to the idea. (114)

Irony here is distinguished from the idea and from the continuity of abstract thought. As Kierkegaard defines that abstract thought properly speaking as dialectic, with reference to Socrates as well as Hegel, it is the case for him that abstract thought necessarily encounters the myths of imagination and the discontinuities of irony, because there is always a limit to how far abstract thought can go, which is what a lot of Kierkegaard's writing is devoted to explore. The discontinuous nature of irony fragments history turning it into myth and literature: 'Irony dealt with historical actuality in the same way. In a twinkling, all history was turned into myth—poetry—legend—fairy tale. Thus irony was free once again' (277). That last quotation is a comment on the Romantic Ironists, but is a part of Kierkegaard's own programme of philosophical writing with the proviso that it is not all of philosophical writing.

The Romantic moves between endless temporary possibilities. In this case, the Romantic is nothing, because the Romantic can become anything. The Romantic must turn the environment, including morality and ethics which are constitutive in actuality, into products of poetic creation and therefore empty them. The discontinuities of irony remove the substance of life, morality and ethics, as everything becomes a discrete idea of subjectivity, and nothing can have any external reality. The Romantics do sometimes recognise that it is a bad thing to deny the reality of everything including morality and ethics. However, they can only express this idea at an aesthetic level. At that level, everything becomes a mood for the Romantic Ironist, so that life breaks down into a series of unconnected moods.

Kierkegaard follows Hegel in regarding Solger as the Romantic Ironist who is most aware of the limits of aesthetic subjectivity, even where we are concerned with an aesthetic work (1989, 322). The power of the aesthetic as poetic appears in the way that the truth appears in the downfall of a person at this point, presumably referring to Aristotle's notion of tragedy as based on fall following recognition of a concealed truth. But what Kierkegaard means by truth as a whole is something more absolute than the truth of a misjudgement, and its consequences, revealed to the hero of tragedy: 'The something more that can come from this dilution in an infinite hope is nothing more or less than the bliss implicit in the perishing of everything, the desolation and the emptiness in which there certainly is far too much peace and quiet' (322). The Romantic position is based on an elevation of the poetic, but leads to poetic failure, as Kierkegaard argues a few pages back in comments on Tieck:

Romantic poetry moves between two poles. On the one side stands the given actuality with all its paltry philistinism; on the other, the ideal actuality with its dimly emerging shapes. These two elements are indispensable to each other. The more actuality is caricatured, the higher the ideal wells up, but the fountain that wells up here does not well up into an eternal life. The very fact, however, that this poetry moves between two opposites shows that in the deeper sense it is not true poetry. In no way is the true ideal in the beyond—it is behind so far as it is the inspiring goal, but at the same time it is within us, and this is its truth. (305)

Kierkegaard goes on to argue that 'because the separate elements stand isolated—or, more correctly, because the separate elements subsist in an isolated endeavour, there can never be any poetic unity' (306). Where the poetic, apparently referring here to all Romantic literary production including novels, is polarised between the actual and the ideal, which is the Romantic ironic position, there is a failure of poetry. Poetry requires unity to be successful poetry and that unity must come from reference to the truth discussed earlier, which is more than dialectic. Clearly, this is the truth of Christianity, or at least when talking about the pre and non-Christian world, some position which contains something close to the basic Christian claims. For Kierkegaard, this claim is centrally one of the unity of the self with itself, which is only achieved finally in the next life, and which we aim at in this life. Grasping that truth must mean encountering the Romantic Ironic absorption of subjectivity with itself and must show that this self-reference, which breaks down into a series of discrete references, is unified by a complete negation of the world. That complete negation is itself close to the Romantic ironic position, but the negation which is truth negates everything from an absolute position, not as the discrete mood of a moment.

For Kierkegaard, Romantic irony revives and transforms Socratic Irony. Socrates is portrayed as beyond ethical and aesthetic categories (1989, 213–214). In *The Concept of Irony*, Kierkegaard presumes a split between Greek culture and Jewish law, equivalent to the opposition of Romantic aesthetics and ethics (1989, 213–214). Socrates' irony of subjectivity is presented as overcoming both ethics and aesthetics in positing ideality. Socrates' is found to be on one side of the dilemma, his irony is the precursor of Romantic irony: the Romantic ironists themselves frequently identified Socratic irony and the Platonic dialogue as precursors. His denial of the substantive aspects of morality in rejection of the state and law, make him negatively critical. The solution Socrates offers is what Kierkegaard seeks: a relationship beyond the dilemma of aesthetics or ethics, law or Romanticism.

The negative condition of the novel is where its possibilities of getting beyond a merely ironic point lie, as was discussed above in relation to Andersen, but going a step beyond. In *The Concept of Irony*, there is a deeper and more extensive exploration of issues raised in *From the Papers of One Still Living*, in which despite the criticisms of Romanticism and the areas of agreement with Hegel, terms are developed for an understanding of the novel as a genre and the value of the form of the novel, even where it does not merit the highest aesthetic ranking. The novel combines myth and poetry, that is epic style monumentalism and unity of voice combine with subjective relativity, in ways that give insight into areas where dialectic and abstract thought are of limited application, where irony is structurally inherent, but in need of limitation to keep some unity of form and world. Poetry can be partly taken as irony and myth can partly be taken as objectivity, which exist in a necessary unity in the novel. Therefore, the novel can partly be experienced as the tension between elements of epic and elements of subjectivism.

Either/Or

Kierkegaard wrote *Either/Or* in the same year as he received his magister's degree, 1842, and published it in 1843. *Either/Or*, Part 1 does not include an explicit philosophy of the novel, but two essays on aesthetic topics are part of the way that the elements of a philosophy of the novel appear across Kierkegaard's writings, and in this respect, *Either/Or* is the continuation of *The Concept of Irony*. The relevant essays are 'The Immediate Erotic Stages or the Musical-Erotic' followed by 'The Tragic in Ancient Drama Reflected in the Tragic in Modern Drama'. It is in the second of these essays that Kierkegaard brings together themes of society and state, religion and literary aesthetics, discussed above in a particularly clear way. In the key passage of his analysis for present purposes, Kierkegaard suggests that Christianity exists in the world of modernity, 'our age', in which remorse replaces pain and guilt replaces sin (1987 I, 149). The public drama of pain and guilt is replaced in the Christian world by inwardness and the subjective (149). Comments on the difference between modern and ancient tragedy are likely to have relevance to the difference between the novel and the epic, an essential issue for the novel since the novel itself is always caught between more objective epic and more subjective poetic aspects. The difference between epic and novel is not entirely the difference between ancient and modern worlds, but there is some connection, and of what is modern in modern tragedy and what is ancient in ancient tragedy do not exclude the subjective reflective elements labelled as modern from ancient tragedy or exclude the objective substantive elements label as ancient from modern tragedy. The same applies to the compassion, guilt and pain of antiquity, as it does for the sin, repentance and transparency of the modern.

From his analysis of tragedy, we can extrapolate that for Kierkegaard the novel as part of the modern-Christian world is characterised by sin, repentance and transparency, and by a shift from the aesthetic to the ethical. This may seem in tension with the aesthetic irony discussed in *The Concept of Irony*, but Romantic irony is a product of the isolation of the aesthetic from the substance of society, which Kierkegaard identifies in his discussion of modern tragedy. The modern literary work has this aesthetic absolute because the aesthetic is not part of the social substance. Literature has become more ethical in the modern world, because of the role of sin, repentance and transparency, replacing pain, sorrow and compassion. The role of pain, sorrow and compassion in antique literature comes from a world in which those are the highest realities, so is aesthetic in the sense that these are immediate experiences.

In the modern novel, the idea of a real person who has pain and sorrow and for whom we feel compassion has been replaced by the narrator or characters who are transparent to the reader in their sin and possible repentance, that is in their ethical condition, as is confirmed by Kierkegaard's discussion of the contemporary novel in *From the Papers of One Still Living* and *A Literary Review*. This is how the novel can be highly reflective. Kierkegaard's thought on tragedy gives an important perspective on the novel, because it suggests that though the novel strongly tends towards the subjective aesthetic ironic, it does so in a world where ethics have become more basic than aesthetics to literature, so that the irony has a background in the ethical struggles and failures of subjectivity, and the sense of subjective responsibility lacking in antiquity. Anxiety, a subjective situation of individuality that Kierkegaard explores shortly afterwards in *The Concept of Anxiety* as essential to the Christian self, replaces sorrow (1987 I, 154–155). Anxiety contains the reflection that belongs to self-aware subjectivity and includes reflection on time, a factor distinguishing the novel from the more timeless and monumental world of epic. The ethical nature of anxiety is fully explored in *The Concept of Anxiety* with regard to the nature of sin, free will and different types of ethics, that is metaphysical and dogmatic, all of which Kierkegaard can be taken as suggesting indirectly, and maybe beyond any conscious intention, is to be found in the novel.

Moving from Kierkegaard's comments in *Either/Or* on tragedy to his comments on music will enable further enrichment of his view of the form of the novel. Kierkegaard takes *Don Giovanni* as the essential opera in 'The Immediate Erotic Steps or the Musical-Erotic'. Here he is making points about philosophical aesthetics, the nature of the erotic and the nature of writing. Kierkegaard does not have much to say about music in general, but he is always concerning with writing, with language and communication in general, and their limits. He finds it necessary to make a detailed discussion about the music, where the relation between music and writing is an obvious issue in opera.

The legend of Don Juan can only be given artistic form with complete success in music, according to Kierkegaard. But that is music with text, in an opera. Kierkegaard refers to stage versions by Molière and Johan Ludvig Heiberg, claiming they bring absurdity into the character of the Don because his seduction is less immediate, more dependent on verbal trickery reducing the demonic force, the immediate force, of the opera version. In that case, Don Juan has to be understood through the category of the interesting and becomes a seducer who reflects. The immediacy and demonic force in opera comes from music, from its status as the art closest to sensual immediacy (1987 I, 92).

Kierkegaard suggests that the Don lacks the consciousness necessary to seduction, and he is completely and absolutely desire and the desire which seduces as an act. The implication is that the Don does not use language to seduce, and that music is necessary to represent the desire which seduces without words. This also gives him a joyfulness lacking in the melancholy of Faust and his one seduction. 'One must apply the word "seducer" to Don Giovanni very cautiously. This is not because Don Giovanni is so perfect, but because he does not fall within ethical categories at all. Therefore, I would rather call him a deceiver, since there is always something more ambiguous in that term' (1987 I, 98). The Don's seductions are so perfect that they are not seductions, and cannot even be labelled in any morally loaded way, which is why he belongs to music.

What Kierkegaard finds in music is a revelation of the movements of desire in the movement between moments of sound. Music brings forth the relation between the essential and accidental in desire, so that it is just as much the phenomenon of indeterminacy as it is the phenomenon of an essential idea. The sensuality of music is pure aesthetic immediacy in comparison with the reflective nature or language. Nevertheless, language is the aesthetic limit of music, according to Kierkegaard. Language and music are the only material forms of art which exist in time (68) and which appeal to the ear (68). Their temporal duration is necessary to their existence as phenomena of experience.

For Kierkegaard, the relation between music and words can be defined in the way we can discover music through the field which is on the boundary of music and language (66). This is necessary because music resists direct expression in language, so we have to define music through dialectic. It is what language is not, while having some common elements with language. Language is the only medium in which the sensuous becomes only an instrument. Language reduces the sensuous to a medium and constantly negates it. But the same is true in music, what is heard has to continually disengage from the sensuous. Language and music are the only media which are addressed to the ear.

Language and music have time as their element. All the other media have space as their element, though Kierkegaard also suggests that opera extends itself in time and space, it has 'a kind of self-extension in time and space' (1987 I, 118). The occurrence of music in time also means the constant negation of the sensuous, since the moment always disappears to be replaced by another moment. All language contains a musical element, some appeal to sound in the construction of phrases. Language is reflection and cannot grasp the immediate as the immediate is indefinite.

Kierkegaard goes on to argue that the relation of the Don and his servant Leporello in the opera emerges from the way that medieval literature creates an individual who is representative of the idea, and often places another individual alongside him in relation to him. This relation is usually comical and is one in which one individual makes up for the other's extreme qualities. These couples include Don Quixote and Sancho Panza, suggesting that the theme is important in the development of the novel, though this is not followed up by Kierkegaard. This is a feature of the way a philosophy of the novel seems to develop accidentally in his writing with no thought of a complete theory avoiding major gaps. The tension between ideal and real has already been in an issue in discussing Kierkegaard on the novel, but less focused on a clear duality of two major characters.

Don Juan has Leporello as his comical attendant. Medieval thought made the conflict between the flesh and the spirit within Christianity into a subject of reflection, which is the origin of literary duality, creating personified forms of both forces. So in the case of Don Giovanni, the Don has become spirit in the abstract sensuality of music, and Loporello has become the less musical fleshly associate.

In the medieval world, sin only appears in aesthetic indifference, in reflection. But Don Juan cannot be defined from the point of view of aesthetic indifference and reflection, so this is the point as which he dies and the music stops. The doubling of the Commendatore in the Stone Statue represents the point of reflection. Doubling undermines the pure moment to moment sensuality of music. Don Juan resists the reproduction of life, referring to the Commendatore's statue coming alive, because he is just affirmation of sensuous desire. Reproduction refers to spirit and negates the immediacy of desire, and as part of drama in a way it is not part of music drama. This is a way in which Kierkegaard defines the end of the opera *Don Giovanni*, the point where music and the purely aesthetic collapses, as well as the Don's demonic desire.

Don Juan is a pure seducer, since his love is sensuous not psychical, and it seduces all, it is undiscriminating in its objects. This distinguishes him from Greek figures like Hercules, who have many women but do not think ahead to the next one. So compared with the Ancient world, the Don lives more in time. His seductions are momentary, but the moment is the sum of moments taking us beyond the moment in the essence of the seducer. The character of the seducer is part of Kierkegaard's preoccupation with the transition from the moment to endurance over time. 'Music is superbly suited to achieve this, since it is much more abstract than language and therefore articulates not the particular, but the universal in all its universality, and it articulates this universality not in the abstraction of reflection but in the concretion of immediacy' (1987 I, 95).

Kierkegaard offers the second servant aria as an example of unreflective desire, that is the list of the women the Don has seduced. Kierkegaard sees something epic here, though music expresses what epic cannot. This is epic in the partly negative sense given by Aristotle to indicate a less pure poetic form than tragedy. The Don becomes epic by continually finishing and being able to begin all over again, which is life as the incoherent sum of moments, alluding to Aristotle on epic form, as discussed in Chap. 2 above. However, the sensuous cannot be purely epic because as it moves within immediacy, it has not reached the point of words. Only music can present it. Music has an element of time in itself but it does not take place in time, except metaphorically, by which Kierkegaard appears to mean that the experience of time in music does not refer to time as extended in the events of life, but in the time of listening to music only. Music cannot express the historical within time and so cannot be epic. So the most lyrical phenomenon is what becomes music, rather than words, but, this is found fully only in opera where there is staging as well as words.

All the elements discussed above of Kierkegaard's analysis of *Don Giovanni* apply to the novel, particularly the Romantic novel, at least in the sense of an attempted pure Romantic novel like *Lucinde* in that it abandons commitment to the articulation of a consistent point of view in language, moving between moments in a way that is beginning to dissolve the narrative into moments of pure poetry, as if trying to be music. The epic and reflective moments that nevertheless arise in *Don Giovanni* must also apply to the Romantic novel, and indeed to some degree to all novels, because Kierkegaard discusses all novels in terms of the Romantic novel. What Kierkegaard explores through opera are the qualities necessary to the greatest possible novel, in the transitional area between language and music, so that the form of the novel always contains its own collapse in trying to become something else, or at least tends to incorporate anxiety about that collapse as will be discussed at greater length in Chap. 9 below in relation to Marcel Proust.

A Literary Review

A Literary Review continues the indirect building up of a philosophy of the novel, as it takes us back to *From the Papers of One Still Living*. Thomasine Gyllembourg is raised from brief treatment to the main focus, though Kierkegaard still only knows her as 'anonymous' and apparently continues to assume a male author. As before the status of the novel as a form is linked with the status of liberal democratic politics, which is just politics for Kierkegaard, reflecting the historical reality that the idea of a political world comes from the erosion of monarchical and traditionalist power by power claiming to rest on representation and rational process. For a detailed account of the complexities of Kierkegaard's views on politics, see *Kierkegaard on Politics* (Stocker 2014). This time, in *A Literary Review*, Kierkegaard refers to the idea of revolution contesting monarchy and creating passion of a kind in an era which lacks passionate connection between individual. As in the 1838 essay, Kierkegaard briefly refers to the commercial world, though more directly when he mentions 'transactions in paper money' (1990, 74) to sum up a social world lacking in the substance of money as valuable specie, as in gold coins, and in which relations are transactional rather than passionate. This all relates to the way he sees the Gyllembourg novel, and largely sees the novel in general, as from of writing that belongs to a world of reflection and temporary connections between individuals. Kierkegaard even repeats the phrase *ecclesia pressa* (52) from *The Papers of One Still Living* though the context is different, more to do with a woman (Mariane) who upholds Christian expectations with regard to marital conduct, more in an ethical than a religious way, than to any direct sense of religious community.

In *A Literary Review*, as in *Either/Or*, the text begins with a playful approach to the Preface. It is in the later work that the Preface underminines any imperative to read the book, rather than a Postscript at the beginning of the main text questioning the Preface, before questioning the essay which forms the main text. In his examination of Gyllembourg's novel, Kierkegaard picks out the role of love affairs in it to bring out the issue of the double existence of humanity, which recurs in various ways across his work.

> Being in love is the culmination of a person's purely human existence, which is a double existence, and for that very reason being in love is simultaneously just as much inwardness as it is a relation directed outwardly to actuality. Happy erotic love is the equilibrium of the relation.

> Less inwardness and a dominant relation to actuality is a less beautiful love; a dominant inwardness and a lesser relation to actuality tends toward unhappy love. (49)

The idea of double existence, as has been noted above in relation to the pagan Norse god Asa-Loki in *The Concept of Irony* can refer to some limit condition of existence in relation to humanity, but is still a way of bringing forth human existence as containing more than the single existence of a thing. Just as the duality of the pagan god leads the reader towards an understanding of the human individual in a religious context, the duality of existence in love leads us towards Christian love of neighbour and of God. The love affair brings out the duality of existence in an individual directed towards intense community with another individual as well as inner self-community, which as we have already seen in Kierkegaard contains the problem of duality and unity, as there is always a self-relation in human consciousness.

Kierkegaard's philosophy of the novel, here as in earlier texts includes the ideas of reflectiveness as essential to the novel, which is positive here as part of defending substance in the individual which is a contrast with reflection as dealt with in *From the Papers of One Still Living*:

> He travelled both in the old world and the new and then returned to his estate. Consequently he is an individuality who has remained constant, but this also demands an element of reflection [*Reflexion*], and of self-reflection [*Reflexion i sig*], and on the other hand this again is a reflexion of the age [*Reflex af Tidsalderen*] which itself lacks decisiveness and has not had enough influence on him to sweep him along. (58)

Though the capacity of the novel for reflection, characters having thoughts about each other and about the world, as does the narrative voice, lacking in the monolithic voice of epic and the inwards directed nature of lyric, the novel is both superficial in the many reflections, but substantial, or at least dealing with character who have personalities of some substance where reflection shows that substance. A negative kind of reflection is referred to later (102) in relation to exhibitionism, self-revelation of a kind which is always a revelation of emptiness. That these possibilities of reflection are something particular to the novel as a form, though discussed in relation to *Two Ages*, which is assigned a place in the possibilities of reflection.

> The novel has as its premise the distinctive totality of the age, and the production is the reflexion of this in domestic life; the mind turns from the production back again to the totality of the age that has been so clearly revealed in this reflexion. But (according to the preface) the author did not intend to describe the age itself; his novel lies somewhere between the presuppose distinctive character of the age and age in reflexion as illustrated by this work. (32)

Kierkegaard reference to *Two Ages* as typical of the age, anticipates the twentieth-century discussions of the novel as something mimetic and realist, which are discussed in Chaps. 5 and 7 below. Though Kierkegaard is here referring to one novel, and not one he is placing on a level with the work of Cervantes and Goethe, he is suggesting something ideal about it as both reflecting an age in an immediate way and presenting reflection on the age, all through the nature of domestic life. So the novel could perhaps be other things, but it can be and it is hinted at its best should be, a reflection of a society at a particular time, a reflection on that reflection and establishing the reflection through a focus on family and home life, where the contours of an age might be thought to be absent. The element of reflection and reflexivity in reflection itself alludes to Romantic irony, even if Kierkegaard does not make the link explicit, and seems to be trying to balance it with the themes of social reality and political ideas.

Conclusion

Kierkegaard presents himself in varying ways as theological thinker and a thinker concerned with aesthetics in an ironic playful sense. We should not ignore the degree to which these two versions of Kierkegaard overlap. We should also not ignore the degree to which he was a historical, social and political thinker. His contributions in these areas are no less rich for being unsystematic. He does not offer himself as a historical thinker, but all of Kierkegaard's writing has very sensitive and careful historical situation, along with use of history. He shows that the novel, as a widely ready literary genre, is itself a product of a world in which subjectivity seems more important compared with community and tradition, where the individual struggles to find harmony with the social world. This goes together with the commercial interests of the age and the interest in political change away from traditionalist monarchy. Kierkegaard does as much as anyone has to show that the novel is historical in bringing perpetual unrest in these areas into not just the themes of the novel, but its whole form and energy. His contribution to the philosophical investigation of the novel is highly underrated. This chapter has aimed to make some contribution to redressing the balance and demonstrating that the philosophy of the novel should go from Idealist and Romantic aesthetics through Kierkegaard to Lukács, with due regard to Nietzsche's literary aesthetics. It is the work of Lukács, introduced through Nietzsche, which form the basis of the next chapter.

References

Crouter, Richard E. 2007. Schleiermacher: Revisiting Kierkegaard's Relationship to Him. In Stewart 2007c.

Fichte, J.G. 1982. *The Science of Knowledge*, trans. and ed. Peter Heath and John Lachs. Cambridge and New York, NY: Cambridge University Press.

Kangas, David, J. 2007. J.G. Fichte: From Transcendental Ego to Existence. In Stewart 2007b.

Kierkegaard, Søren A. 1983. *Fear and Trembling/Repetition*. Kierkegaard's Writings, VI. trans. and ed. Howard V. Hong and Edna H. Hong. Princeton, NJ: Princeton University Press.

Kierkegaard, Søren A. 1987. *Either/Or, Part I & Either/Or, Part II*. Kierkegaard's Writings, III & IV. trans. Howard V. Hong and Edna H. Hong. Princeton, NJ: Princeton University Press.

Kierkegaard, Søren A. 1989. *The Concept of Irony with Continual Reference to Socrates/Notes of Schelling's Berlin Lectures*. Kierkegaard's Writings, II, trans. Howard V. Hong and Edna H. Hong. Princeton, NJ: Princeton University Press.

Kierkegaard, Søren A. 1990. *Early Polemical Writings*. Kierkegaard's Writings, I. trans. Julia Watkin. Princeton, NJ: Princeton University Press.

Kierkegaard, Søren A. 2009. *Upbuilding Discourses in Various Spirits*. Kierkegaard's Writings, XV. trans. and ed. Howard V. Hong and Edna H. Hong. Princeton, NJ: Princeton University Press.

Stewart, John. 2007. Hegel: Kierkegaard's Reading and Use of Hegel's Primary Texts. In Stewart (2007b).

Stocker, Barry. 2014. *Kierkegaard on Politics*. London: Palgrave MacMillan.

5

Lukács on Subjectivity and History (Introduced Through Nietzsche)

Nietzsche: From Tragedy to Novel

Before examining the work of Georg Lukács on the novel, it is important to look at what comes between Kierkegaard and Lukács, though what is taken as most important here is not a treatise on the novel. It is Nietzsche's work on tragedy along with scattered remarks on the novel which is addressed here. Stendhal (pen name of Henri Beyle) and Fyodor Mikhailovich Dostoevsky feature frequently in Nietzsche's letters and particularly in his notebooks, with Stendhal featuring more however. Nietzsche's admiration for Stendhal is a view of him as connected with the French aphorists and essayists, so like them anticipating many of Nietzsche's own insights and claims. There is nothing that amounts to an analysis here, but it does confirm that Nietzsche places himself within a French tradition which integrates essays, aphorisms, reminiscences and novels. There are more substantial but brief remarks in *On the Genealogy of Morality* (in Nietzsche 200) (Essay III, Sect. 6), *Twilight of the Idols* (in Nietzsche 1968) (Sect. 45 of 'Expeditions of an Untimely Man') and *Ecce Homo* (in Nietzsche 2000) (Sect. 3 of 'Why I am so Clever'; Sect. 3 of 'The Case of Wagner').

© The Author(s) 2018
B. Stocker, *Philosophy of the Novel*,
https://doi.org/10.1007/978-3-319-65891-9_5

Remarks in the latter two books refer to Stendhal's status as a psychologist, empiricist and atheist. Nietzsche does not say much about which Stendhal works excited his attention. There is a wide variety including novels most famously the novels *The Red and the Black* and *The Charterhouse of Parma*, along with other novels, memoirs, travel writings, biographies, essays on literary writers and composers. The reference to Stendhal in *Genealogy of Morality*, II.6 certainly refers to *On Love*. Here Nietzsche contrasts Stendhal's idea of beauty as the anticipation of happiness with Immanuel Kant's Idealist theory in *The Critique of the Power of Judgement* (2000), in which beauty is thought of as interest without interest. There are other readings of Kant's aesthetic, but Nietzsche sets up a contrast which contains a recognisable version of Kant on beauty.

Despite the admiration Nietzsche has for Stendhal as a psychologist, and the lesser attention he pays to Dostoevsky, he does indicate in the same section of *Twilight of the Idols* where he mentions Stendhal, that he has a greater admiration for Dostoevsky: '[T]he testimony of Dostoevsky is of importance—Dostoevsky, the only psychologist, by the way, from whom I had anything to learn: he is one of the happiest accidents of my life, even more so than my discovery of Stendhal' (Nietzsche 1968, 99). Nietzsche goes on to indicate that he finds Dostoevsky's account of criminals in a penal colony in *House of the Dead* particularly valuable. This fits with remarks on Dostoevsky in *The Anti-Christ*, Sect. 3: 'One has to regret that no Dostoevsky lived in the neighbourhood of this most interesting *décadent* [Christ]; I mean someone who could feel the thrilling fascination of such a combination of the sublime, the sick and the childish'. In combination with his remarks on Stendhal, we can infer that what Nietzsche most values in the nineteenth-century novel is psychological investigation, extraordinary and disturbed character types, and challenges to religious or any non-empirical way of think, even in a passionately Christian author like Dostoevsky whose work is of course nevertheless full of atheism and existential despair. We can say that Nietzsche finds in the novel tendencies towards psychological observation particularly of extreme types and collapse of moral-metaphysical system. Nietzsche seems to discern a disintegrating aspect in the form of the novel, following on from earlier accounts but suggesting something more radical with regard to the possibility of normal psychology and a structured world, anticipating later developments of the novel, and literary thinkers like Lukács who responded to later developments.

What is more important for the form of the novel is what Nietzsche has to say about the connection between the appearance of the novel and the death of tragedy in *The Birth of Tragedy* (Stocker 2004). It is a lot more concerned with Ancient Greek Tragedy than the novel, but that does not limit its effectiveness in contributing to an understanding of the form of the novel. The *Birth of Tragedy* can also be read as a justification for a way of writing philosophy, a way that appears in this text, and in all Nietzsche's subsequent texts. That way of writing philosophy is the philosophical novel, already posited in Jena. The Romantic origins may have been a source of embarrassment to Nietzsche, since he only mentioned Romanticism to condemn it as hysterical and governed by *ressentiment*, apparently preferring the pose of classical severity itself somewhat questionable given his only early question of the definitions of the classical. In some respects, Nietzsche's approach to literary genre is less rhapsodic and more Hegelian that the Romantic Ironists. *The Birth of Tragedy* emphasises the distinctions between genres and authors, even while appealing to a version of the philosophical novel and the goal of a genre, which includes all genres, though not approvingly. Tragedy itself how is a difficult unity of the opposing forces of the Apolline and the Dionysian, which structure all human experience, so has something of the ambition the Jena Romantics had for the novel. The genre that abolishes itself, because it is the end of all genres, but in a less heroic way. The relevant passages from *The Birth of Tragedy* are paraphrased below.

The tragic unifies the Apollonian and the Dionysian, the epic and the satyr chorus. The Socratic dialectic undermines tragedy through the agency of Euripides. Consciousness, virtue and wisdom are made equivalent so denying the tragic insights, reducing both the Apollonian and the Dionysian to effects rather than forms of being. This appeared in the tragedies of Euripides which bring the spectator on stage. The spectator no longer participates in the music and being of the Dionysian, because the spectator is now just that appearing as a chorus, which merely views action, already explained in the prologue. That spectator is now Socrates, so reducing the tragic to consciousness, virtue and their beauty. The bringing of the spectator onto the stage can be said to create Socrates to allow the dialectic philosopher. The Dionysian now becomes naturalistic effects, and the Apollonian becomes logical schematism (*The Birth of Tragedy*, Sect. 14). The discussion of that reduction occurs just after the discussion of Platonic dialogue in a return to Euripides. Some uncertainty is suggested about whether to regard the Platonic dialogue as the continuation of Euripides decadent tragic or as its overcoming.

However, the Socratic death of tragedy allows the birth of Platonism. Plato the poet, who according to legend burned his poetry under Socrates' influence, can now take on Socratic dialectic as the basis of a philosophical-literary genre (Sect. 14). The daemonic Socrates himself is under the influence of his own inner daemon, the daemon of instinct, which negates Socrates' rationalism. That daemon turns Socrates away from reducing everything to conscious knowledge, according to his cyclopean vision, and to turn towards music. The Socratic rationalism itself turns him into a Cyclops, identified by Homer, and by Aristotle invoking Homer, as what lies on the limits of humanity. An extreme of dialectic leads to a one sidedness which is both godlike and animal like, as is appropriate to the sons of the sea god Poseidon. The Homeric Cyclopes live isolated from each other without law or community, feeding themselves and staying to their own caves. Socrates isolates himself from the Dionysian experience of the contradictions and underlying nothingness of being. He cannot join the Dionysian loss of self, which established an absolute community, and cannot even join the repeated displacements of the Dionysian in the Satyr Chorus or the tragic performance. Socrates daemon is a counter daemon who leads him towards the community, which must rest on something before law and individuation. Now there is the possibility of rising above schematism and naturalistic effects.

The Socratic death of tragedy provides two sources of new philosophical-literary inspiration: the philosopher who plays music; the dialectician who writes dialogues. Socrates returns to the Dionysian, Plato creates a new unity from the genres of Greek literature (Sect. 14). On the one side, the Euripidean tragedy forms the basis of the novel, through the low characters such as the Graeculus, the cunning servant who is a debased form of Odysseus (Sect. 11); on the other side, the Dionysian returns underground in a tradition of rites and excesses. Plato's dialogues form their own basis for the novel, which seems to be an ambiguous legacy. The dialogue rises above the Aesopian fable where it begins, and which was the only literary form Socrates admired, through bringing in all other forms (Sect. 14). Plato's metaphysics was anticipated in the tragic resistance to an image of a particular individual. This seems in contrast to Nietzsche's later condemnation of everything Platonist, but maybe a distinction can be made between their philosophy turned into a system, and their own living and writing of philosophy, which would be compatible with the later self-image of Nietzsche as anti-Plato. It is possible to formulate a Nietzschean goal of philosophical literature after the death of tragedy. A literature which emphasises the plurality of styles within one style, the impossibility of natural forms, the contradictory nature of any naïve approach, the conflict between particularity and universality, the ideal of the hero caught between particularity and universality in necessary crime, the struggle with the empirical self, the struggle with the death and nothingness necessary to rise above mere sensibility and given laws, an individuality torn between itself and community, a representation exploring its unrepresentable origin. Philosophical writing in Nietzsche is dialectic and music, dialogue and poetry, law and intoxication. The Socratic combination of rational criticism and the daemonic is the model and counter model of Nietszcheanism, continuing into its later stages, and suggesting there is something of the philosophical novel in Nietzsche's own way of writing, a topic for Chap. 10.

To translate man back into nature, to become master over the many vain and overly enthusiastic interpretations and connotations that have so far been scrawled and painted over that eternal basic text of *homo natura;* to see to it that man henceforth stands before man as even today, hardened in the discipline of science, he stands before the *rest* of nature, with intrepid Oedipus eyes and sealed Odysseus ears, deaf to the siren songs of old metaphysical bird catchers who have been piping at him all too long, "you are more, you are higher, you are of a different origin!"—that may be a strange and insane task, but it is a *task*. (*Beyond Good and Evil*, 7 'Our Virtues': § 230. Nietzsche 2000, 351–352)

Nietzsche's discussion of the birth and death, and return of tragedy, gives many pointers to philosophical aesthetics and the study of literary genres. The account of universality and particularity, of hero and law, points towards the kind of development of Hegelian concepts that enabled Lukács to an account of the novel in *The Theory of the Novel* (Lukács 1971b). With the help of Nietzsche, Lukács was able to turn Hegelian concepts into an account of hero and world in the novel, as continuation of epic form. Nietzsche's account of Platonic dialogue as a literary genre and in the origins of the novel point towards Bakhtin's account of Socratic dialogue, Menippean satire and polyphonic novel in *Problems of Dostoevsky's Poetics* (Bakhtin 1984b); his account of the place of the Dionysian in European culture and literature point towards Bakhtin's account of the Carnivalesque in his Dostoevsky book and, more particularly, in *Rabelais and His World* (Bakhtin 1984a). At the most general level, through *The Birth of Tragedy*, it is possible to look back to Vico's interpretation of law and history through Homer in *The New Science* (Vico 1984); and forward to Lukács on epic and novel, the appropriation of Homer in Joyce and the philosophical reflection on the novel and genre in *Ulysses* and *Finnegans Wake*. Vico had already provided the suggestion of the recurrence of the early Greek struggle to establish law and language out of the violence and muteness of the earliest stages of humanity. The stages of gods, heroes and peoples will keep returning in the tension between law and force, language and gesture.

As Nietzsche suggests in 'The Uses and Disadvantages of History for Life', we can struggle with the weight of history through a return to the creation of history in Ancient Greece. Nietzsche here refers to a pre-novelistic era, so the novel is the literary form tied up with and burdened by history. It can only be fully recognised as the work of eighteenth-century historical philosophy permeates intellectual and cultural life. The importance of Homeric epic itself can only be fully discussed in the beginning of historical philosophy in Vico's *New Science*. *The Iliad* and *The Odyssey* are the earliest forms of history as well as of the novel, and there is an inevitable return to them as historical thought and the genre of the novel emerge. This is all obliquely present in Nietzsche. In Lukács, we can see how the Nietzschean approach to literary form, and what Nietzsche draws on, feeds into a conscious philosophy of the novel.

Romantic Lukács

The early work of Lukács, particularly with regard to *The Theory of the Novel* (1971b), but also taking into account *Soul and Form* (1974) makes a vital contribution to the philosophical discussion of literary form. In the tradition of German Idealism and Romanticism, literature appears as forms which contain the essential contradictions of consciousness in general, and through stages of history. We can trace this back to Kant's *Critique of the Power of Judgement*, but also to the earlier work of Vico. The role that literature has in *The New Science* makes it an essential form for grasping an intersection of law and language, as they appear in stages of history. Vico most obviously anticipates the overtly historicist approach of Hegel, via Rousseau and Montesquieu, but Kant's apparent formalism should not blind us to the essential historicism present in much of Kant: there are connected assumptions about law and cognitive judgement, which have strong precedents in Vico. From Vico and Kant, we can follow a line of development in the exposition of literary form as a philosophical issue in German Idealism and Romanticism, and the work of Schopenhauer, Kierkegaard and Nietzsche, then Lukács and Benjamin.

From Vico to Lukács, a literature is embedded in historical consciousness, reflecting or expressing the essential capacities of language in the consciousness of an era. The German Idealists and Romantics are all interested in, our troubled, by how literary-aesthetic consciousness is subjective and inward, so expressing essential aspects of individual consciousness, but also supporting the differentiation of subjectivity from objective world. The connection of aesthetic-subjectivity with world may require the world to be seen as determined not only by the rational ideas of reason, but by its subjective inner self-reflection.

This may allow a metaphysical realism in which individual consciousness is determined by an objective, it might also only allow an internal realism in which the reference of our conscious constructs to an outer world is uncertain. The tensions round these questions have developed to the point where it is no longer plausible to conceive of literary history and aesthetic theory as joined in the Idealist enterprise of reducing literary texts to the categories of historical concepts which reflect the inner structure of consciousness. These tensions were already at issue in Kierkegaard and Nietzsche. Nevertheless, we cannot consider questions of literary history and philosophical aesthetics without regard to the Idealist and Historicist gesture, because at some point we must be concerned with what the historical context of literature is and how it refers to the structures of consciousness. Attempts to reduce the philosophy of mind to the categories available for discussing literary genre and form would be misguided and implausible given developments since the time of Lukács, as would attempt to reduce history to those concepts. Reduction of literary history to Idealist speculation cannot survive an interest in the characteristics of consciousness itself, which owe their origins to German Idealism to a very large degree. Literary studies themselves have done so much to incorporate awareness of non-canonical texts, social context and discourse in all its aspects that the work of Lukács at issue here cannot be accepted as the total basis of literary studies. It must also be said that Lukács' work on literature as part of society and history has contributed to those processes.

It must also be noted that the early texts of Lukács are some kind of limit for him, which they had to overcome. For Lukács, the overcoming was an embrace of Marxism and the production of very significant work on Marxist philosophy of history and society, literary history and aesthetic theory, along with an important role in the history of Hungarian Communism, particularly in 1919 and 1956. Lukács' work on the philosophical relation of Marx to Hegel and an associated internal study of Marx's categories transformed the understanding of Marxist philosophy.

Despite all these later achievements, it is assumed here that the most significant work is in earlier texts, which are a culmination before other preoccupations take over. Their importance here is that they are both extraordinary works of historical synthesis which are also full of valuable conceptual analysis. This is reflected in a style of writing, which is daunting but is a literary achievement in itself, an achievement of dialectic, in which the connections between ideas are established through the power of writing, with a sensitivity of style which also allows for precision in the use of concepts. The lack of the explicit political teleology is an advantage from the point of view of grasping texts and genres: maybe the later achievements can be best preserved by reading them from the point of view of earlier texts.

Lukács: *The Theory of the Novel*

In many respects, this is a continuation of Hegel's discussion of epic and novel in the *Aesthetics*. It is somewhat like Hegel, without God in general, and without Christianity in particular. Lukács differs from Hegel in giving weight to the novel as a major branch of literature. The core work for the Idealist Romantic phase of Lukács' work is *The Theory of the Novel* (1971b), so putting philosophy of the novel at the centre of his achievement. It is summarised here, according to its chapter headings in order to provide a way into this remarkably difficult and complex contribution, which is perhaps the greatest single work on the philosophy of the novel. The explication takes the form of extensive paraphrase followed by explanation of the book as a whole.

(Chapter 1: Integrated Civilisations). The happy world is one in which the self is not a stranger to the world, so that the starry sky lights up all paths with the same fire as in the soul. Action has a double meaningfulness: in sense and for the senses. Philosophy is in life or is what determines literature. There is no rift between inside and outside, self and world, soul and deed. Everyone is a philosopher and there is no separate activity of philosophy. In the utopian aim of philosophy, inner impulses of the soul are co-ordinated with forgotten eternal forms. Passion is determined by reason in complete being. There is no experience of the danger and torment of looking for the self or risk of losing it. Transcendental power is experienced in a madness, which reveals what would otherwise be silent. There is no absence of suffering, but there is a correspondence between deeds and the urges of the soul to greatness and completeness. There is no feeling of an abyss in the soul.

Epic belongs to the happy world. The only epics strictly defined are Homer's so the happy world is the Ancient Greek world. The Ancient Greek mind is different from our mind, with a different transcendental topography. Modern thinkers try to find momentary happiness in the Ancient Greek world, of a kind foreign to the essential nature of life in the Ancient Greek world. Others have looked at the suffering in themselves the source of their creativity and looked at the greatness of Ancient Greek literature as the product of the deepest possible inner suffering. From the point of view of the Ancient Greek world, all meaning can be taken in at a glance. Knowledge looks directly at things, creation directly copies eternal visible essences, virtue is the knowledge of paths given to us. Love, the family and the state are the home which fills relations with others with substance (an implicit reference to a Hegelian view of ethical life. Much of what Lukács says has this kind of implicit reliance on Hegel as can be understood, at least to some degree with reference to the discussions of Hegel, along with related and reactive thoughts in Chaps. 3 and 4 above).

For us the spirit is productive, not passively accepting a world where it is at home. Thought now follows an endless approximation, and we have invented the creation of forms. Substance now exists outside ourselves, so that there is a chasm between self and world. The totality of the world is destroyed. Tragedy moves from the epic question how does life become essential, to the question, how does essence become alive. In Plato's philosophy, life loses its being because the truth is in abstract forms. If philosophy shows the world of experience to be arbitrary then tragic destiny appears as a cruel extension of that empirical arbitrariness. Plato unmasked this tragedy as formed by the rift between essence and life, in a move which ended the Greek world. Now the world is only lit by the stars as objects of pure knowledge, disconnected from life and ethics (implicitly starting on the path to the philosophy of Immanuel Kant, who said his philosophy was concerned with the starry sky overhead and the moral law within). Individual actions no longer reflect inner essence as we can no longer say what essence is, we only have the phenomenal self. In this way, the metaphysical unity of the world is destroyed and art is no longer a copy of the world, because that presumes a metaphysical unity which can be transformed into aesthetic unity, art is now independent of the world. The pagan gods have fled, and the Christian church is based on the split between original sin and other worldly salvation. However, the medieval Christian world was able to achieve a new totality, a rounded world, on the basis of a balance between heterogeneous perspectives. Aesthetics became metaphysics, but for the last time. In the modern world, aesthetics can only become metaphysics through turning the aesthetic form into a metaphysical thing. Art is caught in the contradiction between nostalgia for Greek happiness and art's own existence as what can form a conscious sphere only after the break-up of Greek totality. Art can only exist by producing a reduced world of its own, or by showing the impossibility of achieving the object of art and the emptiness of artistic means.

(Chapter 2: The Problems of a Philosophy of Form). Since the loss of Greek totality, there is attempted unity but not the Homeric totality which comes from life. There are shifts in genre resulting from an evolving dialectic of form in search of transcendental conditions to justify its existence. Emergent genres are characterised by transcendental homelessness, exemplified by the modern novel. For the Ancient Greeks, philosophy of history coincided with history so that the genres came and went in a way which appeared absolutely natural. Genres have become much more confused, a mass of experience in which form has become symbolic. Epic hopes to reconcile subjectivity with the substance of the world as object. Tragedy could survive because it already dealt with a split between life and essence. Because tragedy was not suddenly abolished it continues in a nostalgia for the unity of essence and life. However, it cannot get beyond resorting to pure essence or resort to a brief existence in the life left from the original totality. Shakespeare is an example of the latter, and his literature is a failure compared with the great epics and epic-novels. Modern drama has excluded life to retain its aesthetic form, but life keeps returning and showing the limits of a priori schema. The hero as a great figure no longer appears natural and has to rise above normal humanity. Tragedy therefore can now only deal with absolute solitude and silence. The dominant problem becomes that of trust and communication with other humans.

The epic is the form of the extensive totality of life with an empirical 'I', drama is the form of the intensive totality of essence with an intelligible 'I' (another implicit suggestion that literary change is part of the path to Kantian philosophy). Epic is less able to exclude the empirical, and the real world interrupts any utopian promise it carries, so that the epic becomes polarised between what is and what should be (again an implicit reference to Kantian philosophy). The 'should' kills life and reduces the epic to rhetoric as a force of unity. After Homer, the best work is the epic in Virgil and Dante, and then the epic style novels of Cervantes and J.W. Goethe. These works deal with the subjective longing for totality, in which emotion becomes lyricism. The modern novel ends up with Émile Zola who mimics epic monumentality, but can only produce sociological facts and emotionalism, opposed to each other with little unity. The epic looks for unity in subjective wonder and humility before the world. A subjective transcendental synthesis is the basis of unity.

The short story is able to produce a unity of lyricism and objectivity, through the precise and limited range of its world. Arbitrariness and ambiguity can be given form and the story is given unity by mood, the subject of artistic creation. Meaninglessness and the absurd become the form of fiction and are redeemed by eternal form.

(Chapter 3: The Epic and the Novel). Tragic verse creates distance emphasising the hero's solitude; epic verse creates a distance of lightness in which the bonds of the earth are lightened in happiness. Epic deals with the heaviness of being tied to life as brutal materiality. Epic can only be written in verse in a time of lightness, otherwise it is transformed into lyric verse (an implicit reference to the evolution of poetry after the great epics of ancient Greece, ancient Rome and medieval Italy). It is prose which has the plasticity to embrace the contradictions of a world divided between constraint and freedom, heaviness and lightness.

Dante achieves the perfect immanence of the transcendent (presence of the ideal world in the language of this world) in a language which is more lyrical than Homer's and in which absolute immanence is no longer possible, so that sense appears in the sensible. Ethical life has become external postulates, but postulates which are fulfilled. The form of the novel shows a search for totality, in which there is a psychology of the hero. Ethical necessity and real relations are replaced by psychological facts (as we have seen, Nietzsche puts this at the centre of the novel). Crime and madness appear in the hero, as heroism and wisdom are only separated by psychology from them (again what Nietzsche finds important in the novel). Crime and madness are objectifications of transcendental homelessness. Form has become the resolution, and therefore acknowledgement, of the absurd, the lack of direction in life.

A second nature is formed of the conventions where the inner soul can become man (a reference to the German Idealist and Romantic understanding that natural humanity develops a second nature in culture, an idea with strong roots in Jean-Jacques Rousseau and coinciding with the emergence of the novel as a topic of philosophical-aesthetic debate). The second nature is a dead nature of frozen forms, which leads to sentimental attachment to the lost first nature. Man is alienated from both natures, when the second nature emerges. The second nature becomes an alien, sublime and unapproachable law. Living outside a world of ethical substance, the individual becomes purely cognitive looking for an end to willing and wanting (an implicit reference to Arthur Schopenhauer's philosophy and ethics, along with Nietzsche's critique).

(Chapter 4: The Inner Form of the Novel). Dante's world is that of a system of concepts, but concepts which are still visual. The totality of concepts can therefore be constitutive rather than regulative, part of the world not limiting it from outside. A novel systematises totality in abstract terms. The objective world is conventional, and the subjective world is internal. The form giving intention of the novel cannot overcome this opposition or the opposition between systematisation from concrete life. The elements are abstract in Hegel's sense that they are one sided and unconnected. The hero's nostalgia for utopian perfection comes into conflict with factual social structures, and this is shown in the form of an experience that cannot overcome the social facts.

Every art form is the attempted resolution of a metaphysical dissonance which comes from the incompleteness of the resolution attempted by the mood of the novel world and the atmosphere of the characters. The novel has particular dissonance which is the distance between the immanence of being and empirical life. The novel has a world which is objectively incomplete and subjectively is concerned with mature resignation. The novel has an abstract structure in which immanence of meaning is achieved by exposing its absence; the absence of immanent meaning is the meaning of the novel. Dissonance is the form of the novel and is what defines the novel. In other literary forms, ethics precede the individual form, providing its essence and totality, balancing parts in 'justice'. The ethical intention is within the novel in every detail. Other genres appear to have a finished form; the novel exists in its becoming. The novel is what has a problematic. The content of the novel is incomplete, but as form it balances being and becoming and overcomes itself as complete.

The laws of the novel are less definable and formulated than with closed forms, but they still exist in tact and taste which stand apart from ethics and protect the novel from abstraction. These laws enable the novel to achieve epically normative objectivity. Abstraction is avoided if the subject accepts objective reality, otherwise the epic form collapses. This is the self-recognition and self-abolition of subjectivity identified by the Romantic aesthetic philosophers. The normatively creative subject is divided between an interiority which struggles against an alien world and a subjectivity which recognises the mutual necessity of the subjective and objective worlds, in a unified world. Irony makes everything connected and many sided through misunderstandings and cross purposes. However, the relationship is conceptual not organic and still leaves the parts in abstract self-dependence.

The parts require a stronger architecture than epic in order to maintain unity, as the parts are more contingent. The parts of a novel have independent life, which is covered over by ironic (showing the parts to be less than an absolute point of view) compositional tact (avoidance of showing the unintegrated structure of the novel) in something like organic unity, but the organic appearance is always illusory (implicitly suggesting the inadequacy of the Jena Romantic approach to irony in the novel). The novel tries to overcome its lack of inner unity with an outward biographical form, as a way of coping with the dual force of life without completeness and a conceptual system outside life. It is the breakdown of constitutive concepts of art (concepts of art which belong within art), the individual becomes necessary not only as an example but as the bearer of values. Life and system are present in the biographical individual, a problematic individual who unites two spheres. The problematic individual arises from the conflict between the outside world and individual's ideas which have become subjective ideals.

Reality without an immanent ideal appears as nothingness. The immediate result is purely intellectual but has effects on literary form. There is a disharmony between the interiority of the individual and the substratum of actions; and the incompleteness of the world which makes totality impossible. The Romantic ideal of the novel as absolute literature containing all genres is the result of trying to create a whole where totality is impossible, and where ideas regulate reality from outside. The novel shows the struggle of individual from the emptiness of present reality to a self-recognition where a glimpse of meaning—integration—is possible. The novel is composed of discrete parts, and the epic has a continuum in its form. They represent two aspects of infinity: the novel is the bad infinity (a term from Hegel) of limitless addition of disconnected parts; the epic has infinity of range combined with an organic limit. The novel raises up the individual, but turns the individual into mere instrument. The beginning has an importance in the novel which is not present in epic. The novel is structured around the beginning and end of the hero's life. In epic, the beginning and end are just examples of intense moments like others within the epic. For Dante, the beginning and end mark the boundaries from chaos and from pure redemption. With these limits, we find the eternal ecstatic becoming of the *Divine Comedy*. (The suggestion is that time is repetitive and non-developmental in epic; in the novel, it is liner and developmental).

(Chapter 5: The Historico-Philosophical Conditioning of the Novel and Its Significance). The novel is intrinsically paradoxical, constantly integrating the heterogeneous and then abolishing it (Romantic Irony). The only unifying principle is the ethic of creative subjectivity, which is in contradiction with the norm of objectivity. Tact tries to correct the non-objectivity of the novel, establishing a relation between two ethical positions. The novel contains reflection on reflection, the subjectivity of the narrator reflects on the reflective attempt to give form to life. Each stage of reflection is a destruction of a stage of naivety, which turns the novel into a circle where the individual is led to resignation. Demands are seen to be only demands, but their unreality is combined with the unreality of the individual who can give up ideal demands. The child-like world of the epic, where the hero is in the secure world of a familiar god, turns into the adult world of the novel, where the gods have become demonic, because they are fallen gods or gods who have not achieved their domain. In the demonic world, meaning and causality is incomprehensible, and the world has become senseless. Tragedy absorbs everything into the soul and its longing for home, and the demonic and the godlike are the same in a labyrinthine, meaningless reality. Gods appear as fallen from divine transcendence in epic; in the novel, God has abandoned the world. In drama, there is no separation between interiority and the world, everything the soul comes into contact with becomes part of its destiny. However, in modern drama, this stage has not been reached and it is in a styleless investigation of the conditions of the union between soul and world. In epic, the victory of gods over demons is necessary, and the hero is just a centre. In the novel, the victory of the gods is not necessary and individuality becomes all. The novelistic struggle is itself the effect of a demonic challenge to the apparent solidity of modern reality, which is known to be lacking in substance. The novel is a form of negative mysticism (the theological tradition in which we gain knowledge of god by denying knowledge of any particular thing, so that we can overcome all limited forms of knowledge). The negative mysticism is a via *dolorosa* (road of suffering, like Christ's route to the crucifixion) contained in Romantic Irony. All particular perspectives, forms and genres are mentioned in order to be denied. The form of the novel is a demonic way in which the demonic nature of the soul is shown in a godless world, but which also shows us the way to god. This structure of the novel reflects reality as it is. A godless world, in which present reality lacks substance, lacks integration between ideas and world. Dostoevesky is held given a rather redemptive but vague role. His work is referred to as something beyond the novel, maybe as the beginning of what comes after the novel or maybe as what ends the novel as the age of sin. Maybe Bakhtin's *Problems in the Poetics of Dostoevsky*, examined in the next chapter, can be read as a response to the role Lukács ascribes to Dostoevsky.

Commentary on *The Theory of the Novel*

The Theory of the Novel is not exactly a philosophical novel of exploration of form, but it is an impassioned essay with some narrative elements and a melancholy attitude to the passing of time. It conveys a way of understanding the novel as a form through the passion of its engagement and responses, which bring out what is most notable in the novel. In many respects, this is a continuation of Hegel's discussion of epic and novel in the Aesthetics. It is somewhat like Hegel in a more pessimistic version giving weight to the novel as a major branch of literature, unrestrained by philosophy and religion, because the novel shows tensions within consciousness that are not obviously resolved by religion and philosophy, or at least not of the kind Hegel thought made art redundant as a major form of human consciousness.

As we have seen, for Hegel, the novel is a decadent form of the epic and for Lukács, and the Hegelian picture is essentially correct, while not allowing enough to the aesthetic achievement of the form of the novel. However, there are reasons why he has to add to it and reasons why this creates some distance from Hegel's original position. Apart from the lack of God in Lukács, at least in terms of religious traditions and institutions, the continuing development of the novel after Hegel's time inevitably questions Hegel's failure to engage with the novel as an aesthetic form. The issues of God and the development of the novel are linked since the content of the novel cannot be supernatural. Its content is inevitably limited to that of social life and psychological 'reality'. As Lukács notes, Cervantes was a conventional Christian but his fictional world in *Don Quixote* inevitably throws doubt on God and Christianity. Since it throws doubt on the ideal in at length and with great variety of points of views, none of which can rise above a parodic view of the ideal, whether with reference to chivalry or to religion.

For the Romantic Ironists, *Don Quixote* stood as the model of an infinite irony, an interplay of the infinite possible points of view, which together lead us to the absolute since their interplay shows the lack of truth in any particular point of view. For Lukács, this can only be the bad infinite. The novel just keeps adding episodes or points of view without achieving a totality, so to some degree repeating Aristotle's view of epic in comparison with tragedy. The Homeric epic achieved totality since the question does not arise of different points of view, or of any kind of psychological reality distinct from action in a world which is our home. Novalis described philosophy as transcendental homelessness, for Novalis philosophy is tied up with the novel.

The work of the Jena Romantics on the novel as a fusion of poetry and philosophy was rooted in a reading of Kant and Fichte. Lukács claims that for Fichte, the novel is rooted in an age of sin. The Jena idea of the novel is of bad infinity, sin and a subjectivist form of philosophy. Lukács position builds on this. He builds on their discussion of the novel as structured by irony and adds to it, in the context of a less optimistic view of the novel's purpose. It is the form of sin. Sin is not presented in a Christian or theological sense, though that is not necessarily entirely absent. Just as Lukács' discussion of irony and ethics in the novel echoes Kierkegaard's in *The Concept of Irony*, his view of sin and the demonic echoes that of Kierkegaard in Either/Or I, particularly the sections on music and tragedy. Though writing from a strongly Christian point of view and apparent theological conservatism, for Kierkegaard in general sin can be discussed in psychological (*The Sickness unto Death*, Kierkegaard 1980; *Concept of Anxiety* 1981) and aesthetic terms (*Either/Or I*, Kierkegaard 1987). In *The Concept of Irony*, the ironic view of the novel is seen as ethically destructive, since it throws itself back on the pure autonomy and interiority of a self which has no limitation. In *Either/Or*, it is suggested that sin only exists from the Christian point of view, which creates sin by defining certain acts as sinful. Therefore, what is defined as bad by Christianity is not sin strictly speaking if it comes from following nature or the 'aesthetic' interest in the moments of life, rather than in deliberate opposition to Christian principles. Aesthetic or natural 'sin' is daemonic, a subject which follows its nature to the full without regard to the moral law, rather than deliberately engaging in acts of evil. From Kierkegaard's point of view, any reflection at all on the daemonic leads to anxiety, melancholy and sickness of a psychological kind. Kierkegaard constructs a model of the daemonic as aesthetic-natural hedonistic becoming reflective-melancholic sinful, which has clear application to Lukács. The Ancient Homeric world did not know sin according to Lukács, in line with Kierkegaard. There is an antique understanding of the daemonic, but in the Homeric world this cannot outweigh the power of the gods, the totality of the world which prevents disturbance, or the existence of the human individual in harmony with the environment and not opposed to it. Aesthetics only deals with an autonomous and powerful daemonic in the novel since Cervantes.

It is important here that in *The Discourse on Method* and *The Meditations*, Descartes refers to the possibility of a deceiving demon as the source of my world and the need to avoid imagining a fantastic world of knights and enchantment. In Descartes, philosophy should establish itself through a narrative of subjective experience which avoids the daemonic and the fantastic, a concern which suggests that narrative and subjective reflection are both prone to these temptations or fears. It is not just German Idealism and Romantic Irony which risk a collapse in a fantastic daemonic world, the danger goes back to Cervantes and Descartes.

It is very much in Kant that Lukács suggests the origin of the daemonic can be found. The references to Kant are oblique, but it is clear that Lukács finds the Homeric world to be a kind of opposite to Kantian ethics, in which the idea of the moral law is outside the individual and therefore becomes a transcendental ideal. The novel is structured by the absence of the moral idea (and God) from the world of experience. There is no novelistic structure otherwise. It is because of this that the novelistic world is daemonic. The hero is pure subjectivity confronting an objective world, moral law and other subjectivities, which stand outside the starting subjectivity. Once the subjective psychological starting point is accepted, instead of the individual as an actor in a totality, these kinds of separation and opposition cannot be eliminated. The hero is daemonic in relation to the world, and the world is daemonic in relation to the hero. The hero may now be a criminal or a lunatic (both are suggested by the character of Don Quixote) and sees the outer world as alien. That is the point of view of Kantian epistemology and judgement for Lukács. The novel is written as a judgement in which a self synthesises a manifold of intuitions through concepts. The intuitions are chaotic pure sensation. The concepts are abstract products of intellect, and the judgement itself is an imposition by a pure ego of abstract concepts on the materiality of sensation. This is a unity of what cannot be unified once it has been torn asunder. The same problem exists for ethics. The epic is formed by a world view which includes ethical structure in its totality. The novel is formed by the lack of ethical ideals in the world and the need to impose ethical unity from outside. The ethical point of view cannot be imposed from outside. Lukács follows Hegel here. He maybe following Kierkegaard more though, since while Kierkegaard accepts that the modern world has lost the ethical immediacy of the ancient world, he does not accept a mediated unity in the modern world. The ethical if it is outside subjectivity cannot be reunified with it and subjectivity is left on its own, an impossible burden unless it can find the absolute within itself. Unlike Kierkegaard, though Lukács is not very willing to articulate a strong subjectivity. We are just left in a daemonic world.

The structure of the novel in Lukács is determined by isolated and absolute subjectivity. The structure is accordingly ironic, since the experiences of the hero are never felt to come from inside and are not felt as the hero experiencing an inner self. The psychological subjective nature of the hero has other consequences. Since the novelistic world lacks the timeless permanence and totality of the epic world, it must seek other sources of unity. The sense of changelessness and enduring world which unifies epic is replaced in the novel by time and memory. The world can only be formed through the flow of time, and the self can only be formed by memory. The hero experiences a world changing through time and experiences the world as a succession of moments rather than as a constant whole. The world is devalued since it is something that changes and therefore lacks metaphysical substance. The same applies to the understanding of the self, which can only grasp itself through past moments which are lost opportunities. All moments are lost opportunities since every moment is the experience of the world as alien and as the self failing to find itself, or express itself in the world.

Lukács distinguishes between the novel of failure and the more positive novel in the Bildungsroman. However, it is clear that for Lukács the essential category of the novel is the novel of failure and the Bildungsroman, or any other apparently positive novel, is a mask for failure. The discussion of the archetypal examples of the Bildungsroman, Goethe's Wilhelm Meister novels, makes this clear as Lukács describes the positive motifs as damaging to the aesthetic unity and quality of the novel. Comparable points can be found with regard to Dickens and Balzac. Dickens is held to be stuck in a world of social convention alien to inner individuality and preventing his comic invention from achieving a positive vision. Balzac provides for an implicit contrast with Dante, the *Human Comedy* (Balzac's term for his many novels taken as a whole) compared with the *Divine Comedy*. For Lukács, the complex interweaving of themes and characters across novels in Balzac does not create anything like totality or a positive vision. It shows the arbitrariness and formlessness of a novelistic world in which the only connections between individuals are accidental and external even if numerous.

Flaubert's *Sentimental Education* with its passive and introspective hero, and sense of lost ideals with regard to both subjective love and political-historical events, is taken as typical. Tolstoy is considered as the author of modern epics, but while Lukács sees genuinely epic aspects in Tolstoy, particularly with regard to feelings of unity between humans and nature, these are moments in a novelistic structure which can in the end only mourn the loss of unity between humanity and nature. In a rather Hegelian way, Lukács suggests that nature itself becomes gross materiality lacking in spirit, particularly with regard to the place of marriage in Tolstoy as where society and nature converge.

The account of time and memory is set up in relation to Henri Bergson, who discussed these themes in *Matter and Memory* (1991). From this point of view, Bergsonian time and memory is an accurate philosophy of alienated subjective individuality, rather than the basis of a philosophical totality. Cartesian, Kantian and Fichtean subjectivity are shown to collapse into the experience of pure moments and the need to impose unity on them through memory. The novel lacking in a world of objective unity can only unify its own point of view with regard to the psychological moods of the hero, in Lukács' thoughts about subjectivity.

Inevitably the moods are a unity, felt to be imposed from outside, even when dealing with a subjectivist Bergsonian explanation, so this is still and alienated form of unity.

These literary and philosophical meditations were put in a new context, when Lukács became a communist and participated in the short-lived 1919 soviet government of Hungary. Lukács had a new phase as a Marxist thinker, most notable for its contribution to social philosophy, *History and Class Consciousness* (1971a), but also including major work in literary aesthetics and history.

Lukács the Marxist

Lukács' Marxist phase as regards the novel includes a number of works but most famously *The Historical Novel*, a book written in Moscow at the height of Stalinist terror. Stalin does not get any references, so at least the book is free of official ideology to that degree. Marx, Engels and Lenin are frequently invoked. Lenin's political experience of the Russian people shortly before the October Revolution of 1917 is compared to Walter Scott's understanding of the common people at vital moments of Scottish and British history (1969, 45–47) in his relevant novels, an extraordinary conjunction.

> Lenin learns from these reactions with the greatest sensitivity and turns them to account with remarkable speech and precision in the consolidation, substantiation and propagation of the correct political perspective. It would of course be historically wrong if interactions of this kind were portrayed in novels dealing with the Middle Ages, or the seventeenth or eighteenth centuries. Besides, such interactions lay far beyond the horizon of the classical novel. Moreover this example was only meant to illustrate the general structure of the interaction. But though all Scott's heroes acted with a 'false consciousness, this is never a scheme, neither in its content nor its psychology. (Lukács 1969, 47)

The Historical Novel certainly goes beyond examination of Marxism in its sketches of intellectual history in the nineteenth century which indicate the role of Hyppolite Taine, Jakob Burckhardt and Friedrich Nietzsche (who was in personal contact with the two previous figures) in developing connections between elitism, subjectivism, agonism and liberalism which are as useful as far as they go, but are rather constrained by Lukács' framework of the decay of progressive bourgeois thought after 1848. His focus on William Makepeace Thackery and Gustave Flaubert's less widely read historical novels, *The History of Henry Esmond* and *Salammbo*, does give insights into intriguing moments in literary history, but are again rather constrained by the overarching narrative of bourgeois decline. The novels picked out as signs of decline are no less palatable to current literary tastes than the Walter Scott narrative novels given the highest status by Lukács, which rather undermines the decline thesis. Leo Tolstoy's *War and Peace* written after the onset of bourgeois 'decline' is by most standards a greater literary achievement than anything written by Scott. It is nevertheless important to remember that Scott had an enormous influence on nineteenth-century views of the novel and of history, inspiring other 'national' novelists like Alessandro Manzoni and James Fenimore Cooper, and Lukács gives a good overview of how such novels seemed important in dealing with political dilemmas of the time through a view of the past and the development of nation.

Lukács' faith in Scott's closeness to popular feeling is questionable, but his reasoning around the epic possibilities of the novel does give insight into the nature of the genre. The epic, Lukács argues, should concentrate on secondary and imaginary ordinary people in great historical moments in order to create a complete and rounded view of the relation between great events and the people. The central personalities in events distract from the broad social impact and context. The successful historical novel is an example of the novel retaining vital aspects of epic. The action of the *Iliad* does not deal with the final fall of Troy and Achilles is offstage most of the time. The confusion of the Battle of Waterloo in *The Charterhouse of Parma* and of the Battle of Borodino in *War and Peace* serves as Lukács' examples of how to deal with great historical events in literature.

The most significant point here is that of how a novel may acquire an epic aspect, which as Lukács suggests, comes from incorporating real historical events of importance and including military actions, but using them as a background rather than as centre of the novel's action. The insistence on the reality of historical events in novels with epic qualities may seem at odds with the highly fictional nature of events typical in epic, or at least their extreme embellishment as in knightly medieval epics. However, the Homeric epics refer to stories which have some kind of root in Bronze Age battles in which Greeks fought on the Aegean coast of Anatolia. In any case, these epics had such force in defining the collective self-understanding of the ancient Greeks that they acquire a historical reality of their own. Something similar applies to the Romans and Virgil's *Aeneid*.

What is striking about the 'Marxist' Lukács is how far he goes in seeking the epic in modern literature. Scott's historical romances are elevated to Homeric level, which is a strange place for them. Scott was of course a major influence on the nineteenth-century novel, but has not lasted well as a classic author on the level of Homer. For Lukács

> In the entire history of the novel there are scarcely any other works —
> except perhaps those of Cooper and Tolstoy — which come so near to
> the character of the old epos. [...] it is linked not with his interest in his-
> tory as such, but with the specific nature of his historical themes, with
> his selection of those periods and those strata of society which embody
> the old epic self-activity of man, the old epic directness of social life, its
> public spontaneity. This it is that makes Scott a great epic portrayer of
> the 'age of heroes', the age in and from which the true epic grows, in the
> sense of Vico and Hegel. (Lukács 1969, 35)

Lukács' comments are at least partly plausible with regard to the Scott and Scott influenced texts he considers, but he does still leave out what seems 'epic' in various ways about *Don Quixote*, James Joyce's *Ulysses* and *Finnegans Wake*, Herman Melville's *Moby-Dick* and Goethe's *Faust* (a verse drama, but with some novelistic qualities), and which makes them seem like definitive texts in the self-understanding of the nations concerned. Joyce's novels are part of the decline of bourgeois culture anyway for Lukács. *Moby-Dick* is ignored and just does not fit the ascending and decadent categories he has for the novel. A novel, or related verse work like Alexander Pushkin's *Eugene Onegin* or *Faust*, can be focused on concerns other than grand historical (or pseudo-historical) events and have an epic feel from the scope of action and the grandeur of the concerns of central characters, even if in the negative sense of struggling with meaninglessness.

What Lukács does achieve is a sense of the continuing relevance of Vico along with Hegel, though Vico is the really important reference here, as argued in Chap. 2 above. Lukács' view of the definition of epic is constrained by the wish for a literal repetition of the Homeric world, or at least as close as representations of medieval England and early modern Scotland allow. The adherence to Scott, who is likely to seem tendentious to current readers and to have a tedious style for even the most educated reader (surely, even Scott fans concede that his style is hard work), seems an oddity now but is at least a way in which Lukács gets the reader to think about the continuing power of the epic. The limitation is that he does not conceive of how the epic presence may continue in various ways, including in the works mentioned in the paragraph above.

We can be more appreciative of how far the various kinds of epic manifest themselves if we have read *The Historical Novel* and if we have seen its argument for the lasting importance of Vico in identifying an epic pole to literary narrative, a pole never entirely absent from the novel as a form, which always seeks some transcending point of view to organise itself. Lukács' commitment to more Leninist revolutions will stir few people now, but he does draw attention, as Kierkegaard did decades before, to the hopes for transformation that are found in the novel. There is always some sense of seeking a better form of community, which may be below the political threshold, but always connect with the urge towards between laws and institutions. *The Historical Novel* can be read alongside *Studies in European Realism* (1978) for a historical and political view of the novel, which has value but does not rank as an achievement with the creativity and striking style of *The Theory of the Novel*. Lukács was in Moscow as another major literary thinker was working in Russia, Mikhail Mikhailovich Bakhtin, who had his own original views the relations between the form of the novel and the historical world.

References

Bakhtin, Mikhail. 1984a. *Rabelais and His World*, trans. Hélène Iswolsky. Bloomington, IN and Indianapolis, IN: Indiana University Press.

Bakhtin, Mikhail. 1984b. *Problems of Dostoevsky's Poetics*, trans. and ed. Caryl Emerson and Wayne C. Booth. Manchester: Manchester University Press.

Bergson, Henri. 1991. *Matter and Memory*, trans. N.M. Paul and W.S. Palmer. New York, NY: Zone Books.

Kant, Immanuel. 2000. *Critique of the Power of Judgement*, trans. Paul Guyer and Eric Matthews, ed. Paul Guyer. Cambridge and New York, NY: Cambridge University Press.

Kierkegaard, Søren A. 1980. *The Sickness unto Death: A Christian Psychological Exposition for Upbuilding and Awakening*. Kierkegaard's Writings, XIX, trans. Howard V. Hong and Edna H. Hong. Princeton, NJ: Princeton University Press.

Kierkegaard, Søren A. 1981. *Concept of Anxiety: A Simple Psychologically Orienting Deliberation on the Dogmatic Issue of Hereditary Sin*. Kierkegaard's Writings, VIII, ed. Raidar Thomte and Albert B. Anderson. Princeton, NJ: Princeton University Press.

Kierkegaard, Søren A. 1987. *Either/Or, Part I & Either/Or, Part II*. Kierkegaard's Writings, III & IV, trans. Howard V. Hong and Edna H. Hong. Princeton, NJ: Princeton University Press.

Lukács, Georg. 1969. *The Historical Novel*, trans. Hannah and Stanley Mitchell. London: Penguin Books.

Lukács, Georg. 1971a. *History and Class Consciousness: Studies in Marxist Dialectic*, trans. Rodney Livingstone. London: Merlin Press.

Lukács, Georg. 1971b. *The Theory of the Novel: A Historico-Philosophical Essay on the Forms of Great Epic Literature*, trans. Anna Bostock. London: Merlin Press.

Lukács, Georg. 1974. *Soul and Form*, trans. Anna Bostock. London: Merlin Press.

Lukács, Georg. 1978. *Studies in European Realism*, trans. Edith Bone. London: Merlin Press.

Nietzsche, Friedrich. 1968. *Twilight of the Idols/The Anti-Christ*, trans. and ed. R.J. Hollingale. Harmondsworth: Penguin Books.

Nietzsche, Friedrich. 2000. *Basic Writings*, trans. and ed. Walter Kaufmann. New York, NY: Modern Library and Random House.

Stocker, Barry. 2004. From Tragedy to Philosophical Novel. In *Nietzsche and Antiquity: His Reaction and Response to the Classical Tradition*, ed. Paul Bishop. New York, NY and Woodbridge: Camden House and Boydell & Brewer.

Vico, Giambattista. 1984. *The New Science*, trans. Thomas Goddard Bergin and Max Harold Fisch. Ithaca, NY and London: Cornell University Press.

6

Bakhtin, Ethics and Time

Introduction

Mikhail Mikhailovich Bakhtin produced one of the most significant contributions to the philosophy of the novel in the most unlikely of circumstances, as he formulated and expanded on his central ideas in the Soviet Union of the 1930s, a time of state terror against all enemies of the Communist Party and Joseph Stalin, real and imagined, not sparing intellectuals and writers of any kind in any branch of knowledge. Despite this, Bakthin worked on manuscripts that analyse the nature and history of the novel from a perspective that is not obviously rooted in Marxism–Leninism or even Marxism of any kind though many commentators on, and followers of, Bakhtin have been sympathetic to Marxism. Others have thought of Bakhtin more as a Russian populist or a Christian moralist. Soviet Russia at the height of Stalinism was a place where not only Bakhtin made his contribution to thinking about the novel, but also Lukács developed the second phase of his thought on the genre in a more obviously Marxist way.

Scholarship of Bakhtin's writing runs into large areas of complication including the relationship between his thought on language and those

© The Author(s) 2018
B. Stocker, *Philosophy of the Novel*,
https://doi.org/10.1007/978-3-319-65891-9_6

of two friends, Pavel Nikolaevich Medvedev and Valentin Nikolaevich Voloshinov (Morris 1997) many there are the number of uncertainties generated about the arc of his thought due to the circumstance of manuscripts published, or even rescued from storage, decades after their composition, as conditions in the USSR moderated after Stalin's death, together with the decades long progress in Bakhtin's thought, then circulating in Soviet literary circles leading to the emergence of devotees who persuaded Bakhtin to bring manuscripts into print long after he wrote them. This is not the right place to investigate all these complications. The reading of Bakhtin here will concentrate on his texts on literary genre rather than language and speech, when discussed separately from literature, and will treat differences in his thought in an atemporal way as different possibilities emerging from his concepts, rather than as a history of the development of his thought.

Bakhtin on Dostoevsky

Bakhtin's fundamental concerns are with the relations between time and place in literature, the folkish and epic origins of the novel, the multiple precedents for the novel as a genre, the multiple forms of the novel even in its antique origins when it was deemed less elevated as a genre than epic, the multiple versions of the novel as a genre in modern times. While Bakhtin gave importance to Menippean satire, largely referring in Bakhtin to Greek language satires by the second-century Roman Anatolian, Lucian of Samothrace, as a precedent for the novel, it is less important in his account as a whole than some assume on the basis of the central role it has in Chap. 4 of *Problems of Dostoevsky's Poetics* (Bakhtin 1984a), 'Characteristics of Genre and Plot Composition in Dostoevsky's Works', along with references in *Rabelais and His World* (1984b), which tends to assimilate various genres to Menippean satire and assimilate all of this to the carnivalesque. The Greek language of the Lucian satires fits Bakhtin's emphasis on the more demotic nature of Greek culture compared with Roman Latin hierarchies, which comes closer to the polyphony proper to the novel.

Bakhtin's account of Dostoevsky' novels gives them a transcending status amongst modern literature. In his account, Dostoevsky's discourse about the world, ideology, merges with confessional discourse, self-consciousness. Principles of worldview govern concrete personal experiences. The fusion increases the signifying power of self-utterance and increases its internal resistance to external finalisation. The idea helps self-consciousness become sovereign over fixed, stable, and neutral images. Only in polyphony is it possible for an idea to have a direct power to mean. In monologic art, the hero is not self-conscious and becomes just a fixed, final image of reality. Ideas lose the direct power to mean, becoming just an aspect of reality. The idea is separated from the hero and could be placed in the mouth of any character. The monologic worldview is impersonal and imposes the view of the author on characters. There is no other idea which is recognised as an object of representation, and there is a semantic unity of worldview in which a thought is affirmed rather than represented. The affirmed idea is distinguished stylistically from unaffirmed ideas, which lose any independent force and are just psychical facts of one character's mind, or part of social types.

Polyphony shows ideas as beyond affirmation and repudiation. Idealistic philosophy, the unity of consciousness, expresses ideological monologism, the unity of existence. Idealism believes in one unified consciousness: individual, plural consciousnesses are rejected as merely empirical and lacking in cognitive significance. Polyphony sees truth in the plurality of voices. There can be a unified truth without a single consciousness, if that truth emerges from contact between consciousnesses. In this case, the unified truth is full of event potential. The monologic conception of truth and cognition comes about where consciousness is placed above existence and the unity of existence is turned into the unity of consciousness.

The unity of consciousness can be expressed in the spirit of a nation, people, history etc. The Enlightenment was the peak of a European rationalism with a cult of unified and exclusive reason. The main genres of European literature were established at that time and were therefore monologic. In a monologic work, the authorial idea has three functions: the principle for visualising and representing the world; a deduction drawn from the represented material; the ideological position of the main hero. The monologic principle turns the represented world into a voiceless object of deduction. It's works require that formal style and philosophical deductions are formed into one viewpoint. Authorial ideas are not represented, they are what represents. Dostoevsky represented ideas other than his own and was a great artist of the idea. The idea in Dostoevsky is inseparable from the image of a person, a person born of that idea and that person is not a type. The idea is only a fully valid idea where it lives in uninterrupted dialogic interaction with other fully valid ideas. The man in man appears in the idea in the unfinalised core of a hero's personality, transcending thingness. Therefore, the hero of Dostoevsky gives himself up to the unfinalised idea as an unselfish man. The idea is born and lives in contact between voice-consciousnesses, appearing as an interindividual zone of intense struggle amongst consciousnesses. The theoretical side of the idea is inseparable from the ultimate positions of life taken by speakers in then dialogue. The idea acquires the contradictory complexity and living multi-facedness of an idea force, which is born, lives and acts in the great dialogue of an age calling up similar ideas from other ages including the future, in the image of an idea. Idea images come from reality, and prototypes can be found in the theoretical and ideological work of the time.

Dostoevsky uncovered the potential in an existing image idea. He placed ideas in the intersection of different consciousnesses, foreseeing conflicts and links which did not exist in his own time. Dostoevsky's novels are polyphonic, and their ideas cannot be regarded as separable and systematic thoughts. The idea exists as the totality of an integral position in the whole personality, and in the labyrinthine complexity of links between different ideas. Dostoevsky resists the classicist, Enlightenment and Romantic tendencies to create aphorisms, which are self-sufficient thoughts scattered through a work. Bakhtin, here, suggests a point of difference with the Romantic philosophy of the novel discussed in Chap. 3 above.

Dostoevsky's polyphonic novel exceeds the biographical novel. The biographical novel is built on a deep organic unity between the hero and the plot of his life. Dostoevsky's heroes live outside plots and dream of living in a normal life plot. Dostoevsky uses aspects of the adventure novel: the hero has no firm identity; a labyrinthine adventure world is introduced, sympathy with the insulted and injured; the fusion of the ordinary and the extraordinary, the grotesque and the sublime.

A social-psychological novel fixes characters in their place in family and social relations and is not like a polyphonic novel. Dostoevsky is part of the history of genres that is historical poetics. The polyphonic novel comes from a European tradition which combines adventurism, problematic questions and dialogue. At this point, Bakhtin seems closer to a Romantic philosophy of the novel, in the advocacy of fusion and what looks like an absolute genre of all genres. The wish to avoid self-contained aphorisms and fragments is the most obvious point of difference, referring to Bakhtin's dislike of rationalist hierarchy. That is, he opposes any tendency towards a discursive level which is elevated above other voices, which is what he may see as what happens when aphorisms and fragments are given a privileged role.

History of a Genre

In Bakhtin's view of the deep history of the novel in 'Characteristics of Genre and Plot Composition in Dostoevsky's Works' in *Problems of Dostoevsky's Poetics* (Bakhtin 1984a), all that leads up to the modern novel, and all that is most important in the modern novel, is presented through Dostoevsky's novels presumed as the highest examples of the novel, present and guiding in all the best moments of what precedes these novels going back to antiquity. Literary genre reflects stable tendencies in the development of literature, it preserves elements of the archaic in a constant renewal. The Ancient Greeks had a category of the serio-comical including Socratic dialogue (including Plato), Symposiasts (as in Plato's *Symposium*) and Menippean satire. It was counterposed to the serious genres of tragedy, history, epic, rhetoric etc. The serio-comical genres are all saturated with the carnivalistic. One-sided rhetorical seriousness is joined with joyful relativity. The serio-comical is concerned with the living present and breaks down literary distance. They rely on experience and free invention, not legend. Single style is replaced with a multi-styled and hetero-voiced nature. Genres are mixed as are levels of tone. The word starts to appear as represented word rather than representing word, and a leading role is played by the double-voiced word. The novel comes from the combination of epic, rhetoric and the carnivalistic.

The Socratic dialogue is not a rhetorical genre, it is carnivalistic in origin, particularly in its oral stage. The Socratic dialogue originally shows truth as dialogic not ready made, it comes from interaction. Plato's later dialogues degenerate into the dogmatic presentation of a ready-made truth. Socratic dialogue contains syncresis, juxtaposing positions and anacresis, provoking words and opinions from an interlocutor. Socratic characters are ideologists, active in the ideological event of seeking and testing truth. Socratic dialogue emphasises the extraordinary event, the threshold situation where automatism and objectness are penetrating forcing individuals to reveal their deepest personality and thought. There is an embryonic image of the idea in the Socratic dialogues, in the testing of the person who represents an idea. However, the Socratic dialogue is a syncretic philosophical-artistic genre rather than a polyphonic novel.

The Menippean satire comes from the breakdown of the Socratic dialogue and roots in carnivalesque folklore, it includes Boethius' *Consolations of Philosophy*, as suggested in 'Epic and Novel' (Bakhtin 1981, 27) along with various satirical and novelistic forms. Bakhtin here brings a sixth-century work of philosophy, religion and poetry into a discussion of a genre of satire going back a few centuries before the Common Era. This is a part of a problem with the rather expansive way Bakhtin sometimes uses the term 'Menippean satire', it is too expansive. His achievement is really to show how a constellation of texts including Menippean satire properly defined and Boethius' way of mixing genres all feed into what becomes the modern novel.

According to Bakhtin, the Menippea advances beyond Socratic dialogue in: increased comedy and carnival; complete freedom of plot and philosophical invention; the creation of extraordinary situations in order to test a truth; the combination of symbolic and fantastic with slum naturalism; ultimate and universal questions with a practical and ethical basis rather than theoretical philosophy; a three-planed construction which moves between Earth, Olympus and the Underworld; experimental fantasticality which looks at the world from a strange perspective and appears later in Jonathan Swift (in the eighteenth century) and François Rabelais (in the sixteenth century); abnormal moral and psychological states such as split personality, doubles, limitless dreaming, passions on the threshold of madness; scandal scenes and eccentric behaviour which overturn all manners and norms, and the normal course of events, breaching the wholeness of the world and predetermined behaviour; extreme contrasts and paradoxical unions; utopian elements in dreams and journeys; insertion of many genres and extensive parody or objectification; the word as the material of literature; journalistic tendency to reflect the topics of the day. The Menippea comes from an age of breakdown of existing standards, and a Stoic awareness of man as victim of fate, destroying the epic and tragic wholeness of man and fate. The internal dialogicality of thought and speech became an issue in Marcus Aurelius and Augustine. Here we have tried to synthesise the extreme variety of concerns that Bakhtin brings to the deep history of the genre of the novel. The rise of the novel corresponds with the decline of the influence of Stoicism in early modern and Enlightenment Europe. The suggestion that antique Stoicism makes the individual an observer of fate seems one sided as Stoicism suggests a non-commitment to externalities in which the influence of fate is made irrelevant. The Stoic has an inward looking rationality devoid of interest in externalities in Bakhtin's account also, but in the context of antiquity he has a strong basis for the claim that the Stoic inwardness and rationality weakens the hold of existing literary forms.

However, there are some complications around this, which Nussbaum deals with when she discussed Seneca's tragedies in relation to his Stoicism in *The Therapy of Desire* (1994). The main Latin novel of antiquity, the *Metamorphoses* of Apuleius (*The Golden Ass*), is written from a point of view which advocates pagan mystery religion rather than Stoicism. Stoicism did have a strong presence in elite culture until the Christianisation of the Roman Empire, any broad cultural history of antiquity will look at the transition from paganism to more philosophical ethical schools and then Christianity, but the schools include Epicureanism and Pyrrhic Scepticism as well as Stoicism. Mystery religions were important to pre-Christian Romans. Bakhtin is a highly important and effective counter to the kind of idealisation in which the novel emerges as a high literary form on the precedents of Homer, Virgil and Dante alone, but he does engage in his own strongly reductive and sweeping claims. Both Saul of Tarsus/Saint Paul and Saint Augustine of Hippo had Stoic influences, but have to be understood with regard to other influences as well, including other parts of Greek philosophy, Jewish teachings and Manichaeism.

The jump from Stoicism to carnival, and its Roman origins in Saturnalia, is certainly a rather large one. Bakhtin's description of the carnivalesque is syncretic pageantry of a ritualistic sort and is a language of symbolically concrete sensuous forms. Carnival language cannot be translated into a verbal language or abstract concepts, but can be transformed into literature as what has artistic images in a concretely sensuous nature. There is no division between performers and spectators in carnival. It is lived rather than watched, participants are in life turned inside out. Carnival suspends the laws, prohibitions and restriction that give structure and order to ordinary life. Hierarchical structure and inequality including terror, reverence, piety and etiquette are suspended, distance between people is suspended, and there is free and familiar contact between people. There is a new mode of interrelationships between people on the carnival square. Eccentricity as the latent side of human nature is revealed. Carnivalistic misalliances unify what was self-enclosed and distinct. The sacred is united with the profane, the high with the low, the great with the insignificant, and the wise with the stupid. There is a carnivalistic category of profanation, which includes obscenities linked with the reproduction of the earth and the body, blasphemous parodies of sacred texts and sayings.

These are concretely sensuous ritual-pageant thoughts, which have been formed by thousands of years of existence amongst the broadest masses and have a formal, genre-shaping influence on literature. It has influenced literature in the appearance of the dialogic and in the destruction of epic and tragic distance. At this point, Bakhtin suggests a rather Viconian move, as discussed in chapter two above, from a literature above normal humanity to a more human world. In Bakhtin's account, literature becomes familiar, so that the author is familiar with his characters. Carnivalistic acts are part of the transformation and the primary act is the mock crowning and decrowning of the carnival king. That act is the form of the core of the carnival sense of the world, the pathos of shifts and changes, of death and renewal. The carnival is the festival of all-annihilating and all-renewing time. The crowing and decrowning is a dualistic ambivalent ritual, which expresses the inevitability and the creative power of the shift-and-renewal, the joyful relativity of order. The carnival king is the opposite of a real king in social status, giving joyful ambiguity to authority. The symbols of kingly authority acquire a two-levelled meaning.

In Bakhtin's continuing account in 'Characteristics of Genre' in *Problems in Dostoevsky's Poetics*, death and birth are contained in each other. There is no absolute affirmation or negation, but constant shifts and renewals in a dualistic unity. The crowning/decrowning ritual determines an ambivalent and two-levelled decrowning for artistic images and whole works. Without ambivalence, there is only the negative exposure of a moral, sociopolitical or journalistic kind. Carnival images are dualistic uniting change and crisis, birth and death, blessing and curse, praise and abuse, youth and old age, top and bottom, face and backside, stupidity and wisdom often expressed through paired images. Eccentricity appears in the reverse use of objects, violating the norms of everyday life. Carnival laughter is deeply ambiguous and is linked with the oldest ritual laughter. Laughter was directed towards the highest worldly and other worldly power in order to force them to renew themselves through ridicule. Ritual laughter is connected with death, rebirth and the reproductive act. Laughter fuses ridicule with rejoicing in reaction to crises in the life of the following: the sun, a deity, the world, and the man. The tradition of ritual laughter allowed the medieval practice of the parody of sacred texts. Parody is integral to Menippean satire and is a carnivalistic form alien to the pure genres of epic and tragedy. Parody is the ambivalence of a world turned inside out and is represented in *Don Quixote* (1984a, 128) which is far removed from formal literary parody of purely literary texts. The speech life of European peoples contains whole layers of carnivalistic language, particularly abuse and ridicule.

The Renaissance saw a major invasion of literary genre by the carnivalistic: Rabelais, Erasmus, Shakespeare, Cervantes. After the Renaissance, however, the carnivalistic broke up into festive court masquerades, chamber masquerade, farcical comic antics, the circus, bull fights and theatre subculture. Before then carnival was unmediated, but from the seventeenth century on carnival became a literary tradition of carnivalisation. So the Renaissance contains some kind of authentic literary carnivalesque, but the Latinate-Roman hierarchies, formalities and abstractions reemerge in the seventeenth century.

On the crowning/uncrowning ritual of carnivalesque, Bakhtin argues that some of Plato's Socratic dialogues follow the crowning/decrowning structure, contain misalliances of thoughts and images, a reduced from of carnival laughter in Socratic irony; the image of Socrates is ambivalent, beautiful and ugly in the *Symposium*, Socrates speaks of himself in carnivalistic terms as a pander and midwife. Carnivalistic heroes are different from those of epic legend, as carnival debases the hero, humanise him and familiarise him while leaving the heroic core: Faust, Gargantua, Don Quixote etc. The carnivalistic allows a connection between a philosophical idea and the artistic image of adventure. Here, Bakhtin gives the examples of Boethius' *Consolations* and Voltaire's *Candide*, (Bakhtin 1984a, 134) though in the preceding essay 'The Idea in Dostoevsky' *Candide* is referred to as an empty novel of ideological deduction (83). The genres of Christian literature are contained in the *New Testament* and influence a medieval literature which is Menippean in the sense of a testing of hero and belief, but at the expense of the dialogic element. The Menippean satire also appears in the nineteenth-century philosophical fairytales of E.T.A. Hoffman (137) confirming that Bakhtin takes the Menippean to the extreme as a presence in all works where some plurality of voice and ideas is present.

Dostoevsky's novels and short stories contain the Menippean and carnivalistic elements of dialogism within sololiquies, a hero living outside norms, concentration on thresholds (doorways, entrance halls etc.) and large rooms as carnivalistic, doubles, extreme dreaming, scandal, misalliances, characters as bearers of ideas who are tested in testing the ideas, the inseparability of the idea from the character as whole, the confrontation of ideas, the existence of ideas in a dialogic situation not as abstractions, use of various genres, parody, reversals, eccentric escapades and mystifications. The influence of the carnivalistic in Dostoevsky partly comes from Renaissance literature including Shakespeare and Cervantes, in the carnival sense of the world, the forms for visualising the world and man, and the godlike freedom in approaching them. The study of carnivalisation in literature goes beyond the influence of individual works. There is a study of the tradition as a whole, the influence of a generic tradition where the discourse of language is more important that it's repeatable use in a particular context.

Dostoevsky's literature in Bakhtin's account includes the carnivalistic scandal and dethrowning as a symbolic tearing to pieces, a sacrificial dismemberment into parts where the parts of the dismembered body are enumerated. Carnival laughter appears in Dostoevsky in reduced form, where the laughter is contained in the confrontation of voices not as direct laughter. There is a general catharsis in Dostoevsky, which is much broader than tragic catharsis in Aristotle: nothing conclusive has yet taken place in the world, the ultimate word of the world and about the world has not yet been spoken, the world is open and free, everything is still in the future and will always be in the future. In Dostoevsky the fates of people, their experiences and ideas are pushed to their limits, everything is passing over into its opposite. The logic of dreams in Dostoevsky enables carnivalistic fusion of opposites, laughter and decrowning, thresholds to appear as places of crisis. In the comfortably inhabitable space of home, away from the threshold, there can be a biographical life in biographical time.

Dostoevsky leaps over biographical time. On the threshold and the carnival square, there is only crisis time in which a moment is equal to vast amounts of time. Stories about gambling by Russians in exile enables Dostoevsky to refer to characters separated from the norms of their own country leading lives of constant scandal, and gambling is itself carnivalistic in relying on fortune and chance. Gamblers and convicts become similar in this life taken out of life, in a time which is like the threshold of death in which characters are in hell, referring back to the carnivalistic transitions between this world and the underworld which itself combines the Christian hell and more pagan conceptions. Dostoevsky relativises everything that disunifies people and gives a false seriousness to life. Carnivalised time appears in Dostoevsky as the time of a day, which is not the time of tragic unity but is close. It is even further from biographical and historical time, it is a time of an unlimited number of radical shifts and metamorphoses. All that is disunified and distant is brought together at a single spatial and temporal point.

The boundaries of Menippean satire in Bakhtin are strikingly vague with just Lucian and Varro at the centre and Socratic dialogues alongside the *Metamorphoses of Apuleius*, also known as *The Golden Ass*, a bit further towards the circumference. Plato's dialogues are assumed to follow a carnivalesque approach to the confrontation of ideas and the character of Socrates. The dialogue is presented as rooted in a testing of ideas in an extreme public confrontation more concerned with the contest than the truth, while Socrates is presented as the carnivalesque unity of opposites, ugliness and beauty in particular. Bakhtin does not present anthropological and historical evidence of this and it is maybe an indirect tribute to Nietzsche's view of tragedy as contest between Dionysian and Apolline rather than a historically well-based claim. The carnivalesque, including its presence in the 'Mineppean' could be taken as an expression of the Dionysian across European culture. Bakhtin is more concerned with ancient comedy than ancient tragedy, but this does not reduce the sense that Bakhtin draws on Nietzsche's thoughts about the irrational and conflictual side of ancient literature.

Whether or not, it is plausible to place Plato's dialogues in a line of descent from the carnivalesque, Bakhtin has other ancient sources for the novel and he is not alone in seeing a line from Socratic dialogue to the modern novel, as this claim is shared even if in different articulations with Friedrich Schlegel and Nietzsche, as we have seen above in Chaps. 3 and 5. In Schlegel, the suggestion is made in a very affirmative way for Plato and the novel, while in Nietzsche the suggestion is one in which dialogue and novel are both regarded as beneath tragedy.

Other suggestions for the ancient sources of the novel, in 'Epic and Novel' (in Bakhtin 1981) include the Sophistic novel, biography, the Greek novel, comedies, hagiography, confession and epic. In this account, Xenophon looks like a major precursor of the modern novelist through his Socratic dialogues (*Symposium* and *Apology*) and his biography of the Persian King Cyrus (*Cyropedia*). The inclusion of epic gives the novel an origin in the most elevated kind of literature and means that Bakhtin shares some ground with earlier accounts of the novel as the descendent of the epic genre, particularly Homer. Bakhtin's own understanding of epic gives it a common grounding with folk literature. Epic is more elevated than Rabelais' *Gargantua and Pantagruel* which has a dominating role in Bakhtin's account of the origin of the modern novel, particularly through *Rabelais and His World,* so allowing for the idea of the novel as the fallen or more reflective version of epic.

What unifies epic and folklore is the shared chronotype. The 'chrono-type' combines the Ancient Greek words for space and time in Bakhtin's writing to allow for the ways in which genre is tied to organisation of space and time. In both epic and folklore, time and space go beyond normal measurable and experienced forms. The hero is ageless and cam cross enormous distances without any real time elapsing, which is part of the unity between time and space in folklore and epic: the hero trav-els enormous distances and endures many adventures without ageing. In both genres, characters are types and face mythical forces as opposed to the individualised psychologising and realist social context that emerges in the novel.

The *Metamorphoses of Apuleius* [better known as *The Golden* Ass], one of the few novels surviving from antiquity and the only one in Latin marks a step beyond the Greek or Sophistic romance or novel for Bakhtin. Now, time has more content to it and is not reversible. Lucius, the hero of *The Metamorphoses of Apuleius*, goes through ordeals in which he becomes more worthy so the time taken and the nature of the incidents in that time is not accidental. The incidents come from myth rather than a random series of unlikely events. The chrono-type has changed from the Greek novel. These characteristics are not completely absent in novels. Bakhtin identifies the *Metamorphoses of Apuleius* as full of material which comes from mythical religious concep-tions of a journey towards a life free of the chance entanglements and misfortunes of social reality. Bakhtin places the unpleasant social reality of the *Metamorphoses of Apuleius* in a continuum with the descent into the hell of Odysseus in the *Odyssey* and Aeneas in the *Aeneid*. The con-trast between the protected life at the end of Apuleius' novel, as the ini-tiate of a religious cult, and the unpleasant scenes he observes as an ass is a transformation of the contrast between the normal life of Odysseus and Aeneas and what they experience in their descent into Hades. The contrast Bakhtin refers to in the epics is between the lives of heroes close to the gods, descended from them and guided by them, and the lives of souls in the afterworld deprived of any experience of the world of the living. The contrast is between an experience of nature given super-natural qualities and an underworld of supernatural status where there is a longing for the worldliness of the living, in the sense that they live in a world rather a place of darkness and experience at some limit close to unconsciousness. Any kind of descent of the hero in a novel into unpleasant social reality or anything close to death, like a visit to a graveyard, is a transformation of the epic descent echoed in the realist and particularly the naturalist aspects of the modern novel. So in this respect, Bakhtin challenges the tradition of looking at the ancient epics as displaying a harmonious world in which the individual is at home and the hero exists at a purely heroic level.

Bakhtin emphasises the existence of ancient Greek novels as well as epics in 'Epic and Novel'. In his account, the Greek novel is a genre of fantastic journeys (echoed in many of the tales of the *Arabian Nights*) in which a young couple are in love, are separated, travel to many places in journeys which should take many years, but during which they never age. They survive shipwrecks which appear to kill the rest of the passengers, though everyone reappears at some point. They narrowly avoid death by some unlikely stroke of good fortune. Inevitably, the young couple survive unharmed return home and are married. Bakhtin sees this branch of ancient literature, which only survives in a very few examples as leaving an important legacy in the modern novel, particularly through Voltaire's *Candide*. In the eighteenth-century novel, Candide travels very widely, including a journey across the Atlantic Ocean, survives dangers and at the end of many such incidents is unified with his love partner. However, in Voltaire's world, the couple have aged so their reunion is a parody of the Greek novel.

Parody is fundamental to Bakhtin's conception of the novel. The earliest novels, or novel related forms, have a parodic relation with epic. While Voltaire parodied the old genre of Greek novels, though maybe through a more direct concern with fantastic stories in novels of the seventeenth and eighteenth centuries (for example *Gil Blas*). He notes the role of parody in the English novel of the eighteenth century in relation to Samuel Richardson's *Pamela*. Henry Fielding stands out as the parodic counterpart to Richardson, due to his direct parody of *Pamela* in *Shamela* and the relation *Tom Jones* has with the Richardson world of virtue defended and triumphant.

Bakhtin's emphasis on the Greek novel has another place in his world view extending beyond questions of literary genre. The tradition of the Greek Novel feeds into the Byzantine novel. Since Byzantine was a work applied to the eastern Roman Empire after its fall in 1453 and with pejorative overtones, it is perhaps not the ideal term to use in any context except to refer to the western imagination of a decadent later Roman Empire centred on the Bosphorus, however, its wide use is probably now beyond reversal. It should at least be noted here that the Greek novelistic tradition continued in the Greek speaking part of the Roman Empire through the loss of the west, including Rome itself, after Constantinople had become the primary capital city. The tradition continues though a continuing Roman Empire which after the Emperor Justinian, probably the last Latinate Emperor, in the sixth century, becomes a Greek empire continuing the name and political tradition of Rome. Having tried to clear away some of the accretions to the image of the late Roman Empire, it can be noted that Greek literature and philosophy in Greek carries on through the Middle Ages in a context where Greek is a living language in a way that Latin is not. Latin divides between the mother tongues of Italian, French, Provençal, Castilian, Catalan, Portuguese, Romanian and so on, with Latin itself surviving as a language of religion and scholarship. It is a living language in the sense that the scholarly and religious communities use it as a means of transnational communication, write in Latin and conduct religious services in Latin. However, it is not the language of significant literature any more than it is the language of communication between the common people.

Language of the Novel

In the *Essays*, Michel de Montaigne may have gone to the extreme in 'Apology for Raymond Sebond' (an ironic title) in mocking the philosopher Sebond for writing 'Latin', which is Spanish with Latinate word endings, and many Renaissance writers went to the extreme in mocking the philosophy of the 'Schools', but it is clear enough that medieval Latin lacked in literary achievements and in creating a broad fluent speaking community, even within the spheres of scholarship and church. In religion and scholarship, the Latin Catholic west had created a linguistic hierarchy in which the church used a language unknown to its adherents who spoke in languages not used for official church purposes. Even Dante's Tuscan Italian was in some way beneath the level of church and scholarship and that is certainly the case for the speech of the labourers, artisans and farmers of Tuscany.

The everyday language of the Roman Empire in the east was Greek as was the language of state, church and learning. The same ways of using Greek did not apply to the church and to everyday life, but at least this was a gap in the kind of Greek used, not a gap in comprehensibility. There was not the same hierarchy between languages as in the west, and to the language of the Orthodox Greek east was that of the speech of the common people. The same applied when Orthodox Christianity spread to the Bulgars and Slavs, most significantly for Bakhtin to the Russians. The language of the people was the language of the church, and of the Bible which was not available in the west except in Latin until the Hussite and Lollard movements of the fifteenth century and was not widely available until the sixteenth-century Reformation. The Russian novel does not emerge until the eighteenth century, so by then the linguistic hierarchy issue was not the same in the west. From Bakhtin's point of view, though, the Greek–Russian unity of people and church leaves traces in the novelistic tradition, particularly in the work of Fyodor Dostoevsky.

The western Latin Catholic tradition of language hierarchy is challenged in the novelistic tradition by François Rabelais and that has pan-European significance which reaches Russia in Bakhtin's account so it is not that Bakhtin puts forward grandiloquent claims for Russian or a broader Orthodox Graeco-Slavic exceptionalism in the context of cultural separatism. He does certainly see a different path for Russia where the genre of the novel has emerged more directly from folk literature and produced a Dostoevsky who brings the genre of the novel to a particular height which has populism at its base, the populism of a culture where the folk tale is not linguistically separated from religious discourse, where the church is part of the people in a way that the Latin speaking Catholic priests cannot follow. What Rabelais sees in Dostoevsky is a literature shaped by a populism that cannot be the same in the west, where the spiritual life was above the people.

Linguistic hierarchies are an issue in Russian literature. Bakhtin himself points to the different class-based linguistic registers Ivan Turgenev deploys in *Fathers and Sons*, which also refer to ideological struggles. Dostoevsky was an aggressive despiser of Turgenev for reasons connected with his western learning political liberalism and a literary style, which might be considered that of a well read and cultured member of the gentry. Bakhtin does not support the more aggressively slavophile, autocratic and traditionalist aspects of Dostoevsky's thinking, which he relegates to opinions that are undermined by the pluralism of his novels. There is still a literary core in Dostoevsky which is a product of Russian populism and Orthodoxy, or at least a way of understanding them. The idea that the Orthodox church grants a spiritual freedom unknown in Catholicism is an important part of Dostoevsky's assumptions and is at the centre of his well-known and widely anthologised Grand Inquisitor passage in *The Brothers Karamazov*. The Inquisition marks a Catholic tendency to coerce in faith apparently lacking in Orthodoxy. Even Dostoevsky's religious inclinations are associated with parody, Christ returning in *The Idiot,* and the ambiguity of grace and salvation. The murderer Raskolnikov in *Crime and Punishment* finds a way to God through his sin and may be closer to real faith than some habitual believers who have never transgressed in such a way.

Bakhtin does not directly commit himself to an ideology, or a world view, and he lived through times when it was dangerous to have a view on such things deviating from state backed ideology. It does appear, from the reading of his texts and the Russian understanding of him, that he had leanings towards a version of Russian populism, emphasising the plurality and openness of language in which scandal and conflict have a place and in which these qualities of popular life are more important that the nature of the political regime. This might or might not be best understood in combination with some form of revisionist Marxism, or Marburg Neo-Kantianism or religious populism: what is most interesting about Bakhtin is how he understands the novel in terms of social and linguistic events, varying across culture and history, with its own ethical and social force.

Carnival

The Dostoevsky book emphasises polyphony, the plurality of voices. In some way, Dostoevsky is the inheritor of the Menippean satire, the genre of abrupt transitions, shocks and combined voices. Different ideological points of view emerge in the novels and are able to speak fully, for and against Christianity, nihilism, revolution. Speaking in a free way creates scandal. The scandal has an element of the carnivalesque about it, the challenging of norms and hierarchies. In the multiplicity of voices, sometimes emerging with destructive force, the monologue of the author's point of view disappears. Ideas come into competition and conflict and the hero's point of view of loses any privileged status. Dostoevsky's achievements are very distinctive though they also show what is distinctive about the novel as a genre. The plurality of voice and ideas refers to a view of language as constituted by a plurality of style. Bakhtin rejects any linguistic view he associates with an ideal form of language. Wilhelm von Humboldt is criticised on this account (1981, 271) as is Ferdinand de Saussure (264) in 'Discourse in the Novel' (in Bakhtin 1981). There is some ambiguity about language which expresses itself in differences of style. The contextual nature of meaning encourages ambiguity and the fusion of ideas in competition. There is something sacral in the polyphony resembling the sacral nature of the carnivalesque.

The carnival is an exploration of the abundance of ways in which people play a social role and fit into a hierarchy. The carnival inverts hierarchy as the slave becomes king for a day. The inversions of power and the mocking may have dangerous potentials for violence and cruelty, but the true carnival always affirms life rather than death and destruction. Bakhtin partly explains this in relation to contrasts in literature. The late medieval or Renaissance stories of Giovanni Boccaccio's *Decameron* (198, 200) are embedded in a carnival spirit which mingles life and death, but always celebrates the triumph of life.

Bakhtin establishes a contrast with the nineteenth-century stories of Edgar Allen Poe, particularly 'The Cask of Amontillado', which has a carnival setting (199–200). The anonymous narrator lures a certain Fortunado against whom he seeks revenge for obscure reasons, to the surreally extensive underground tombs of his villa, on the grounds that he needs an authority in wine to test a supposed pipe of Amontillado for its authenticity. Fortunado is dressed as a carnival fool and is lured to death by entombment. His laughter, however, is the last thing the narrator hears from him. For Bakhtin, Poe's story is the negative side of carnival in which life and death, laughter and despair come together, with a triumph of death and despair. The story is one of oppositions which do not mix and, therefore, are already part of death. Roland Barthes has a similar approach to Poe's 'The Facts in the Case of M. Valdemar', in 'Textual Analysis of Poe's "Valdemar"' (Barthes 1981) even if in the context of different interests.

For Bakhtin, if we separate life and death, then death has already triumphed as formal separation between opposites is death in dissolution as opposed to the organic unity in which death is part of life as a cycle of rebirth and renewal. The relation between the narrator of Poe's story and his victim Fortunado is itself an incidence of doubling, a major part of the carnivalesque for Bakhtin. The double creates uncertainty about identity as the two could be said to one and when they act on each other, one is acting in relation to the same one, or it can be said that the possibility of the self-contained one is undermined by an inevitable possibility of doubling.

Bakhtin notes the importance of the double in *Don Quixote* though the union of the Don and Sancho is more the union of opposites than the doubling of one at least at the surface level. There is evidently a sense that the Don is the imagination and Sancho is the common sense (or similar oppositions) of one person. Going back the discussion in Chap. 4 above, for Kierkegaard, this kind of double refers to the difficulty Christianity has in accepting the sensual in any way and only as the lower gross part of existence, a doubling which continues in *Don Giovanni* where the Don represents a kind of sensuality that is abstract and ideal, beyond speech, while his servant Loporello presents a kind of pragmatic common sense sensuality. There is no reason to assert a direct influence of Kierkegaard on Bakhtin in this matter, but we can say the power of the simultaneous doubling and opposition of two characters at the centre of *Don Quixote* leaves a deep impression on later literature and philosophy of literature.

Precursors and Beginnings of the Novel

Bakthin's view of the origins of the novel extends a major role to medieval Romance and epic, which he identifies, uncontroversially, as genres which tend to converge. *Don Quixote* might be regarded as a parodic play on this convergence. Bakhtin goes beyond the line that goes from epic and Romance in Romance languages to the role of Wolfram von Eschenbach's thirteenth-century epic and romance *Parzifal,* which he regards as novelistic and a major precursor to the Germanic novel, though *Simplicissimus* in the seventeenth century is uncontroversially the earliest example he gives of the German novel proper. The search for identity and the uncertainties about reality in *Parzifal* provide instances of what may be more proper to the genre of the novel than to romance or epic, particularly at their most pure. *Parzifal* is discussed in this way in 'Forms of Time and Chronotope in the Novel' V. 'The Chivalric Romance', X 'Concluding Remarks' and 'Discourse in the Novel' (in Bakhtin 1981).

Bakhtin gives a major role to the *Bildungsroman* in the modern novel as the way in which the hero can find a place in the world, drawing on earlier novelistic types of the road and the test. The road, the physical journey, has had an important role in the novel in providing an opportunity for incident and encounter with difference aspects of society. *Don Quixote* provides a prime example as the Don travels with Sancho Panza and sees every aspect of Spanish society from galley slaves to dukes. *Parzifal* provides an example of how the test enters the novelistic genre via the tests endured by the knight errant in chivalric literature. Bakhtin's thought here can be continued through religious literature like John Bunyan's seventeenth allegory of salvation, *The Pilgrim's Progress,* which we can then see as feeding into the *Bildungsroman.* That is the novel which has a narrative of personal growth, discovery, self-discovery and education of every kind, particularly associated with J.W. Goethe's Wilhelm Meister novels: *Wilhelm Meister's Apprenticeship, Wilhelm Meister's Journeyman Years.* The *Bildungsroman* suits a literature of psychology, self-discovery and inner perfection, which is a necessary part of the novelistic concentration of the self. This view of the *Bildungsroman* is built up across 'Forms of Time and of the Chronotope in the Novel' and 'Discourse in the Novel'.

Another important element of the modern novel for Bakhtin is the idyll, which is the topic of 'Forms of Time and Chronotope in the Novel', section IX 'The Idyllic Chronotope in the Novel'. The idyll provides a particularly clear example of the way the modern novel builds on complexity. The idyll exists in contrast to the time of the modern novel in the sense of timelessness in the rural place close to the rhythms of nature, where nothing changes and clock time never matters much. The contrast with city life is a strong theme in many modern novels. Bakhtin offers Jean-Jacques Rousseau's *New Eloise* as a major example (1981, 230–231), implicitly linking this literary device with Rousseau's version of Enlightenment thought on the place of nature and a history of preceding thought and literary examples, of which Virgil's *Georgics* is probably the first great instance. Bakhtin explicitly takes the theme of the novelistic idyll forward to the place of the servant Françoise in Marcel Proust's *In Search of Lost Time* (235).

François Rabelais' *Gargantua and Pantagruel* serves as Bakhtin's first example of the modern novel, not only in *Rabelais and His World* (1984b), but also in 'Forms of Time and Chronotope in the Novel', section VII 'The Rabelaisian Chronotope' (in Bakhtin 1981). Bakhtin presumably does not find it a perfect example of the modern novel since he suggests that Book V does not fit. The issue of the first instance is always going to be difficult since the work appointed as the paradigm should both stand apart from later works in the series as the point of reference and be part of that series. These are not obviously harmonious criteria since the first in the series lacks precedents while the later ones have novelistic precedents, marking them out as distinct from the first in the series.

The role of romance, epic, ancient novels and other forms as precedents may offer one solution to the need for the novel which is a proper novel to play off previous examples of the genre, to work within an established genre, but then the question arises of why these precedents are not authentic examples of the genre, which surely should not be restricted by consideration of its place in time over other criteria. There is always the possibility of seeing some earlier, later or maybe contemporaneous work as more typical or as the one which has no precedent. Apart from these abstract considerations, an argument can be made that *Gargantua and Pantegruel* are too shapeless (even without Book V) and too fantastic in incident as well as structure to be considered a novel.

Don Quixote certainly attracts more commentary on its claimed status as the original than Rabelais' work and a more obvious presence in later literature, as it can be seen in the many allusions to it in well-known novels over centuries. Henry Fielding's refers to it in *Tom Jones* where Tom's travels with Benjamin Partridge parody Don Quixote and Sancho Panza. His less widely read novel *Joseph Andrews* sets itself up explicitly as modelled on Cervantes' novel. Another eighteenth-century English classic, *Tristram Shandy* by Laurence Sterne, refers to *Don Quixote* by means of a horse called Rocinante, as it is the Don's animal. In the twentieth century, Jorge Luis Borges made *Don Quixote* and its recreation the theme of his well-known story 'The *Don Quixote* of Pierre Menard'. More recently, Graham Greene's novel *Monsignor Quixote* makes an obvious reference and is structured round a modern day Quixote, Sancho and a car named Rocinante. Shaftesbury, Hegel, Schlegel, Schelling, Kierkegaard, Lukács and others have taken *Don Quixote* as the starting point. Bakhtin has a good case for taking Rabelais as the starting point given his own interest in placing the modern novel in a broad historical context which also has the merit of undermining the idea of a simple beginning in *Don Quixote*, along with the possibility of any such beginning.

Humanist Metaphysics

'The image of man is always intrinsically chronotopic' (Bakhtin 1981, 85). Bakhtin offers a humanist metaphysics in which humanity is what it can be represented in forms of the unity of time and space. As this is a claim about the image, representation, rather than the real nature of humanity, this is not metaphysics in the primary sense. However, a necessary image is a necessary aspect of what it is an image of, even if that still leaves questions about the real nature, the deep structure of what is presented as an image. The idea of a necessary image may be compatible with more than one primary metaphysical vision, but it certainly suggests a metaphysics of some sort at the primary level as the determiner of the necessary image.

Bakhtin offers an implicit metaphysics of how humans appear in cultural representation. Given the anthropological significance he gives to the novel and storytelling, as tied to myth, carnival and dialogical language, essential aspects of culture, the chronotype looks like a term of the metaphysics of culture. This is metaphysical pluralism in the sense that Bakhtin allows for different chronotypes, but the fusion of time and space is unavoidable and the elevated status of Dostoevsky suggests a metaphysics which underlies the variable metaphysics of other story telling forms. It is a humanist metaphysics since this is a goal for humanity rather than a discussion of non-human structures of reality. It combines a claim about which literary genre, and examples of literature, best capture the structures of human cultural existence with a claim about which is ethically preferable. The claim that the forms of activity most compatible with the full activity of the human individual is an ethical guide and is nothing new; the idea goes back to Plato at least and is dominant in antique ethics in its discussion of the good life.

According to Aristotelian categorisation, we should regard the ethical discussion as prudential rather than theoretical and therefore as a secondary part of philosophy, but even so it is tied to Aristotle's metaphysics which we understand in some part through reflection on what it is about ethics that refers to the nature of humans. Bakthin does not offer a grand metaphysical system, but what he says about culture is suggestive of a metaphysics of the structures of representation. Since humans produce their own representations, the human has a particular status here which can be taken in humanistic or religious terms. The humanist and theological metaphysics of representation is one metaphysics at the level of culture where we are not concerned with questions of existence, but fits best of all with the convergence of humanistic theology and sacralised humanism. It also fits with a politics of community in which the interactions of individuals are more the starting point than individuals. Though modernist individualism does not exclude an interactive understanding of individuality, Bakhtin's interest in heightened moments of communal awareness in public space of some kind, suggests a critical approach to any individualist contractualist view of the political and social world.

In his taxonomy of antique forerunners of the modern novel, in 'Forms of Time and Chronotope in the Novel' (in Bakhtin 1981), biography comes as the third stage after the Greek Romance and the Adventure. The adventure itself provides a precedent for the novels of the road and the ordeal. Biography includes Petrarch, Suetonius, the letters of Cicero and the *Confessions* of Augustine. The place of Augustine has some interest given Bakhtin's leanings towards the cultural benefits of Greek Orthodox Christianity. Augustine, wrote in Latin, was from the very Romanised province of Africa and has a very elevated significance for the Catholic church, extending to its Protestant breakaways. Augustine has a high place for the Orthodox church, but is not as important as in the Latin Catholic tradition. The sense of an interior self develops in a very significant way through Augustine, perhaps in implicit contrast with the communalism of Orthodox culture. The self develops in the western tradition while the east is more concerned with the unified community of the people. That at least may be useful context for Bakhtin's understanding of the elevated standing he gives Dostoevsky's writing.

Rabelais appears in Bakhtin's literary philosophy as the last expression of a medieval culture, with antique origins, of inversion, transformation, the grotesque, the material body and laughter in communal experience. For Bakhtin, this is imagination, but collective imagination and a form of imagination which was a substantial part of medieval which had a large number of festival days. The phenomenon cannot be investigated by current anthropology, because that itself rests on bourgeois individualism. The carnival is a form of non-individualist existence which became pushed aside and repressed after the Renaissance. This repression reaches an extreme in the Enlightenment during which Voltaire takes a particularly negative view of Rabelais referring to *Gargantua and Pantagruel* as eight times too long (Bakhtin 1984b, 116–118). The Romantics, however, revived Rabelais, though with less emphasis than Cervantes and Shakespeare. As Bakhtin points out, Laurence Sterne developed a 'subjective grotesque' in *Tristram Shandy* (44–47). Friedrich Schlegel and Jean Paul (Paul Friedrich Richter) contributed to the revival of the Renaissance writers and the grotesque. Goethe's literature reflects this evolution.

From Carnival to Polyphony

While Bakhtin regards the carnival as inaccessible to social science as well as established forms of literary criticism, he does think that has been absorbed into literary culture including the kind of literary criticism most related to literary creation, Romantic criticism. Rabelais takes discussion of historical meanings of the components of *Gargantua and Pantegruel* as the wrong kind of literary criticism, which cannot explain the richness of meaning in the novel. The decline of Rabelais' literary reputation also relates to the replacement of parody with mere satire, which is an expression of superiority. It is the seventeenth-century essayist Jean de La Bruyère (one of Nietzsche's heroes) who is associated with a downgrade of Rabelais (1984b, 107–110) on the road to Voltaire's dismissive attitude towards Rabelaisian 'barbarism', someone identified by Adam Smith, for example, as a major figure in the development of literary style. After the Romantics, the historian Jules Michelet, as well as the novelist Victor Hugo stand out as admirers of Rabelais who see the necessity of the grotesque in literature, so at this point Bakhtin aligns himself with nineteenth-century historicism and realist novels. Michelet was the translator of Vico into French, so as often we can sense some afterlife of Vico in the philosophy of the novel. One way of looking at Bakhtin is that he turns the Viconian ideas of a human stage of history and a lower classes despised by the hero-aristocrats in the heroic stage of history, into a cross historical interest in the way that anti-hierarchical forms of ritual and literature keep coming up from the mass of the population.

It may be that Bakhtin saw aspects of carnival in the Stalinist purges, which included denunciation from above and an overturning of hierarchy in the sense that denunciation could overthrown a high-ranking person, creating an opening for the denouncer, but this is not his attitude to carnival as such which is devoted to laughter, life and reproduction. Even casting people into Hell becomes part of life for carnival, as it is associated with images in which what contain hell is a pregnant woman, something associated with the renewal of life. The mockery and overthrown in the carnival is done with laughter and as part of life, not as a pretext for the destruction of life. There is a case for reading

Bakhtin on the carnivalesque with care so that we do not ignore any destructive aspects that Bakhtin saw, particularly given his experience of a society of denunciation which often served to remove people from power.

On the whole, though the carnival in Bakhtin is the context for a celebratory account of Rabelais, in which carnival is taken up by Rabelais and comprises what is necessary to life in his literary work. It provides a social and ethical guidance for the novel in presenting free interaction. The place where there is pluralism of voices and speech is best for creating the atmosphere of carnival. Though, this might seem like a celebration of pluralism under a tolerant state or a state fragmented into the governments of many small communities there is less idyllic aspect. If we consider the possibility of dark undertones in Bakhtin, it should also be remembered that the Roman Empire, where carnival began as Saturnalia, was a power structure destroying what resisted it, though it certainly had plurality of spoken languages. Tsarist Russia, like Bolshevik and Stalinist Russia and the USSR, was and is very pluralistic in spoken languages, but dealt with localism and linguistic variation from the point of view of Russia as national, autocratic and Orthodox in Tsarist times and as unified behind the party state with its dictatorial leader in the Soviet Communist era. Bakhtin's celebration of pluralism does not itself mean a rejection of political autocracy and homogenising state policies. If we take Bakhtin's celebration of Dostoevsky's political views, and it is not at all clear we should, we could see a Bakhtin who believes in a carnivalesque life-oriented popular culture best contained and nurtured within Russian autocracy in politics and Orthodoxy in the state church. Bakhtin at the very least leaves this possibility open.

Bakhtin suggests a line from carnival and Rabelais to Fyodor Dostoevsky, which passes through Cervantes, Sterne and Romanticism, but which is much more pure as an expression of polyphony and dialogism. Dostoevsky's fiction, particularly the novels, is given a unique status within Russian literature, but also within world literature so that something unique is established about Russian literature and culture. Something is also established about what is valuable about carnival. Bakhtin wishes to avoid the 'liberalisation' as we might call it, or Enlightenment rationalisation of the themes of carnival, laughter, parody and the grotesque, which he sees growing from the time of Cervantes. Nevertheless, his idealisation of Dostoevsky's novels creates an ambiguous situation since surely they are embedded in the liberal bourgeois individualist background of other novels. There are distinct individuals in the Dostoevsky novels with individual motive and thoughts, distinguishing these novels from the Rabelaisian.

The elevation of Dostoevsky must lead to some reassessment about what is valuable in carnival, as the conflict of ideologies (something that can only exist in the bourgeois world of constructed world views in politics and elsewhere) predominates in these novels along with responsiveness of individuals to the discourse of those with whom they interact. This is the Dostoevsky of Bakhtin's thought, which cannot be the same as what comes out of reading Dostoevsky particularly given Bakhtin's strong intellectual framework. It is anyway an important response to Dostoevsky's fiction telling us something about what it can inspire. What it inspires in Bakhtin is, in part, the idea of individuals whose discourse is formed by reaction to discourse of other individuals, which they then must imitate and incorporate to some degree even in the act of opposing it. This applies to spoken dialogue, but just as much to inner dialogue, and this is maybe the more important issue as it suggests that the inner self is formed through dialogue. The inner voice also allows for some idea of confession and a relation with God, though Bakhtin suggests this more in relation to confession as a genre than in relation to any religious ideas.

There is something both communal and sacred about the inner self, which is presumably how Bakhtin thinks Dostoevsky overcame liberal individualism. There is no isolated self-contained independent, self no matter how far we look into the inner side of consciousness. Dialogue is constant both within characters, who mingle words heard and read that come from other characters, and between characters in the novel as a whole. The constant dialogue and the unity of selves within the dialogue provide an alternative to liberal individuation. The double has a related importance in Dostoevsky, which can be seen in the novel *The Double*, as well as the way the characters form pairs in other Dostoevsky novels.

The variety of voices in Dostoevsky's novels makes them polyphonic. They are polyphonic as opposed to monological because there is no privileged voice or logos. The author's voice enters into Dostoevsky's novels, but not as the superior voice, just one voice amongst many. The same applies to the voice of the hero. From Bakhtin's point of view, the clash of ideologies seen in such personalised terms undermines the abstraction of ideology. The polyphony and dialogism have roots in style. Style in the writing of the voice of any character has some element of stereotype in it. The stereotype constructed in style can be repeated and become the object of repetition. It is very difficult to avoid some elements of this and given Bakhtin's suspicion of individualism, and it may not be a bad thing because it shows the ways that selves exist in ways that cannot be understood as unique individuation. The dialogue and polyphony are carnivalesque, while existing as literature rather than carnival and as more pure literature than Rabelais. It is a world of shifting voices merging, copying, splitting, imitating and rejecting in a process which creates fusion rather than preserving separation. These characteristics suggest populism whether or not populism is presented as an ideology. The constant presence of dialogue, within and between characters, also suggests an ethical presupposition in communication. Populism, or communitarian and communalist thought, might be said to be based on the merger of the politics of the ethically superior people with an anti-individualist ethics, so we should not assume that Bakhtin's dialogism and polyphony are the framework for inclusive and open social ethics or politics.

The status Bakhtin gives to Dostoevsky's novels means there are two categories of novels: polyphonic and monological, though overall it looks like a novel properly speaking should be polyphonic while the epics, or maybe epic elements in the novel, are monological. Rabelais and then Cervantes, followed by Sterne and German Jena Romantics, appear to exist between these poles. The polyphonic novel can be taken as the inner essence and goal of the novel, which always has some polyphonic characteristics and is suited to polyphony in a way that drama is not because of the direct presentation of discourse in plays. Significantly, Bakhtin compares Dante with Dostoevsky. They are said to both present a plurality of visions, thinking in Dante's case of the three parts of the *Divine Comedy*, with a variety of spaces interacting. Dostoevsky makes the spaces simultaneous not successive, so creating a chronotype of simultaneity in time and space, though Bakhtin does make this explicit. Dostoevsky appears to be an advance then on the Tuscan epic, for reasons which include the use of simultaneity rather than succession as a principle.

Bakhtin's sense of the ethical possibilities of the novel, the history of the genre, its location with regard to social life including carnival, the complexities of the genre, the relation between epic and novel, the different sources of the novel, the relation between the folkloric and the literary are all part of a labyrinthine approach to the novel. It is surely not easy to turn all these components of Bakhtin's literary thought into a single system of thought about the ethics, history and form of the novel.

What emerges overall, or at least what is selected as most important here, is that our literary experience is tied to structures of time and of ethical commitment. The timeless work of literature, where the characters stand outside time is apposite to a world where individual ethical choice is not so important. The work of literature where time is a constraint as is space belongs to a world of ethical choice. It is a world where there might be an ethical polyphonic aspect to politics. The ethical choice is ideally stimulated by a variety of voices. If we hear all ethical voices than we are more ethically educated and more able to make a decision which fits with the world of interacting individuals.

Despite the importance of ethics in Bakhtin, his ethical evaluations are not always clear. How do the worlds of Dostoevsky, Rabelais, early Christian literature and Platonic dialogue compare? We should be able to compare them, so that is ethically important, but we must also make a choice. In some degree, there is a trade-off. The release of energy in carnival, from deep inside the community is part of a world of shared ethical concern, but unreflectively and aggressively. The Platonic dialogue is intellectually admirable, but too abstract. Christian literature may still be too didactic. Though there is no obvious superiority of Dostoevsky to all the other aspects of the novel, his novels have the best balance of intellectual engagement, strong individuality combines with strong community, and the most morally engaged open dialogues. Bakhtin avoided political discussion and may have regarded the whole sphere with disdain. Nevertheless, he does describe a public sphere which must influence any politics going on if the politics is open. Given the values Bakhtin does put forward, he is surely bound to try to introduce or at least allow for lively polyphony in politics. The political forms are uncertain, but the underlying communal interaction is clear, itself presenting a politically valuable pressure on the state and on political institutions. Both communal and individual values are strong in Bakhtin, so his view of the novel, amongst other things may suggest a way between communitarian aspects and liberal aspects of political thought, though maybe not so much as a middle of the road compromise, but may be as a way of maximising both. Bakhtin largely writes in a way which suggests authentic community is placed over individualism, so the idea of maximising individualism and community together may not have been a point of reference for him, but it is one way of thinking about his legacy.

From Bakhtin's point of view, we can certainly see the need for an anthropological approach to history where the conflicting views of individuals are important. This is not necessarily a naive populism, because Bakhtin allows for ethical criticism of popular and traditional forms of literature and of life. There are moments that look like a dogmatic anti-political traditionalist populism in which human metaphysics is defined by the 'chronotypes' of popular literature. Bakhtin makes us think about these issues and why both poles can exist in interpretation of his work. As the novel is at the centre of these philosophical investigations, he certainly shows the philosophical importance of the novel in relation to social ethics, ethics of communication and the ethical foundation of politics. His view of the novel as a genre defined by philosophy is an idealisation, which is also over inclusive so unstable, but a productive and provocative idealisation which should encourage the philosophy of the novel to engage with the dynamism of the novel in terms of contested ideas, challenges to authority, experience of time and space as concrete and the plurality of the word.

The next chapter will be focused on the relation of the novel to the idea of mimesis in literature along with the political aspects of the novel. The discussion will continue from this chapter in that it will deal with the idea of the deep history of the novel, along with the political and ethical assumptions and entanglements that emerge in the aesthetics of the novel.

References

Bakhtin, Mikhail. 1981. *The Dialogic Imagination: Four Essays*, trans. Caryl Emerson and Michael Holquist. Austin, TX: University of Texas Press.

Bakhtin, Mikhail. 1984a. *Problems of Dostoevsky's Poetics*, trans. and ed. Caryl Emerson and Wayne C. Booth. Manchester: Manchester University Press.

Bakhtin, Mikhail. 1984b. *Rabelais and His World,* trans. Hélène Iswolsky. Bloomington, IN and Indianapolis, IN: Indiana University Press.

Barthes, Roland. 1981. Textual Analysis of Poe's "Valdemar". In *Untying the Text: A Post-Structuralist Reader*, ed. Robert Young. London: Routledge and Kegan Paul.

Morris, Pam (ed.). 1997. *The Bakhtin Reader: Selected Writings of Bakhtin, Medvedev, Voloshinov*. London and Oxford: Bloomsbury Academic.

Nussbaum, Martha C. 1994. *The Therapy of Desire: Theory and Practice in Hellenistic Ethics*. Princeton, NJ: Princeton University Press.

7

Mimesis, Humanism and History

Auerbach on Mimesis

A major expression of historicism referring directly back to Vico, can be found in Erich Auerbach, which at the most general level makes him comparable with Bakhtin, though they otherwise have rather different approaches. Though not expressing a Marxist orientation, Auerbach's version of historicism exercised considerable influence on Marxist and Marxist leaning literary criticism through his student Frederic Jameson, his presence in Edward Said's *Beginnings* and Hayden White's 1996 essay, 'Auerbach's Literary History: Figural Causation and Modernist Historicism' (in White 1999). In the case of Said and White, Auerbach's central interest in Vico's *New Science* is also passed on Vico is discussed in the final chapter of *Beginnings*, 'Conclusion: Vico in His Work and This' while White includes two essays on Vico in *Tropics of Discourse* (1978) 'The Tropics of Discourse: The Deep Structure of the *New Science*', and 'What is Living and What is Dead in Croce's Criticism of Vico'. These appearances of Vico in major texts of literary and cultural criticism have not ended Vico's rather marginal position in philosophy of literature, along with all the other fields where he is of

© The Author(s) 2018
B. Stocker, *Philosophy of the Novel*,
https://doi.org/10.1007/978-3-319-65891-9_7

great relevance, but does suggest the importance of Vico's point. It also suggests that those with Marxist inclinations have found it increasingly difficult to sustain a view of history, philosophy of history and the history of literary genres in purely Marxist terms. The after Auerbach version of Marxist theories of the novel rests like Lukács' work on a very Weberian view of the social world, with less of the late Lukács' attempt to pass into a self-enclosed form of Marxism.

Auberbach had a strong interest in Vico and he never completely leaves behind Vico's elevation of epic, even while he investigates a variety of literary narratives. Dante's *Divine Comedy* has approximately the role for Auerbach that the Homeric epics have for Vico and the idea of Dante as a kind of second Homer owes something to Vico himself. Auerbach has a far more to say than Vico about the forms of literary narrative that follow his ideal epic, but like Vico's attitude to Aesop's fables, he sees less of interest in later work. He does not deny enormous value to that work, but he remains within a longing for the unities that Dante hoped for, that is a Europe unified politically under one Emperor, unified religiously under the Pope, and unified by a common culture within those institutional constraints. Since the novel is a form conditioned by the fragments of earlier myth, epic and romance, this is a way of thinking in which Auerbach is able to uncover something about the nature of the genre of the novel.

Auerbach's central work is the ambitiously titled *Mimesis: The Representation of Reality in Western Literature* (1968), written during World War II in Istanbul, where he moved in reaction to the National Socialist take over of Germany, to take up a chair at the University of Istanbul. Comments Maurice Blanchot makes about Hermann Broch writing *The Death of Virgil* in a spirt of crisis of the west, discussed in the next chapter below, apply to Auerbach writing in exile from Germany in what was the eastern Rome, a place with a perpetually ambiguous relation with the 'West' if west means western and central Europe as it usually does, though of course there is every reason for taking Byzantium-Constantinople-Istanbul as at the heart of Europe. Auerbach opens *Mimesis* with discussions of Homer and the *Hebrew Bible* in the chapter on 'Odysseus' Scar'. This opening has a very commonsensical assumption that the *Bible* and Homeric epic are at the origins of European literature and culture. There is some play on this idea in the *Ulysses* of James Joyce, himself drawing on Matthew Arnold's discussion of Hebraism and Hellenism in *Culture and Anarchy* (2006) and other Greek-Jewish interactions, as noted by Jacques Derrida in 'Violence and Metaphysics' (in Derrida 1978).

The arc of *Mimesis* is one to some degree inspired by Vico (Auerbach 1949), that is of a movement from literary language structured by hierarchy and clear identities to a world in which both horizontal separations in status and vertical separations in origin are steadily undermined over time into a world described at the end of the book in the chapter on 'The Brown Stocking', with a strong air of cultural pessimism. His comments on Dante in Chap. 8 'Farinata and Cavalcante' along with *Dante: Poet of the Secular World* (2007) suggest that he sees in literary history moments when a great universal vision of a human world might come into reality, as in Dante's hope of a universal Emperor and Church foreshadowed in *The Divine Comedy*. For Auerbach, Dante's vision is a noble failure which gives way to the inferior self-interested vision of Petrarch, who whatever his level of literary talent does not have such great goals. As said about the background to Auerbach and his generation of German thinkers:

> It is specifically Romania [Roman lands] that makes intelligible and provides a centre for the enormous grouping of literatures produced worldwide; Romania underpins Europe, just as (in a curiously regressive way) the Church and the Holy Roman Empire guarantee the integrity of the core European literatures. At a still deeper level, it is from the Christian Incarnation that Western realistic literature as we know it emerges. This tenaciously advanced thesis explained Dante's supreme importance to Auerbach, Curtius, Vossler, and Spitzer. (Said 1994, 52)

Of course the Emperor that Dante referred to was the Holy Roman Emperor, the effective Emperor of Germany who had lands in Italy for a large part of the Middle Ages and in principle acted as a universal authority, reviving antique Roman imperium, in partnership with the Pope. The point for considerations on the novel is that the novel since Rabelais becomes the form in which literature fails to reach beyond

Petrarch to Dante. The novel quite authentically invokes a world where hierarchy is weakening, but where nothing fills the new social space to match the highest human goals in which there is some common political, aesthetic and spiritual elevation. Though he praises the 'high style' in Rabelais (284), he considers him incapable of tragedy and therefore hardly worthy of consideration in *Mimesis*, though it is not clear that Auerbach only or even largely considers texts containing tragedy.

> The riches of his style are not without their limits; the grotesque frame in itself excludes deep feeling and high tragedy; and it is not probable he could have attained to them. Hence it might be doubted whether he has rightfully been given a place in our study, since what we are tracing is the combination of the everyday with tragic seriousness. (182)

It does turn out two chapters on that Auerbach considers *Don Quixote* to be lacking tragic stature, so that is both starting points for the modern European novel. Cervantes has even, apparently, failed to be critical of the social reality exposed in the journeys of Quixote and Sancho Panza.

> But to conceive of Don Quixote's madness in symbolic and tragic terms seems to me forced. That can be read into the text; it is not there of itself. So universal and multilayered, so noncritical and nonproblematic a gaiety in the portrayal of everyday reality has not been attempted in European letters. I cannot imagine where and when it might have been attempted. (358)

Cervantes' novel fails to achieve tragic weight, but still remains as a monument of a greatness that cannot be matched in later novels. European culture stands in its shadow, even as *Don Quixote* stands in the shadow of the *Divine Comedy*. Auerbach surveys the history of European narrative with a mixture of concern that the common people have not been included in a properly dignified way and that cultural greatness keeps coming a bit more elusive. The cultural decline coincides with the growth of egalitarian moral sympathy, but this universalism undermines the cultural forms necessary for the effective communication of properly moral sympathy.

Adorno and Humanist History Questioned

Theodor Adorno had an approximately similar background to that of Auerbach in the philological and philosophical interests of German high culture and academia in the early twentieth century. However, while Auerbach was oriented towards a nostalgia for the lost utopia of Dante, Adorno was oriented towards the lost utopia of the Marxist revolution. The revolution that failed to happen in the west and created tyranny in the east. Given Adorno's strong leanings towards high cultural tradition and disdain for the culture industry, there is some resemblance with Auerbach's inclination towards a Dante style European utopia of political and aesthetic unity and grandeur. Loss of aesthetic possibility and a sense that there were more aesthetic possibilities in the pre-capitalist or pre-class world (Adorno is not clear in distinguishing these two) are prevalent modes in Adorno's thought. Though in accordance with Adorno's apparent Marxism, rather detached from political movements and economic class analysis, he offers criticism of some of the grand moments in the history of European culture, in *Negative Dialectics*, mixed with grand hopes like this:

> Even in music— as in all art, presumably—the impulse animating the first bar will not be fulfilled at once, but only in further articulation. To this extent, however much it may be phenomenal as a totality, music is a critique of phenomenality, of the appearance that the substance is present here and now. Such a mediate role befits philosophy no less. When it presumes to say things forthwith it invites Hegel's verdict on empty profundity. Mouthing profundities will no more make a man profound than narrating the metaphysical views of its characters will make a novel metaphysical. *Negative Dialectics* (Adorno 1973, 16)

The idea of Enlightenment is taken beyond the idea of a historically located eighteenth-century movement to a general tendency across history to impose reason on myth. Adorno's view of this tendency is that it follows the model of Shamanic, referred to as animism in *Dialectic of Enlightenment* (with Horkheimer 1986), struggling with natural forces through mimicry. Shamanism becomes myth which is itself a kind of Enlightenment in relation to the earlier forms of 'magical' relation with the world. The *Odyssey* is seen as narrative struggling with myth, but creating new myth. This should mean a new kind of shamanism, if disguised, though Adorno usually does not trace this line of descent all the way back. Adorno refers to myth as repetitive and undifferentiated, suggesting that the sea in the Odyssey is the expression of the capture of the narrative by this force, or the force of the narrative in re-creating myth. This is one of the points at which Adorno seems to be verging on musical language, thinking for example of how late Romantic music is sometimes described as oceanic. This may remind us of how Kierkegaard thinks of music at the limits of language, as discussed in Chap. 4 above. Sensuality and immediacy are best expressed in music, so Adorno brings the immediacy and sensibility of the world through musicality.

In *Dialectic of Enlightenment*, Adorno goes onto a discussion of the Marquis de Sade, where he makes a predictable connection with de Laclos' *Dangerous Liaisons*, but more importantly suggests that de Sade's 'libertine' fictions are the model of the novel. Though since he offers de Laclos as a similar writer, investigation of this possibly superior literary figure as a model might be preferable, though it is not the option taken by Adorno. Richardson's Clarissa seems relevant here as well. We might investigate these issues through Kierkegaard's 'Diary of a Seducer' and long essay on Don Giovanni in *Either/Or*. Since Adorno's first book was on Kierkegaard (1989), there may be some influence, though he never makes it clear.

What Adorno suggests with regard to de Sade is that the pleasure in cruelty, particularly directed at the helpless, is the counterpart to Kantian ethics, defined with regard to the categorical imperative, and is the counterpart to republican revolution, as it appeared in France from 1789 to 1799, and particularly from 1792 to 1794. Sade appeals to republicanism and its eighteenth-century legitimation through nature. On these points Sade is close to Jean-Jacques Rousseau, but distant in

regarding equality as unnatural. From Enlightenment and republicanism, de Sade derives a view of 'value' as what comes from the exercise
of desire in cruelty over someone else. This excavation of the truly natural in ethics, Enlightenment and republicanism turns them into myth,
or exposes their mythical foundations. The repetition and similarity of
erotic cruelty in Sade's libertine fictions are the recreation of myth.

Roughly speaking the later Adorno texts on the novel tend to add to
the understanding of the form after Sade, with particular attention to
Honoré de Balzac and Marcel Proust, along with Fyodor Mikhailovich
Dostoevsky, Franz Kafka, James Joyce, Robert Musil and other figures
of the late nineteenth and early twentieth centuries. Adorno takes the
French novel as the novel of bourgeois capitalism, associating Balzac
with the 'enrichissez vous' slogan of early nineteenth-century France.
That is a phrase attributed to François Guizot, the leading French poli-
tician of the upper class liberal era of the July Orléanist monarchy that
is 1830–1848. Guizot's aphorism refers to the high property qualifica-
tion associated with voting rights at the time and Guizot's belief that
those who wanted full political rights should work to earn them in the
economic sphere. Guizot was a very important contributor to nineteenth-century liberalism despite his downfall, influencing Alexis de
Tocqueville and William Ewart Gladstone, so one of the most important intellectual liberals of the century and one of the most important
political liberals. There are reasons then for Adorno to take Orléanist
France, as significant for the nineteenth-century bourgeois world.

It still requires some explanation that France of the 1830s and 1840s
era remains so strongly Adorno's model of bourgeois capitalism, despite
the German economic take off of the late nineteenth century, and the
obvious constant role of Britain throughout the century as a centre of
imperial, industrial, trading and financial capitalism. Orléanist France
was just one part of the new capitalist world at one time. The explanation is that culture dominates here, in the centrality of the French
novel to the European tradition, stretching from the seventeenth century into the 1950s. Arguments can be made for the centrality of the
Russian tradition, but its most influential moments are clearly from the
nineteenth century and the tradition was strongly conditioned by the
Francophone capacities of the Russian aristocracy and intelligentsia. The

British tradition perhaps can equal the French tradition as the source of world literature since the nineteenth century, but the greatest peak of the tradition, at least in the early twentieth century, was in the work of the Irishman James Joyce. Samuel Beckett another great product of the tradition was another Irishman and wrote his greatest works in French. The German tradition has some of its greatest works, certainly of the early twentieth century (Franz Kafka and Robert Musil) in Austria and what is now the Czech Republic. In comparison the French tradition, as know to most people, is very largely contained within France, and beyond that is often focused on Paris, or if not, usually on a provincial life contrasted with Paris, so seems to be more of a tradition focused on the central aspects of the life of a well-defined nation. Many qualifications could be made of the observations made in the last few sentences and many questions could be raised about the value of these kinds of generalisations, but they are recognisable generalisations, connected with the attitude that European novelists and thinkers about the novel have taken towards the history of the genre.

Despite Adorno's various criticisms of Lukács' literary aesthetics after he became a Communist, he seems rather close to Lukács' assumptions, after he turned Communist, of a progressive bourgeoisie up to 1848, which marks the end of Orléanist France, allied with the lower classes, and a reactionary bourgeoise allied with aristocracy and royalism after 1848. Adorno criticisms really just offer a variation on the picture Lukács offers in *The Historical Novel* and *Studies in European Realism* of progressive novels before 1848 and reactionary novels after 1848, in what is roughly an intermediate position between Leninist Lukács and the idealist-romantic Lukács of Theory of the Novel, closer to Weber than Marx.

What Adorno offers in his between Marx and Weber approach, with strong traces of German Idealism and Romanticism, is an interest in the administered society as an addition to Marxist categories. To some degree this takes the space occupied by monopoly state capitalism in Marxist theory. The pessimism of the early twentieth-century modernist novels is seen as the product of the total negativity of a society in which everything is administered. This overlaps with Weberian accounts of bureaucracy, as well as the accounts in traditionalist conservative thought (Carl Schmitt) and Austrian liberal-ordoliberal claims to a continuation of nineteenth-century liberalism (Friedrich Hayek), of the administrative state intervening in the lifeworld in a much more constant and pervasive way than earlier state forms. We can think here of Foucault's account of biopolitics and of the continuities in thought between Marx, Weber, the Frankfurt School and ordoliberalism. All of these approaches are prone to pessimism about the possibility of meaningful autonomy under a state administration more developed than in any previous society. We see an aspect of Adorno's approach here in the tendency to find ideal moments of some 'pure' nature in the novel, going right back as we have seen to Homeric epic.

> Kant's Platonism (in Phaedo, the soul was something similar to the idea) is an epistemological echo of the eminently bourgeois affirmation of personal unity in itself, at the expense of its substance—an affirmation which ultimately left the name of personality to no one but the "strong man." The rank of the good is usurped by the formal achievement of integration, but this achievement is a priori anything but formal; it is substantial, the sedimented control of man's inner nature. The suggestion is that—regardless of the dubiety of "being oneself"—the more of a personality one is, the better he must be.

> Great eighteenth-century novelists had their suspicions about that. Fielding's Tom Jones, the foundling, an "instinctual character" in the psychological sense, stands for the individual unmaimed by conventions and promptly turns comical. (*Negative Dialectics*. Adorno 1973, 293)

The last great period of literature from Adorno's point of view is what happens in literature from Proust to Beckett in the deepening realisation that some freedom has particular constraints in the modern world.

> And yet it is tempting to look for sense, not in life at large, but in the fulfilled moments—in the moments of present existence that make up for its refusal to tolerate anything outside it.

> Incomparable power flows from Proust the metaphysicist because he surrendered to this temptation with the unbridled urge to happiness of no other man, with no wish to hold back his ego. Yet in the course of

his novel the incorruptible Proust confirmed that even this fullness, the instant saved by remembrance, is not it. For all his proximity to the realm of experience of Bergson, who built a theory on the conception of life as meaningful in its concretion, Proust was an heir to the French novel of disillusionment and as such a critic of Bergsonianism. The talk of the fullness of life—a lucus a non lucendo even where it radiates— is rendered idle by its immeasurable discrepancy with death. Since death is irrevocable, it is ideological to assert that a meaning might rise in the light of fragmentary, albeit genuine, experience. This is why one of the central points of his work, the death of Bergotte, finds Proust helping, gropingly, to express hope for a resurrection— against all the philosophy of life, yet without seeking cover from the positive religions. (Adorno 1973, 378)

The contrast in Adorno between the realism of exaggeration and hyperbole in Balzac and the endurance of disillusion in Beckett is not very far from Lukács' understanding. In Adorno's view, Balzac deals with a world in which human relations are absent, but it is still possible to give life to human relations in literature through the colourful presentation of capitalist production and ambitions. Adorno distances himself from the view of Balzac offered by Engels and elaborated on by Lukács, in which Balzac is a political progressive in his presentation of harsh reality, even if he was a monarchist conservative in politics. However, what Adorno offers is really a more aestheticised version of the same claim, in which Balzac's style and imagination take him beyond immediate reality. What should underly Balzac is the Sadean sense of triumph enjoying its own power over others and this can be found, but the very French centred view of literary history leaves a very rigid view of the development of the novel, rigid even with French literary history.

The sense of growing pessimism associated with first industrial capitalism and then the administered society in Adorno extends to the capacity of literature itself. According to Adorno, Dostoevsky's achievements as a psychologist (emphasised by Nietzsche) are rendered futile by the slightly later development of psychoanalysis. Adorno seems to reveal a kind of naive positivism here despite all his apparently completely different positions. It is a kind of brutalist positivism to think that all insights in non-scientific texts are made irrelevant by scientific advance and equally positivistic to think literature can be reduced to systematic scientific observation and theorising in any way. This approach in Adorno combines with the nihilism of administered society to explain the appearance of a literature that seems to only explore its own impossibility. Proust appears as the last representative of an aesthetics of beauty where love and natural metaphors provide unity and harmony. *Aesthetic Theory* (2002) suggests that art is a tour de force of the unification of diverse material and Proust seems to represent a last stage of a tour de force which can give an impression of beauty and a metaphysical essence that Adorno suggests can be defined with regard to Proust's cousin, Henri Bergson.

> There is one variant that should not be missing from the excessively narrow initial questions in the Critique of Pure Reason, and that is the question how a thinking obliged to relinquish tradition might preserve and transform tradition. For this and nothing else is the mental experience. It was plumbed by Bergson in philosophy, and even more by Proust in the novel, though both men were kept under the spell of immediacy by their disgust with the bourgeois timelessness that will use conceptual mechanics to anticipate the end of life. Yet philosophy's methexis in tradition would only be a definite denial of tradition. Philosophy rests on the texts it criticizes. They are brought to it by the tradition they embody, and it is in dealing with them that the conduct of philosophy becomes commensurable with tradition. This justifies the move from philosophy to exegesis, which exalts neither the interpretation nor the symbol into an absolute but seeks the truth where thinking secularizes the irretrievable archetype of sacred texts. *Negative Dialectics* (Adorno 1973, 54–55)

Even in *In Search of Lost Time*, Adorno sees the sources of nihilism, the French novel of disillusion (which Adorno takes back to Balzac but could be taken back to Marie-Madeleine de Lafayette's *Princess of Cleves* in the late seventeenth century, along with La Rochefoucauld's *Maxims* of the same era and milieu or the recollections of the court of Louis XIV by the Duc de Saint-Simon) in the awareness of death and the 'ideology' of any belief system that denies its power. Beckett, implicitly, exists on an opposite pole to Proust while also following up his most nihilistic tendencies where the suffering of administrative society reaches an extreme, which is even represented as post-apocalyptic with regard to *Endgame*. However, the negativity itself is held to be utopian through the suggestion that there must be something better than the catastrophe revealed in Beckett's literature. Any writing creates monotony and repetition, going back to Homer, while utopia is taken to be the reversion to nature that Adorno sees in the lotus eaters episode of Homer's *Odyssey*. This advocacy of a state of willlessness itself has strong overtones of nihilism so that Adorno's overall aesthetic historical philosophy tends towards an interaction of two kinds of nihilism: abandonment of will and rationalist-administrative will without value, between Schopenhauer and Weber.

The importance of de Sade is not so great in the later texts, but the nihilistic nature of desire taken as an end in itself can be seen as part of Adorno's later literary philosophy. The political conclusions are difficult to discern. There is much more sense of lived politics in Adorno's account of the nineteenth century. The time in which he was writing and living, despite the extreme dramas of mid-twentieth-century Europe is flattened out into the domination of the administered society. The Holocaust is present in Adorno's thought, but its function in his thought is to express the already existing catastrophe of the administered society. The political philosophy appears to be quietist relying on an extra-historical transformation which might release utopia from the catastrophe.

In *Dialectic of Enlightenment*, 'The Concept of Enlightenment', there is a reference to Giambattista Vico (1986, 22), which suggests that philosophical concepts come from the Athenian market place. This is surely a misinterpretation of the progress in Vico from concrete universals in Homer's heroic poetry to the abstract universals of the human world of Athens, which has trade and markets, but not greatly emphasised by Vico in comparison with law, language, religion and literature. His account of Homer does suggest a link between human world and trade. Adorno presents Odysseus as the first bourgeois individual in a struggle with myth. Epic is not myth, there is implicitly a struggle between narrative and myth. The Lotus Eaters episode in *The Odyssey* can be taken as an encounter with world of life before production. The journey of Odysseus is a story of production and of separation from myths with threaten individualistic rationality. The Cyclops episode establishes the importance of the name and individuality, in which the name both gives and takes away individuality. There is a struggle with matriarchal myth, in Circe, Calypso and Sirens episodes and in the Hades episode, which is the oldest part of the epic, according to Adorno.

Juliette is Sade's main voice with regard to the domination inherent in republicanism and bourgeois legality. Her role can be compared with that of Circe, who Adorno suggests shifts from dominating to dominated. Sade is put in the context of Nietzsche and of Laclos. Laclos for the rationalisation of desire and cruelty, Nietzsche for the pleasure of cruelty towards the weak and trapped. From this point of view, Rousseau can be defined as inhuman for defending equality. Humans are driven by pleasure which is best gained as the dominating party in sadism in a limitlessness of desire. Sade and Nietzsche correspond with Kant's categorical imperative in their idea of a supreme law.

There is a Reason-Enlightenment struggle with myth but this produces myth. The Enlightenment representatives struggle with mimesis as magic (presumably underlying later suggestions in Adorno of the loss of mimesis in twentieth-century art, as it creates what it demands reality should imitate). Magic tries to conquer nature by imitating it, becoming then like what it tries to control. This seems to be Adorno's view of myth and the attempts of narrative-reason to overcome myth. From *Dialectic of Enlightenment*, it could be said that the epic is the struggle with myth and magic, along with the demonic powers created by the struggle as imitation, while the novel is the pursuit of desire and cruelty as a law. Mythical dangers keep returning in the Odyssey as in the need for Odysseus to make another journey to appease Poseidon and avert that mythical-divine force.

Adorno's thoughts on Homer and epic are expanded in 'On Epic Naiveté' (in Adorno 1991) where he suggests that the epic narrative has a blindness, which is why Homer is thought of as blind, in relation to events presumably related to its attempted detachment from myth. Narrative stops being narrative as in the Achilles' shield in Homer's *Iliad* and as in the need Goethe feels to interrupt his novels to provide a story. Images, the archaeological and metaphor tend to take over the novel. This is the result of a writing (presumably also

Enlightenment) struggle with the undifferentiated and repetitive nature of myth in which the writing itself incorporates those qualities, so that material takes over from syntax. From Goethe onwards bourgeois literature feels the need to create a normality which it cannot maintain.

These thoughts about the relation between epic and modern literature are followed up in 'The Position of the Narrator in the Contemporary Novel' (in Adorno 1991). The novel in the administered society refers to the lack of differentiated reality and subjectivity in administered society. Proust, Kafka, Musil, Joyce and so on are narrating the lack of subjective vision in the administered world in negative epics. The novel is the form of bourgeois society, dealing with disenchantment from the time of Cervantes and since. The novel becomes hollowed out as mass communication and the culture industry take over the role of reportage still lingering in Proust. The psychological insights of Dostoevsky become insignificant because of later developments in psychology and psychoanalysis.

It could be added to what Adorno says here that the epic has always been an epic of negativity for him, the failure to escape from the mythical world of power, undifferentiated mass and repetition. Essays on Balzac and Proust give us Adorno's views on the progress of liberalism from heroic age to decay intertwined with his literary history. In 'Reading Balzac' (in Adorno 1991), Adorno suggests that Balzac prefers truth to realism. He refers to a world of a bourgeois illusion in which the individual is self-sufficient, uninfluenced by the environment, which is brought into question. It is the world of capitalism in decline (after the defeat of the 1848 revolutions presumably) where individuals do not fit functions and wear masks. Adorno alludes to the German obscurity of Romanticism versus the Latin clarity of Balzac which connects with Enlightenment utopia, so indicating reservations about Romanticism. The bourgeois world of Balzac is of *ruthless self-enrichment*, where profit always has an element of guilt because it is never purely legal. Nothing is as it seems, the factory conceals human relations. Overcoming this is why Balzac lacks realism. The power of wealth is represented in grotesque individuals acting in ways that come from Sade, according to Adorno.

In 'Short Commentaries on Proust' (in Adorno 1991), Adorno proclaims the end of liberal society. It has become a world which claims to be harmonious but is disharmonious in deterministic ways. Proust's mythology creates physical-natural metaphor for human relations showing their alienated nature at the end of liberalism, so that Proust only shows love despite himself. Adorno seems to find Proust as displaying a world more alienated than it is, or some of his comments go in that direction.

Benjamin and Sacred Marxism

The relation between the thought of Adorno and Benjamin is a large topic going beyond the scope of the present book. There is a personal and institutional relationship in that Adorno and the Frankfurt Institute gave money to Benjamin, while Benjamin and Adorno did have intellectual and personal interaction. More significantly they both share an intellectual background deeply familiar with German Idealist Philosophy and Romantic aesthetics, along with nineteenth-century German oriented philosophy and the major literary texts of European culture. They both combined Marxist leaning politics with strong awareness of other political and social theory traditions. Non-Marxist French and German sociology and political thought are often in the background. Benjamin is distinguished from Adorno at the general level by a greater appreciation of popular culture and a strong interest in sacred tradition, particularly Jewish, combined with the most committed kind of revolutionarism, as in the thought of Georges Sorel (1999), for whom revolution and anti-liberal politics was as much an end in itself as a means. A Kantian wariness of instrumentalism in ethics can be found in Adorno as well as Benjamin, along with a related suspicion of distinctions between theoretical concepts and observation of reality, but in the case of Adorno is much more part of a systematic examination of philosophy, which cannot be found in Benjamin.

Benjamin did not write an extended text on the genre of the novel, but several essays referring to the novel, and related genres, add up a considerable contribution to the philosophy of the novel. These are essays on Fyodor Mikhailovich Dostoevsky (in Benjamin 1996),

Nikolai Semyonovich Leskov (in Benjamin 2006a), J.W. Goethe (in Benjamin 1996, 2005), Franz Kafka (in Benjamin 2005, 2006a) and Marcel Proust (in Benjamin 2005) in which Benjamin explores the nature of the novel in relation to epic, fairy tale, folktale, parable, novella and short story. A major part of his approach to the form of the novel is the struggle with myth. That is the mythical forces which shape less reflective forms of fiction, in which characters are archetypes and action is predetermined fate. The novel, as a form, is structured by interaction between subjective points of view and subjective reflection.

'Goethe's *Elective Affinities*' (in 1996) provides Benjamin with the opportunity to show how characters and choice emerge from myth in the novel, but are also tied to myth in a way that the novella is not. The form of the novella allows for a sudden resolution of the dilemmas of choice in love and moral relations which form the subject matter of Goethe's novel. The novel exists more as struggling with mythical forces. This goes back to the daemonic aspects of Don Quixote in Cervantes' novel. Remarks on Gustave Flaubert and Proust build up the discussion of reflection and memory in the novel. These are novels where memory and then forgetting are at the centre, in the description of subjectivity where memory itself is erased by the obsession with the recollection of the past. Benjamin argues that the reflective subjectivity of *In Search of Lost Time* suggests the end of a civilisation in which community and friendship are disappearing. Here Benjamin's revolutionary and messianic interests intersect with his aesthetic categories.

In 'Franz Kafka' (in Benjamin 2005) 'Review of Brod's *Franz* Kafka' (in 2006a), 'Letter to Gerschom Scholem on Franz Kafka' (in 2006a), Benjamin's is more concerned with the relation between parable and novel, drawing on Jewish heritage, so that we can see *The Trial* and *The Castle* as in some way parables of the judgement of the human individual who is always guilty. The morally questionable nature of the judges and accusers in Kafka, the extreme naturalism of his style, removes his novels from pure religious parable, but still leave the reader caught in a world of irremovable moral guilt. This idea of the novel as caught up in a relation with other genres is at the heart of Benjamin's essay on Leskov, 'The Storyteller: Observations on the Works of Nikola Leskov' (in Benjamin 2006a). This essentially deals with short stories, but in doing so, brings up the ways in which the short story can belong to the world of folk wisdom and the novel cannot. The short story can have the epic qualities that come from being embedded in the world that the novel must leave behind in its focus on subjectivity. The short story and its predecessors in folktales can convey mythical repetition as well as a world which is self-contained and timeless, all impossible for the novel.

A complete look at Benjamin's literary aesthetics means looking at *The Origin of German Tragic Drama* (1985). It is a treatise on literary aesthetics which has as much to do with Cervantes' the novelist as with Caldéron the tragedian, Grimmelshausen as with the mournings plays of seventeenth-century Germany. It is as much as anything a work of early twentieth-century literary aesthetics concerned with the twentieth-century politics and literature as much as the early modern period. The emptiness of the sovereignty of the prince Benjamin identifies in mourning plays (or tragic dramas, from two ways of translating '*das Trauerspiel*') belongs to sovereignty in the age of Bolshevik and fascist revolution as Benjamin's 1920 essay, 'Reflections on Violence' suggests in its questioning of natural law and positive law. Franz Kafka and Marcel Proust are just as much in Benjamin's thoughts about the loss of traditional social foundations as any work of tragedy. *The Origin of German Tragic Drama* looms over Benjamin's comparatively brief writing on the novel and has to be taken into consideration.

Benjamin looks back at the Baroque through the nineteenth-century developments in literary aesthetics. Both are writing through the framework provided by German Idealism and Romanticism, though with more explicit attention to Nietzsche in Benjamin. There are strong overtones of the Hegelian phenomenology of extreme subjectivity as unhappy consciousness, beautiful soul and the law of the heart in their account of Modern aesthetics. The Modern in both cases starts in the age of Shakespeare, Cervantes and Calderón and is explicitly recognised through the concepts of German Idealism and Romanticism. *The Origin of German Tragic Drama* opens with an 'Epistemo-Critical Prologue' which defends a form of Hegelianism and echoes the 'Preface' and 'Introduction' to the *Phenomenology of Spirit*. Benjamin's Hegel influenced themes include: the relation of history to nature, the lack of immediate unity in modern literature, the daemonic experience the individual has of itself and the world. Benjamin is also following on from Lukács in this use of Hegel influenced understanding. Both use the daemonic in a way which combines the Ancient Greek and Christian overtones: humans have a daemon, or sprit by nature; and the daemonic world is the evil world. This requires us to hold both the pagan definition and the Christian definition at the same time. Benjamin provides an account of Ancient Tragedy in terms of the daemonic. He refers to the tragedy as a legal and ethical event in which there is a struggle against demonic forces, the demonism of law as it exists. A rather less idyllic account of Homer is suggested here than in Hegel, since the world in which human, natural and divine law are one must be the daemonic world which the tragic hero is taken as resisting. Benjamin suggests that the split between natural and human is already taking place in Homer, in a 'quote' attributed to Schelling but not sourced, which suggests that the *Iliad* refers to the natural world and the *Odyssey* refers to the human world. That might take us in the direction of Adorno and Horkheimer's discussion of Odysseus in *Dialectic of Enlightenment*, and builds on an idea going back to Vico that *The Iliad* and *The Odyssey* are systematically distinct in the worlds they portray.

Nevertheless there is a common presupposition between Lukács and Benjamin with regard to the immediate unity of form in ancient literature compared with modern literature. For Benjamin, this distinction is focused on the distinction between Tragedy and Tragic Drama/ Mourning play. The hero is an active hero in tragedy struggling against daemonic law on the stage of law. What Benjamin refers to is the time of the emergence of the modern novel. The kind of drama Benjamin addresses emerges in London in the 1580 s in the tragedies of Christoper Marlowe, so between Rabelais' *Gargantua and Pantagruel* and Cervantes' *Don Quixtote*. What Benjamin says about early modern tragic drama is concerned with religious changes and political changes, which make the human world seem labyrinthine and arbitrary. This connects with the way the novel moves in a human world of complex interaction and levels, away from the unity and elevated register of the heroic epic.

An account of law is articulated in 'Critique of Violence' (in Benjamin 1996) where both natural and positive law are condemned as violent.

Tragic drama exists in a world of positive law compared with the natural law of tragedy. Benjamin largely explains this with reference to political sovereignty and the work of Carl Schmitt. For Schmitt, at least in *Political Theology*, the sovereign decides when there is a state of emergency, or in the exact words of the translation 'Sovereign is he who decides on the exception' (Schmitt 2005, 5). Benjamin points to the early Modern historical context as one which makes clear such a definition of sovereignty, and Schmitt refers to that historical context. In contrast with the Middle Ages, the Baroque era deprives the sovereign of any ground in divine or natural law. The Reformation and Counter-Reformation have undermined the claims to natural and divine law as the source of state sovereignty. The Lutheran Reformation emphasises the lack of grace, the absence of God in the natural and human world. The Catholic Counter-Reformation continues with that point of view as it both resists Protestantism and reforms Catholicism, inevitably occupying some of the same ground as Protestant reform. According to Benjamin, there is an aesthetically significant distinction between Reformation and Counter-Reformation. Catholicism continues to hold to a view of salvation through good works and the possibility of grace in the natural world.

Benjamin takes the Spanish tragic drama of Pedro Calderón de la Barca as the high point and the Lutheran 'mourning plays' as a drama of decline. However, tragic drama itself is analysed as a concept with primary reference to the mourning play. The intimacy of the divine and the natural in Calderón allowed by Catholic theology appears aesthetically in the predominance of reflection in Calderón. Even the Catholic Counter-Reformation deprives sovereignty of divine and natural support, because it still opposes historical humanity to the natural world and opposes both to the divine. The emphasis on religious purity, of inner spiritual life, still separates the spiritual self from the natural world, the history of humanity from the natural world and deprives sovereignty of a support in the unity of the divine and natural. The distinctions between natural, human and divine echo Lukács. The sovereign is faced with a lack of legitimacy other than the pure decisions of sovereignty itself. The sovereign is insecure since there is no reason for subjects to obey the sovereign. Lacking legal legitimacy, the sovereign can now only be a despot. Lacking legitimacy in the eyes of subjects, the sovereign is also in constant danger as there is no restraint on the over-throw of sovereign except for naked force. The sovereign is always on the verge of a fall and execution, in which case the sovereign becomes a martyr figure and even Christ like. Christ is combined with Herod. Herod appears in many mourning plays as the example of evil sovereignty, the monarch who tried to have the Christ child murdered. The baroque sovereign is despot and martyr, Herod and Christ in one. That sovereign is the essential hero of tragic drama. The sovereign is in the position of mourning, particularly from the Lutheran point of view. The sovereign point of view is of a history which is chaotic, labyrinthine and not rooted in nature or guided by divine purpose. The melancholic and even daemonic nature of the world is evident in *Don Quixote.* The search for unity with nature in allegory is not so evident in novelistic style of the early modern period, but the issue of human unity with and separation from nature is central to the development of the novel. Benjamin's concerns with fragmented allegorical style in seventeenth-century drama draw on the novelistic style and concerns of the early twentieth century. The loss of meaning and strangeness of reality in Kafka, where a human can become 'natural' as a giant insect, or die like a dog as at the end of *The Trial.* Writing as a constant prose poem in Proust, in which history, nature, memory and transcendence mingle. There is another kind of extended prose poem in Joyce intermingling cultural history with extremes of aestheticism and natural material detail. In Kafka, the alien, malevolent and even daemonic nature of law and institutions prevails, while in Proust and Joyce history becomes overwhelming but also chaotic and unguided by any purpose in the state, in nature, or the divine.

Rather than try to fix bits of *The Origin of German Tragic Drama* individually with particular twentieth-century concerns or particular aesthetics of the novel concerns, a mixture of paraphrase and summary will show how Benjamin's work on tragedy fits into the flow of this chapter, and this book as a whole.

The sovereign is satanic-daemonic as despot-Herod, but also satanic-daemonic as the melancholic hero. Satan is identified by Benjamin as the melancholic, the lord of the abyss and the prince of darkness as a state of mind. The reality of the world is Satanic after the Reformation and Counter-Reformation, in the sense of a sadness and melancholia given a lack of grace in history or nature. That is the point of the quotation from Blaise Pascal (Benjamin 1985, 142), which refers to the sadness of the soul that cannot look at itself or anything outside itself. Martin Luther himself is identified with satanic melancholia, as Benjamin suggests that his later life was darkened by his own renunciation of salvation through good works. Salvation through divine grace alone must lead to despair with humanity and with nature, which lacks any means to salvation. The aesthetic form of tragic drama is seen in terms of melancholia and the separation of the divine, the historical and the natural. The separation which means that humanity must be seen as creaturely, (an important point for Auerbach in *Mimesis*), because lacking in the kind of daemonic strength the Ancient Greek world suggested. Creaturely humanity is fallen satanic humanity, gazing inward with melancholia at emptiness and lacking the force of the tragic hero, who is not constrained by the creaturely limits felt by Baroque humanity.

The aesthetic elements of mourning and melancholia can be found in allegory, fragmentation, in pendants and the importance of physical props. It is allegory that is decisive here. The language of Baroque drama is held to be typically allegorical by Benjamin. The allegory appears in the way that human concerns and divine references are expressed in relation to nature. The separation from nature is experienced in literary aesthetics through a compulsion to bring nature into language, something where Benjamin finds a precursor for modernist literary aesthetics in the Baroque. Sentences which bring metaphors of nature constantly to the fore are nevertheless denatured. The reading of such sentences or the observation of their enactment can only be alienating. Baroque language is constantly stretching itself into incorporating natural images so making itself appear all the less natural and melancholic in relation to the absence of nature. The allegorical sentence is a fragmented sentence in a fragmented world.

Benjamin had addressed Romantic philosophy of literature and art in his doctoral dissertation 'The Concept of Criticism in German Romanticism' (in Benjamin 1996) in which he regards Friedrich Schlegel and other Romantics as placing criticisms above the literary work, so expressing views about what a work should be not what it is.

Nevertheless, *The Origin of German Tragic Drama* does rely on a view of baroque drama best understood with reference to Romantic literary aesthetics and Benjamin's reaction to the development of the novel since Goethe. The boundaries of the philosophy of the novel are not completely self-evident and while not all the interesting borderline cases can be explored, Benjamin's general influence makes him worthy of such investigation, as has already been done for *The Birth of Tragedy* in Chap. 5 above and Kierkegaard's essay on *Don Giovanni* discussed in Chap. 4 above. *The Origin of German Tragic Drama* has shaped literary aesthetics, including the aesthetics of the novel far more than Benjamin's doctorate and at least as much as his essays devoted to particular novelists.

Benjamin's account is explicitly linked with the role of allegory in Friedrich Schlegel (1985, 214), and references to the Jena Romantics appear in various contexts in *The Origin of German Tragic Drama*, so we can see that he opens up a general situation for literary aesthetics since the seventeenth century, in conjunction with a body of work which is the first to elevate the form of the novel. For the Jena Romantics, the fragment is an expression of the relative nature of any point of view and the need for an aphoristic sentence structure which emphasises simultaneous contradiction and unity. *The Origin of German Tragic Drama*, rest on Idealist and Romantic categories in general, reworking ideas from Schelling, Hegel and Schlegel.

Ancient tragedy is not alienated from nature in the same way as tragic drama, according to Benjamin. Benjamin refers (1985, 101–104) to a passage in Nietzsche, from *The Birth of Tragedy*, which sees the setting of ancient tragedy as a version of mountains and a valley. Benjamin's account of the hero of ancient tragedy fighting the law of the daemonic-divine clearly draws on Nietzsche's suggestion that the hero is always a version of Prometheus, a hero transgressing divine law in a human struggle. This is the hero as mad and as criminal read back into the Ancient Greek world. Benjamin refers to Nietzsche, in order to find something like Lukács novelistic hero emerging in the ancient Greek world. Like Lukács, Benjamin cannot see the modern hero as an ethical hero. For Benjamin, one thing which distinguishes the tragic hero from the hero of tragedy is a prohibition on images. That prohibition most directly refers to God, but it refers to any kind of divine-ethical content.

The modern literary-aesthetic rests on a prohibition not found in the antique world. That is an effect of Romanticism in Hegel's definition. The acts of the hero of tragic drama cannot have positive ethical consequences, since that would require the forbidden representation of the ethical. The hero of the tragic drama can only contemplate the ethical emptiness of the world, a position of daemonic melancholia rather than ethical struggle.

What we find read back into the sixteenth and seventeenth centuries is the Kantian view of morality as abstract universal law outside the accidents and self-interested actions of history and outside natural empirical humanity. For Benjamin, Kantian morality is a positive reference. The separation of ethical law from the empirical world is necessary to show the ethical emptiness of the world and the need for redemption. From a purely Kantian point of view, Benjamin believes we can understand the contingency and violence of any law, natural or positive. The sovereignty described by Schmitt is welcomed by Benjamin as a way of showing the emptiness of bourgeois sovereignty and any form of rational sovereignty.

The Marxist approach of Adorno and Benjamin to narrative forms, inflected by Kantian ethics and Judaic Messianism, exists as an expression of a Germanic tradition of literary criticism, hermeneutics, aesthetic philosophy and classical philology from Baumgarten to Nietzsche through Lessing, German Idealism, German Romanticism, Marx and Nietzsche. There is a correspondence of Auerbach with Lukács, Adorno and Benjamin here. Lukács' pre-Marxist *The Theory of the Novel* makes the connection particularly obvious. Auerbach, Lukács, Adorno and Benjamin are not all saying the same thing by any means, but a Marxist disappointment with the cultural world, with the failure of the masses, maybe defined as the working class, to adopt the appropriate kind of redemptive literature and world view. Though Benjamin was a pioneer of the study and appreciation of mass culture, there is a distinct disappointment in his thinking that the working class is influenced by aesthetic politics rather than political art expressed in the 'Work of Art in the Age of Its Technological Reproducibility' (in Benjamin 2006b). Benjamin's attitude towards the loss of the aura of the poet when he writes on Baudelaire in a number of essays (in Benjamin 2006b) and on mechanical reproduction is distinctly ambiguous, there is definitely something to mourn in the loss of aura as well as celebration of the loss of hierarchy. Benjamin like Adorno was developing his literary aesthetics as the October Revolution failed to spread beyond Russia and led to inward looking autocracy within Soviet Russia. The rise of Fascism and Naziism increased their pessimism as did the greater interest of the proletariat in entertainment than in redemption through revolution. Both have a literary aesthetics conditioned by the failure of revolutionary history. In Benjamin's case this leads to a hope for a more theological kind of revolution, as can be seen in 'On the Concept of History', also known as 'Theses on the Philosophy of History' (in Benjamin 2006b). Adorno moves towards purely metaphysical-aesthetic ways of thinking about revolution arising from the negativity of contemporary reality, best understood through art.

A Political Conclusion

The pessimistic tone of *The Theory of the Novel* suggests a deeper source of the disappointment in Benjamin and Adorno. For Lukács, there is already melancholy at the loss of epic unity and then at the subjective reflection dominating literature from Gustave Flaubert's *Sentimental Education* onwards. This could have political origins in the disappointment in Germany of the *Kaissereich*, the revived German empire that had its first version in the Middle Ages, from the Franco-Prussian War of 1870 to the collapse of Germany at the end of World War I in 1918. A disappointment that can be found in Nietzsche and Weber who have a shared concern with the loss of value and the possibility of nihilism in the modern world. The *Kaissereich* not providing a positive alternative for Weber and Nietzsche though both had nationalist German inclinations. For Nietzsche, the ideal of Empire on the Roman model, and repeated by medieval German Emperors and then by Napoleon still has allure, while for Max Weber there is the hope of a President in a democracy who is both elected and charismatic (Weber 1994), itself an echo of the claims of the Roman Emperors as explained by Vico. Adorno and Benjamin write in the context of a disappointment in the new German

Empire, anxieties about nihilism and cultural decline, which they hope will be answered by Marxist politics, but not in any immediately apparent form. Auerbach never made the transition to Marxism, but provides a strong point of reference to those adhering to Marxism or at least wishing to continue some major elements of it.

Like Auerbach, these are writers classified more as critics than philosophers, but both engage with philosophy, Vico and Michel Foucault in the case of Edward Said (1985), Marxist aesthetics in the case of Jameson, and bring philosophical understanding to their literary and cultural criticism. Both are notably more political in their writing than Auerbach, who in this way has had just as much influence on Marxist and Marxist leaning literary aesthetics as any Marxist thinker. At the deepest level, there has been a movement from Auerbach's historicist approach to the internal history of literature and style to a more political form of historicism, in which a mixture of Marx and other philosophies of history dominate literary criticism. The work of Jameson and Said on philosophical aspects of history, literature and politics can be compared with Hayden White's work in this area, which is partly formed by an encounter with Vico as well as Marxism, along with Kenneth Burke and the American Pragmatist tradition in philosophy. Jameson's *The Political Unconscious* (1981) mixes Marxist concerns with narratological, structural and discourse Analytic concerns in ways that may undermine the Marxist historical approach or at least come into tension with it, raising general issues of the relation between history and philosophy or theory. Jameson's work here marks a high point of the idea of a field of literary theory integrating Marxism, psychoanalysis, narratology and linguistics. Franco Moretti's work on the *Bildungsroman* (2000) and the novel (2013) connect with this stream of thought and particularly overlaps with Jameson's later work in considering the difficulties of defining a positive *Bildungsroman* (2013) particularly in the ideologically fractured world since the late twentieth century in which heroic liberalism has looked as troubled as Marxism. The time in which Marxism begins to attain a melancholic aspect, after the Bolshevik Revolution, follows on from and even takes from the more pessimistic reflections of Max Weber on modernity as bureaucratic and conditioned by empty legal-rationalism, which has strong parallels in the traditionalist-conservative thought of Carl Schmitt, drawn upon by Benjamin, and the Austrian School of economics, most known through Friedrich Hayek, which regrets the shift towards stage interventionism and a related 'New Liberalism' in the late nineteenth century. All these currents of thought see some major loss in the growth of the state, legislation and administration, along with corporate interests allied to the state, into civil society and personal autonomy.

References

Adorno, Theodor. 1973. *Negative Dialectics*, trans. E.B. Ashton. London: Routledge and Kegan Paul.

Adorno, Theodor. 1989. *Kierkegaard: Construction of the Aesthetics*, trans. Robert Hullot-Kentor. Minneapolis, MN: University of Minnesota Press.

Adorno, Theodor. 1991. *Notes to Literature, Volume One*, trans. Shierry Weber Nicholsen. ed. Rolf Tiedeman. New York and Chichester: Columbia University Press.

Adorno, Theodor. 2002. *Aesthetic Theory*, trans. and ed. Robert Hullot-Kentor. London and New York: Continuum.

Adorno, Theodor, and Max Horkheimer. 1986. *Dialectic of Enlightenment*, trans. John Cumming. London and New York: Verso.

Arnold, Matthew. 2006. *Culture and Anarchy*, ed. Jane Garnett. Oxford and New York: Oxford University Press.

Auerbach, Erich. 1949. Vico and Aesthetic Historicism. *The Journal of Aesthetics and Art Criticism* VIII(2), 110–118.

Auerbach, Erich. 1968. *Mimesis: The Representation of Reality in Western Literature*, trans. Willard R. Trask. Princeton, NJ: Princeton University Press.

Auerbach, Erich. 2007. *Dante, Poet of the Secular World*, trans. Ralph Manheim. New York: New York Review of Books.

Benjamin, Walter. 1985. *The Origin of German Tragic Drama*, trans. John Osborne. London and New York: Verso Books.

Benjamin, Walter. 1996. *Selected Writings, Volume 1: 1913–1926*, ed. Marcus Bullock and Michael W. Jennings. Cambridge, MA and London: Harvard University Press.

Benjamin, Walter. 2005. *Selected Writings, Volume 2. Part 2: 1931–1934*, ed. Michael W. Jennings, Howard Eiland, and Gary Smith. Cambridge, MA and London: Harvard University Press.

Benjamin, Walter. 2006a. *Selected Writings, Volume 3: 1935–1938,* ed. Michael W. Jennings and Howard Eiland. Cambridge, MA and London: Harvard University Press.

Benjamin, Walter. 2006b. *Selected Writings, Volume 4: 1938–1940,* ed. Howard Eiland and Michael W. Jennings. Cambridge, MA and London: Harvard University Press.

Derrida, Jacques. 1978. *Writing and Difference.* trans. Alan Bass. Chicago, IL: University of Chicago Press.

Jameson, Fredric. 1981. *The Political Unconscious: Narrative as a Socially Symbolic Act.* Ithaca: Cornell University Press.

Jameson, Frederic. 2013. *The Antinomies of Realism.* London and New York: Verso.

Moretti, Franco. 2000. *The Way of the World: The* Bildungsroman *in European Culture,* trans. Albert Sbragia. London and New York: Verso.

Moretti, Franco. 2013. *The Bourgeois: Between History and Literature.* London and New York.

Said, Edward W. 1985. *Beginnings: Intention and Method.* New York: Columbia University Press.

Said, Edward W. 1994. *Culture and Imperialism.* London: Vintage.

Schmitt, Carl. 2005. *Political Theology: Four Chapters on the Concept of Sovereignty,* trans. George Schwab. Chicago IL: University of Chicago Press.

Sorel, Georges. 1999. *Reflections on Violence,* ed. Jeremy Jennings. Cambridge: Cambridge University Press.

Weber, Max. 1994. The Profession and Vocation of Politics. In *Weber: Political Writings,* trans. Ronald Speirs, ed. Peter Lassman. Cambridge and New York: Cambridge University Press.

White, Hayden. 1978. *Tropics of Discourse: Essays in Cultural Criticism.* Baltimore, MD: Johns Hopkins University Press.

White, Hayden. 1999. *Figural Realism: Studies in the Mimesis Effect.* Baltimore, MD: Johns Hopkins University Press.

8

Mimetic Limits Desire, Death and the Sacred

Introduction

The philosophy of the novel as we have seen it so far is very focused on narrative and the overall structure of the novel, along with the humanistic ethical and historical with a teleological emphasis on the ethical hopes associated with the novelistic portrayal of individuals and societies. Friedrich Schlegel elevates the novel to an expression of the highest possibilities of human creativity, integrating philosophical and literary aesthetic capacities. Kierkegaard has a less idealised view of the novel, but he not only recognises it as having a particular status in the individualist bourgeois society of his time but also incorporates it into his own writing. In doing so, he suggests that some kind of engagement with the genre of the novel is necessary for grasping the cultural and ethical aspects of the society. Most importantly, the novel is necessary to deal with the paradoxes that Kierkegaard claims must come into human life experience, when we think at all about experience; and which bring us to the level of religion as the fullest possibility of individuality. In Lukács, the individual encounters its loss of a transcendental home, in the development of literature along with society, since the Homeric

© The Author(s) 2018
B. Stocker, *Philosophy of the Novel*,
https://doi.org/10.1007/978-3-319-65891-9_8

epic. The awareness of loss is itself awareness of a home and an orientation of literary aesthetics to the idea of such a home in nostalgia for it. His later Marxist viewpoint refers to the need for social transformation for the fully human to be realised. Bakhtin has an ideal of polyphony and dialogism as a human goal, as the realisation of human essence, which probably has a version of Russian religious populism guiding it, but the broad humanist ethical orientation is still there whether we take Bakhtin as an Orthodox Christian populist, a revisionist Marxist or something else. Hegel' suspicion of the novel reflects his metaphysical humanist goals for literary aesthetics. The absoluteness of humanist ethics is ambiguous as well. The ideal itself suggests a challenge to immediate and everyday awareness. The challenge questions the contents and goals of consciousness. The teleological ideal for humans may question humans as they are. Marxism has been taken as a source of criticism of humanism, at least by Louis Althusser.

The ambiguity about teleological humanist metaphysic, with regard to whether it orientates or criticises humanism experience, is brought out by Jacques Derrida in 'The Ends of Man' (in *Margins of Philosophy*. Derrida 1982). Derrida himself was drawing on various criticisms of humanism and anti-humanist positions. A more broad and detailed account of this issue in Derrida and others can be found in the author's *Derrida on Deconstruction* (Stocker 2006). The obvious beginning for this is in Nietzsche who did reject humanism as a continuation of, or substitute for, theology. Nietzsche develops an alternative position which includes: suggestions that there are two kinds of morality (slave and master); a focus on the biological and physiological aspects of human psychology along with the ways in with psychological drives are not themselves consciously willed; the idea of an eternal return which takes away the primacy of a human life and its possible orientation to historical progress as a substitute for theology; emphasis on the ways that the human individual can disperse between different moments and states; questioning of the historical conditioning of humanity which does not live in the action of the moment; a view of artistic experience as experience of forces beneath and beyond human consciousness; asserting the tendency of humanity towards nihilism placed in the context of the conflicting roles of will and nihilism;

the non-moral and even extremely cruel origin of moral principles and legal institutions; the chance driven and violent origins of the state; and proposing the Overman who is beyond the Last Man and the limits of humanity. These aspects of Nietzsche's thoughts do not themselves completely deny the possibility of humanism. The idea of the Overman itself can be taken as a kind of displaced theology or humanism, though whether it should be is another matter. Derrida's discussion of humanism along with his discussions of Nietzsche in *Spurs* (1979), *Ear of the Other* (1985) and *Politics of Friendship* (1997) explore the ambiguities of Nietzsche's anti-humanism and anti-metaphysics, along with the inevitable paradoxes of any such position which is bound to use language and concepts embedded in humanism and theology.

We will return to Derrida's thoughts about literature later. His reflections on humanism and metaphysics provide a way of showing the progress from nineteenth-century philosophy to a twentieth-century aesthetics pressing at the limits of humanism and thereby the limits of imitation, or mimesis, in literature. This can be found in a number of texts including *Dissemination* (Derrida 1981) and with reference to visual arts in *The Truth in Painting* (1987). This has been central to the discussions of literature since Plato, where it is regarded with suspicion, and Aristotle, where it has a more honoured role. The centrality of the idea to thinking about narrative fiction and novel is recognised in Auerbach' *Mimesis* as discussed in the last chapter. This tradition includes the idea of an imitation of reality which can be regarded as 'humanist'.

The aesthetics of Adorno and Benjamin as discussed in the last chapter provide some challenges to humanist mimesis, with the emphasis on the experience of a disintegrating bourgeois life world, which is a prelude to the apocalypse and contains a kind of apocalypse in itself in the detachment of literature from production, and its awareness of nihilism. Again, we might see a kind of humanism or theology here and the theology is quite explicit in Benjamin, but representation of the human world and assumptions of humane values guiding literature are brought into question. There is certainly some idea of a reconciled or redeemed humanity after some transcending political event, combining Marxist political revolution with ethical or theological ideas.

Bataille

Something more insistingly anti-humanist can be found in the work of Georges Bataille, which opens up ideas about the sacral, violence, death and the limits of representation taken up by other thinkers to be considered in this chapter, particularly Maurice Blanchot and René Girard, along with Jacques Lacan, Michel Foucault and Jacques Derrida. It is a very French line of thought in contrast to the more Germanic line of Hegelianism and Marxism in Lukács along with thinkers considered in the last chapter, also contrasting with the particularly Russian aspects of Bakhtin's thought. These are not absolute distinctions and if, for example, we go back to the time of the Enlightenment, we might roughly thinking equate France with rationalist calm and Germany with more subjectivist and emotionally stimulating thought. Bataille was of course drawing on Nietzsche and French thought related to Bataille drew on Hegel, Husserl, Heidegger and Freud. While it would therefore be wrong to suppose essential national aspects of national literary culture and aesthetic thought down generations and centuries, it is important to note that ways of thinking do cluster at particular times in particular national cultures, often driven by a sense of difference from a neighbouring culture. Even now, Foucault and the Frankfurt School stand for distinctive French and German approaches in contemporary work in philosophy, social science and the humanities. While it is a gross over-simplification to simply present the complexity of intellectual life in France and Germany in this way, there is enough truth in it for it to be recognisable and to drive some inquiries.

Bataille's work covers literary writing, critical writing in literary and cultural spheres and a domain of inquiry into the relations between different drafts of the same work. Here the concentration will be on the work most directed to literary criticism, which is his book of 1957 *Literature and Evil* (Bataille 2012) a small part of Bataille's writing, but a notable event in the history of literary criticism. It is not entirely devoted to the genre of the novel and makes no attempt to discuss the genre or any specific aspects of the novel as a form. The book explores ways in which good is challenged in literature, good referring to the contained consciousness and activity of an individual who has restrained desire sufficiently to operate as a 'normal' person. The normality arises from rather more disturbing realities with regard to the taboos and violence that underly normality. The existence of society is itself premised on prohibition and the sacred, with the destruction of what crosses the border. The border itself is only maintained by the force of what normality tries to contain: death, violence and negativity. Bataille begins with a chapter devoted to Emily Brontë, largely with regard to her novel *Wuthering Heights*, though some attention is also paid to her poetry. Bataille takes the childhood love between Catherine Earnshaw and Heathcliff as a part of the kingdom of childhood, a kingdom which is denied by adult normality. The whole world of dreams and childhood is relegated within the social order so that it can only be seen as evil if it resists agreed moral law. Dreams and childhood consciousness, along with uncontrolled desire in general, never disappear so are always there as possible evil. The prohibitions against them rely on the violence and irrational fear condemned as evil. Bataille refers to Jansenism as an evidence of the ambiguity of religion on these points. Jansenism refers to a seventeenth-century movement within French Catholicism, inspired by the commentaries of the Belgian Bishop Cornelius Jansenius on Augustine. His work was condemned as heretical by the Papacy, but nevertheless the Jansenist movement had a strong influence which lasted into the eighteenth century and maybe later, as a sensibility at least. Those who followed Jansenist ideas to some degree in the seventeenth century included the tragedian Jean Racine and the thinker Blaise Pascal. Pascal has been mentioned a few times in this book already, because his work is an important crossover between philosophy and literature, providing a major inspiration for Nietzsche's approach to philosophy. Pascal's work crossed between science, maths (Stocker 2000), practical inventions, literature, religious controversy and philosophy. All of these have some place in his most widely read book *Pensées*, an unfinished work consisting of fragments on a large number of topics. This is how Jansenism is best known to most people, or at least writing influenced by Jansenism, since Pascal may not have been a pure Jansenist. Racine's tragedies are the other way in which many have absorbed Jansenism (Goldman 2016), though there are questions about the relationship between Racine's plays and Jansenist thought. The sense of the domination of human motives by desire and the inevitably of tragic events in Racine's drama is usually taken to be Jansenist in sensibility at least. Jansenism refers to the depravity of humanity unable to seek salvation except by unmerited grace from God, a grace offered to few. The sensibility developed from this in Pascal, and others, refers to the fragility of reason prone to be lost in paradox and the weakness of human will, which is constantly subordinated to desire rather than a will to follow God and salvation. The dominance of desire in individual motives creates a human world of compromised Christianity surrounded by self-interest and laws built on the balance of self-interests rather than pure law.

This diversion into the seventeenth-century religious thought is offered partly to clarify Bataille, but is as long as it is because this bit of cultural history is fundamental to the development of French literature, including the novel. Pascal's fragments, along with the epistemic uncertainties and moral fallibilities, inform the style and preoccupation of the French novel. His fragments anticipate the aphorisms of La Rochefoucauld and the character sketches of La Bruyère, which have their own considerable impact on the development of the novel. Lucien Goldman's discussion of the relation between Pascal and French tragedy, *The Hidden God* (2016), is itself a classic of literary criticism.

Bataille's fleeting reference cannot be taken as chance or as trivial. It is an invocation of a world in which human society is based on violence and desire, only interrupted by a sacred violence which is the only source of justice. Derrida was concerned with this last point in *The Force of Law* (in Derrida 2002) showing the continuing significance of Pascal's legacy in the kind of philosophy that puts literature at the centre. Pascal gives both indications of the bourgeois world of self-directed actions and desires generally thought central to the development of the novel as a major literary genre, while he also suggests an absolute alternative of the most pure forms of religious experience and expectation, suggestive of a sacred violent destruction of the bourgeois order. A way of thinking which has echoes in the Frankfurt School criticism has been discussed in the last chapter. While Adorno and Benjamin do not come from a Catholic background, and certainly not from Jansenist inflected French Catholicism, the permeation of European culture by Pascal, and

Pascal influenced work, which includes Jean-Jacques Rousseau, Alexis de Tocqueville and Georges Sorel, gives a path of influence into Adorno and Benjamin. They were both certainly strongly influenced by Kant's ethics, which has some rigourist similarities with Jansenism, possibly reaching Kant through Rousseau, though the common roots of French Jansenism and Prussian Pietist Protestantism in Augustine should also be considered here.

The Jansenist insights may become dispersed in ways that make it difficult to distinguish them from broadly similar insights from Augustinian Christianity, something important for Kierkegaard though most noticeable in *The Concept of Anxiety* (1981), rather than the texts considered in Chap. 4 on Kierkegaard above. However, Bataille shows the importance of a Jansenist current of thought and sensibility, in culture and thought, until his own time, informing literary aesthetics amongst other things. Jansenism, particularly Pascal, influenced almost everything through Rousseau including: the development of the novel; liberal, political and social thoughts as well as historiography through Tocqueville; twentieth-century revolutionaries of left and right through Sorel ('Georges Sorel: A Jansenist Marxism' in Kolakowski 1978), one of the almost forgotten thinkers of the twentieth century who is nevertheless present in Benjamin's work on law and revolution in 'Critique of Violence', as discussed in the last chapter. Sorel also provides a connection back to Vico, in his essay 'Étude sur Vico' (in Sorel 2007). So we can simply reflect on the existence of a line which goes through from Vico through Sorel to the kind of sacral revolutionary thought which formed Bataille's political ideas. In Bataille's literary thought we can see some expression of a desire for political revolution as a rupture with normality of various kinds articulated in relation to literary classics not directly concerned with politics, including *Wuthering Heights* by Emily Brontë.

In *Wuthering Heights*, the desires that Heathcliff and Catherine retain from childhood can be seen in Jansenist inflected terms as evidence of human evil. However, they can be seen as evidence of a Jansenist style wish for an absolute rupture in which the innocence of desire can triumph over the cruelty of normality, so that what is evil for normality is pure good. This is the implication of Bataille's own insertion of Jansenism as an issue into his discussion of Brontë. The implication of what he says is that the evil experienced by normality is good transcending a pseudo-good. Bataille does not overtly say this, but this is the unavoidable conclusion of his discussion of good and evil in literature. The kingdom of childhood is innocence of some kind which presses against adult compromises as a violent negation. Catherine's socially prudent marriage, which is not against all her emotions, must nevertheless be assaulted viciously and sadistically, through her husband. Heathcliff has an extreme, even fanatical purity of love, but a purity which leads to death and negation. Bataille argues that the purity of love must coincide with death and negativity as it must exceed the limits of goodness. The suggestion is that the desire, the hope for a pure passion, which drives literature has some echoes of Jansenist hope for salvation in the development of the novel, though particularly the French novel. The British novel itself took a lot of its energy from John Bunyan's *The Pilgrim's Progress*, a seventeenth-century Protestant work of spiritual trials. However, the British novel, or the English language novel in general, has not had the sort of religious interpretation in central texts of criticism as the French novel. Of course, the Protestant influences on novelists since Defoe is acknowledged (Watt 1972). Northrop Frye was an influential liberal Protestant thinker about literary forms, but there is nothing in his work (*Anatomy of Criticism*. Frye 1957) that adds up to an investigation of the sacred and evil in the novel. He addresses its appearance in some poetry as an extreme and external force. Bataille achieves this in a non-systematic way, followed by Blanchot in a more abstracted philosophical approach and receiving a fully Catholic treatment in Girard. The role of Catholic sensibility in James Joyce's novels, a culmination of some kind of the English language novel, partly complicates the picture as does the plurality of Protestant positions, but there is some value in making a pragmatic distinction between Protestant English literary culture and Catholic French culture. This distinction mostly refers to the criticism rather than the literature, but the Marquis de Sade does represent an element in French literature which has no obvious equivalent in English literature, or any other literature. Sade's achievement covers a kind of literary essayistic philosophy as well as his novels, so he may be the real precursor of Bataille.

Bataille's other explorations of the novel stay within the German and French traditions, moving through the Marquis de Sade, Marcel Proust and Franz Kafka. With Sade, Bataille's interest is not just in the exhaustive coverage of immorality, corruption of virtue and cruelty in his work. There is a tradition of writing about more in Sade in France, which includes Foucault, Lacan and Camus as well as Bataille. For Bataille, what underlies the erotic and violent extremism, at its most challenging in *120 Days of Sodom* in his view, is Sade's preoccupation with the mobility of desire. He himself felt overwhelmed by this and preferred to be imprisoned at least for a while in Bataille's reading of the situation. It is the mobility which is the real evil, as evil lacks anything except the negation of the laws and forms which good invokes. Bataille brings this into politics, as he points both to Sade's apparent radicalism in the French Revolution and his ambiguity when questioned about his politics, where he may say he wants a limited form of monarchy rather than a pure republican revolution. Sade's imprisonment in the Bastille fortress and the role he played in provoking the storming of the fortress on 14 July 1789, through lurid exaggerations of what was going on inside, dramatises this overabundant ambiguous mobile desire, providing an equivalent for the erotic stagings in the novels.

The theme of politics and literature continues through Marcel Proust, and here Bataille is particularly concerned with the main literary work, *In Search of Lost Time*, which will be the topic of Chap. 9. What Bataille refers to there is the role of sadism, a thirst for cruelty which is part of good since it is the expression of love. Vinteuil's daughter humiliates him through her female lover during his life and insults his image just after his death, while the narrator, in a more implied way, humiliates his mother with a disreputable love affair. The narrator's love of the mother is central to *In Search of Lost Time*, just as preserving the memory of her composer father will be Mlle Vinteuil's primary concern after his death. Love and goodness themselves require a thirst for sadism, for inflicting pain on the object of love, indicating again how for Bataille 'Lawful' drives are themselves founded on evil. The trajectory from Sade to Proust suggests something particularly French about the role of evil in literature even if it is not unique to French literary tradition.

The exploration of Kafka, again refers just as much to life as the novels, though in this case letters and diaries create a continuity between 'life' and writing. The focus here is on the evil of someone who wishes to devote his life to writing rather than work and marriage. His evil is that he wants to detach himself from the world of obligations, connected with economic and social survival to pursue a solitary vocation which has no use. As Bataille emphasises, the evidence of letters and diaries is that Kafka felt indifferent to family, fiancées and work, longing to be on his own, dreading marriage as the loss of solitude and freedom. The novels show K in *The Trial* and Joseph K in *The Castle*, both floating free of responsibility while longing for some kind of respectability and acceptance by the law. In *The Trial*, the judicial persecution of K is no more than the shame he feels and the desire for acceptance, while living the self-directed life which makes him open to accusation. In *The Castle*, Joseph K is more active in seeking the approval of the law and has more clearly left a family while he struggles to reach the castle by a village, in a journey towards law in which he is always acting against law in the sense that he is selfish and floats free of personal obligations. The castle and its lords are themselves completely banal, and so are unworthy of interest except with regard to Joseph K's fervour to be with the law while outside it, casting himself deeper into immorality, abandoning connections with better people in favour of people he thinks have some kind of power to help him into the castle. Again we see the ambiguity of evil, which both opposes law as it is experienced normally, but seeks some kind of higher law which excuses evil.

Blanchot

Bataille's discussion of Kafka is startlingly similar to that of Blanchot in *The Space of Literature* (1982), first published in 1955, two years before *Literature and Evil*. Blanchot is discussed after Bataille here, because his most important book with regard to the genre of the novel, *The Book to Come* (2003) was published in 1959. It seems likely this was due to collaboration and discussion rather than intellectual theft and the publication dates are probably incidental in relation to the formulation of the ideas. This overlap does indicate the continuity between two approaches which also have major differences. Both Bataille and Blanchot emphasise the extremity and limits in which the mimetic aspect of the novel is subordinated to the experience of limits of representation, to the attempt to experience what cannot be experienced and cannot be put into words. The experience of the limit is always the experience of the loss of the ability to experience, something Bataille argues is true of both sexual climax and death. In Blanchot, death is more the issue than sexual activity or sadism. Negativity is discussed as an inner experience of limits rather than destructive behaviour of individuals.

While there is considerable overlap between the discussion of Kafka in *Literature and Evil* and in *The Space of Literature*, there are some distinctive points in the Blanchot book. The issue of graven images appears in Blanchot's book, referring to the Jewish prohibition of images of God which might be considered to cast doubt on all image-creating activity, including the writing of fiction. The ambiguity Bataille identifies in Kafka's search for the law, while breaking the law, exists in Blanchot's account in a search for pure law while bringing impurity into the world through images. An account which seems to parallel Arnold Schoenberg's presentation of a conflict between image making and image destruction at the heart of Judaism in his opera *Moses and Aaron*. From this point of view, we can see the novel as something always more or less struggling with the tension between representation and the truths that cannot be represented. The novelist may not be concerned with the Hebrew Bible prohibition, but is certainly concerned with a combination of representation, thought and speech which are in tension. Direct speech is an activity not representation, while thought is neither. The novel is driven by desire, generally erotic at the most manifest level, though ambition, power, a recovery of lost innocence and ideological goals may play a role. In any case, dealing with death is also a constant preoccupation as what is sought or feared or as what a character may wish to impose on someone else, along with issues of mourning and loss resulting from death. In Blanchot, attention is directed towards death, whether in itself or through its place in desire.

In *The Book to Come*, Blanchot makes *The Odyssey* the beginning of the novel as Odysseus is the character unworthy of *The Iliad* and therefore unworthy of epic. Blanchot seems to declare the epic dead after its first instantiation. The underlying point is that the novel refers to a reflection on storytelling absent from the epic, which tells a story in an immediate unfolding way. It would be a mistake to see the *Iliad* in this way. The heroes are aware of living on in memory of heroes, that is in song, but Blanchot says something about literary narrative by drawing attention to ways in which *The Odyssey* might be taken as a reflection on *The Iliad*. He refers to the Sirens episode of the *Odyssey* in which Odysseus deals with the danger of monsters who lure sailors to death with their beautiful song, by getting his men to plug their ears while sailing past. They are ordered to tie him to the mast so that he can listen in safety to their tempting song. It seems that they sing the *Iliad*, certainly a story of the Trojan War featuring Odysseus. What Blanchot emphasises is the non-event of the episode. Odysseus hears nothing transformative. Blanchot suggests that this shows how literary narrative builds on moments of apparent non-significance, on this occasion, storytelling itself. Storytelling is the power of nothingness which leads the narrative on apparently drifting between moments of non-significance. Literature is the experience of nothingness. The novel is the most thorough version of this experience in which the reader (or listener as with Odysseus) is detached from the world and from community.

The discussion of long fictional narrative continues in Part One of *The Book to Come*, 'The Song of the Sirens' in the chapter on 'The Experience of Proust', so joining Homer and Proust implicitly as the greatest figures of long narrative fiction, or at least implying that they are at the heart of any discussion of epic and novel. There is a lot of overlap between the discussion of Proust in Blanchot with Bataille's discussion in *Literature and Evil*, and both give attention to *Jean Santeuil* as the prelude to *In Search of Lost Time*, though Blanchot gives more attention to the *roman fleuve* itself. The drift of nothingness that Blanchot associates with Homer's Sirens is at the heart of Proust's writing in which the nothingness is explored as imagination, time and memory. It is significant that Blanchot jumps from Homer to Proust, rather than James Joyce, though the title *Ulysses* refers to Odysseus in Latinate form. On first publication, in a literary magazine, chapters from *Ulysses* were given titles from episodes in *The Odyssey*. This was not done in the book version, but Joyce appears to have encouraged circulation of Homeric titles and parallels in a commentary by Stuart Gilbert (1955), then had doubts about it, while also authorising a Viconain reading of *Finnegans Wake* in its draft form as *Work in Progress* (Beckett et al. 1929). This appropriately sums up the tension between novel as an epic version of myth and poetic subjectivity. Joyce appears in *The Book to Come* but not in a sustained analysis and largely in relation to

Herman Broch, though that becomes another way of connecting the modern novel with its antique epic forerunners in Part Three. It looks as if Blanchot considered Proust's work to be at the centre of what the novel is, so a successor to Homer as the centre of epic, more so than then Joycean play with Homeric antecedents.

In Part Three, 'On An Art Without Future', Blanchot suggests that Homer broke epic (2003, 107), presumably in the relation of the *Odyssey* to the *Iliad* through the Sirens episodes, and this break is repeated through several breaks made with the form of the novel by the early twentieth century innovative masterpieces of Virginia Woolf, James Joyce, Herman Broch, Robert Musil, Thomas Mann, André Gide and Jean-Paul Sartre. It is these works which have turned the novel into an art without a future, though as the epic continued after Homer apparently broke it, this seems like an ambiguous remark.

We know that Blanchot thought the epic carried on after Homer, even if broken in the form it had in *The Iliad*, because he writes on Publius Vergilius Maro through Broch's novel, *The Death of Virgil*. The issue of broken epic is repeated there around the issue of why Virgil wanted to destroy the manuscript of the *Aeneid*, which was unfinished at his death. Blanchot takes this up in relation to his dealings with the Emperor Augustus and the command to write poetry celebrating Rome under Augustus, through an epic connecting the origins of Rome with Aeneas' flight from Troy. He believes that Broch unifies thought and work with a success lacking in *The Sleepwalkers*, though this is a book with a wider audience, in English at least. What Broch pursues is a unity of opposites and a pursuit of reason, which turns into unreason. There is a historical context both for Broch and for the Virgil of the novel, unified around the loss of the West. The loss for Virgil is the end of Rome as it existed before Augustus, in a transcending rebirth, a new star looking to the West. Blanchot does not say so very directly, and it is not at the centre of Broch's writing, but the issue here is surely for Blanchot's contextualisation, at least in part, is that the *Aeneid*, was written in the context of the loss of republican liberty. Blanchot emphasises that Broch was writing in the 1930s and surely means to draw attention to Naziism and Fascism as the twentieth-century death of the West as a parallel to Augustus' messianic view of himself, communicated though Virgil as the messiah of a new order, providing an inspiration for the fascism of Broch's time. The other issue indirectly present, but no less powerful for that, and Blanchot does write on the drawing power of what is not seen, is that the *Aeneid* is in significant degree an emulation of Homeric epics, but for a pious hero guided by a messianic prophetic state project not present to Homeric heroes. At the level of epic form, the *Aeneid* is the imitation which breaks what is imitated through its awareness of the end. This is the mood of twentieth-century literature in Blanchot's analysis, even if the political threat to the West declined because of World War Two. Afterwards, the mood lingers in a culture of novels conscious of broken form.

Though Blanchot's thought is notable for its focus on an individual encounter with death, negativity and the limits of inner experience, it should also be noted that he has a great deal to say about historical context, which means political context to some degree, as well as very broad claims about the overarching development of literary forms. Derrrida's essay 'The Law of Genre' (1980) is an admirable reading of Blanchot with regard to his own short fictional narrative *Madness of the Day*, but is not the kind of reading which invites awareness of the role of political and historical context, along with cultural narrative, that can be found in much of Blanchot's writing. In *The Book to Come*, we also see a lot of biographical context, which is how Blanchot sets up the relation between *The Death of Virgil* and the politics of the 1930s.

The Derridean point that Blanchot challenges distinctions of genre (and gender, it is the same word in French, *genre*) is right for many contexts of reading Blanchot, but should not obscure the degree to which Blanchot at times is a historian and a biographer putting a philosophy of literature into context, rather than an austere anti-representationalist, a writer collapsing distinctions between philosophy and its literary object, or between ways of writing, as he often is. Even the very conventional looking history and biography is directed towards explorations of the limits of mimesis with regard to external reality and the previous examples of the genre. Imitation is loss as the new work transforms and breaks the earlier work, questioning its seemingly unconscious unity, while writing itself is always directed by the experience of writing along with the connected experiences of death, negation, unrepresentability and time.

This point is emphasised in the subsequent chapter 'The Turn of the Screw' in which Blanchot explores the issue of indeterminacy in Henry James' novella of a governess relating the reported and bizarre, even supernatural, experiences of the children in her care:

> The wonderful and terrible movement that the deed of writing exercises on truth, torment, torture, violence that finally lead to death, in which everything seems to be revealed, in which everything, however, falls back into the doubt and void of the shadows. (Blanchot 2003, 133)

Girard

Girard offers a more systematic approach to the novel than is found in Bataille and Blanchot, embedded in his systematic work on anthropological and religious philosophy, in relation to violence, sacrifice and the sacred. The work on the novel, in *Deceit, Desire and the Novel* (1965) is largely focused on the French tradition since *The Princess of Cleves*, but also taking into account Cervantes and Dostoevsky. The discussion in Girard is not just of the novel, but of other forms of writing, particularly the memoirs of Louis de Rouvroy, duc de Saint-Simon, which are discussed by Auerbach in Chapter 16 of *Mimesis* (1968), 'The Interrupted Supper' and feature in Proust's *In Search of Lost Time*. For Girard, Saint-Simon sets up a theme of a struggle to be at the centre of the social world, which connects with Girard's biggest theme, that of mimetic desire, the desire to both be and destroy a rival for the social centre and also a rival in love.

Though the main focus is the French tradition, Cervantes is brought in largely with reference to the story of Lothario in *Don Quixote*. His good friend pushes him into becoming the lover of his wife through his insistence that his friend tests his wife's fidelity to the extreme. Dostoevsky is brought in largely with reference to a short story on a similar theme to that of the Lothario story. Dostoevsky is also featured in *Deceit, Desire and the Novel*, with regard to the danger of humans becoming gods to each other. The French novels discussed by Girard all encounter this temptation, along with the issues amorous jealousy, which leads to the most extreme mimetic desire and violence, but find a way out of it though moments in which mimetic desire has ended, a sacral moment of acceptance of God, maybe indirectly through social scenes which hint at Catholic communion or through moments of the transcendence of ego in which the futility of mimetic desire is realised.

Girard's approach is both productive and reductive, leading him sometimes to emphasising the superiority of little known moments in the writing of the novelist concerned, which favour Girard's thesis. Girard also offers a powerful way of thinking about how a novel, not only in structure, but also in the details of telling and style, in his concerns with social and amorous rivalry, raising issues of the nature of the ego and its experience of a world of competing others, and of conflicting desire.

Compared with Bataille and Blanchot, there is a lot of emphasis on a moral-religious narrative and social realism, but as there is also an emphasis on the transcending and sacrificial moments of the novel, along with the disruption of reason by desire, so there is convergence with the approach in Bataille and Blanchot. Girard does not share their interest in disrupting literary mimesis and his thought is Catholic-Humanist in orientation. Nevertheless, his work on mimesis builds up to more anthropological work on mimetic violence in *Violence and the Sacred* (1977), where a kind of Christian Humanism is combined with a theory of mimetic rivalry leading to violence at the basis of society, constantly seeking a scapegoat until God turns himself into scapegoat as Christ in the Gospels. This does not end the reign of violence in human history though; it may even be the beginning of the drive towards an absolute moment of violence in the Christian apocalypse.

This partly emerges as a preoccupation in Girard's work on Carl von Clausewitz, the author of *On War* (1984) and one of the greats in the philosophy of violence through his work on military thought, now turned into an ancillary of apocalyptic theology. An examination of Girard's thought on Clausewitz, and Clausewitz' own thought, leads us to see the difficulties Girard has in restraining violence within the Christian Humanism he advocates. The Christian Humanism itself focuses on moments of sacred unity between individuals, so disrupting the human world. This disruption can be taken back to Bataille on evil, Blanchot on death and the role of violence in Vico's thought to see how Girard occupies a significant place on the limit between humanist ethical literature embedded in the form of the novel and a literature of uncontrollable violence embedded in the form of the novel. Girard's work on Carl von Clausewitz is presented through conversations with Benoît Chantre, in *Achever Clausewitz*, translated into English as *Battling to the End* (2010). The change in title is unfortunate in concealing the original tribute to the importance of Clausewitz and more generally to the philosophy of war as part of social and political philosophy in Girard, so casting light on his literary philosophy. The most important theme in Girard's discussion of Clausewitz is the struggle for recognition through the use of violence, as it relates to Girard's own work on mimetic violence. A second theme for Girard, connected with the first one, is that of the trinity in *On War*, discussed in a passage that takes up less than a page and forms part 28 of Chap. 1, 'The Consequences for Theory'. The three elements of the trinity are: primordial violence (*der ursprünglichen Gewaltsamkeit*), a blind natural force; hatred (*dem Haß*) the play of chance and probability in which creativity appears; and enmity (*der Feindschaft*), which is subordinate to political reason. They correspond, though not in a completely discrete way (and the categories of the trinity are to be understood as interactive and 'dialectical' rather than as discrete concepts), with: the people (*Volke*), the commander (*Feldherrn*) and the army (*Heer*), and the government (*Regierung*). The primordial violence-people pole relates to passions inherent in the people. The enmity-commander and army pole relate to the play of courage and talent which itself comes from both probability and chance and the character of the commander. The enmity-government pole related to politics. The three parts of the trinity all have their own laws, but also interact and Clausewitz refers to a 'paradoxical trinity'.

The Clausewitzian trinity is one way for Girard to continue his earlier work on the distinct status of Christianity as an escape from mimetic violence, sacrifice and myth. In the earlier work on the novel, desire is seen as structured by competition with an other who is also ourself. This conditions the nature of novelistic love, sometimes leading to overt violence and always structured by a destructive attitude to both the competitor and the object of desire, this also structures an associated quest for authenticity in French literature, which cannot be achieved because of the mimetic nature of desire, except in a more or less disguised moment of sacral escape from ambition and earthly love into altruistic self-abnegation. This gives a Giardian way of understanding the tradition of the French novel and a way of looking at the form of the novel in general.

In *Violence and the Sacred*, the structuring of society is thought of as taking place around recognition of similarity. Here recognition means a comparison in which we wish to both become and destroy our opposite. The combination of identification and destruction produces scapegoats and myths of punitive divinities, from which human societies only escape through the idea of a God who sacrifices himself, so ending the idea of a scapegoat, so introducing a way of limiting mimetic violence that does not resort to the murder of someone assigned the burden of enemy status. Girard's interest in Clausewitz may suggest some instability in this notion that Girard recognises in him, or attributes to him a Pascalian sense that without divine justice there is only force, the force used in war, and also finds an apocalyptic force in Clausewitz, which leads us to the topic of recognition and violence in Clausewitz, war as a duel to determine the dominant will.

In the first book of *On War*, Clausewitz builds up the idea of a war as the imposition of will through violence in a rivalry of two wills, a duel between two nations. Clausewitz is not just assuming an essential will of a nation, abstracted from difference and conflict within that nation. The capacity for a provisionally single will to be created from the elements of a society and a state is necessary for the conduct of war, and therefore for the continuation of the state and the people of that state so long as the social world is a world in which state interests are pursued through violence.

Girard's interest in Clausewitz itself partly stems from the way in which that thought in *On War* can be taken up in relation to the Christian idea of the apocalypse. The ambiguous point at which the limits on Satanic violence collapses preparing the return of Christ. Girard suggests that Clausewitz' own rather dutiful more than passionate Christianity, focused on a providential rather than interventionist deity who works through the details of history rather than miraculous interruptions. This can be seen as part of a theology in which participation in immanent violence is part of bringing the Second Coming, taking us into the violence which Girard defines as mimetic, in the sense that it is defined as driven by identity, but which is anti-mimetic in another sense because representation disappears in literature if the central drive is destructive identification. Clausewitz' thoughts on violence and war can be taken up from a theological point of view, as Girard does, which we could also think of in a deconstructive way. That is around Derrida's readings of Benjamin, Pascal, law and force, justice and divinity, theology and writing and so on, leading us to the primacy of violence in the laws of the novel, as discussed in the previous chapters with regard to Lukács and Benjamin. As with Kierkegaard, Nietzsche and Benjamin, there is a case to be made here for the importance to the philosophy of the novel of philosophical work in neighbouring fields. This is maybe a more extreme case. Clausewitz writes on war, not literary aesthetics. However, war has strongly aesthetic aspects in Clausewitz' account and is understood with reference to the categories of German Idealist philosophy, so is concerned with ideal and real, subjectivity and world, rationality and empirical materialist.

Clausewitz' remarks on 'savage' war and the violence of the people also suggest how his thought might be taken up with regard to partisan war, something that leads into a collapse of the huaön legal state, as expected by Vico in the end of any cycle of history. Clausewitz' own particular orientation is towards the struggle with chance and probability that he associates with the commander, who is between the rationality of the state and the violence of the people. Girard has a strong interest in the idea and history of Europe focused on France and Germany with regard to their mimetic rivalries, which picks up on the central conflict for Clausewitz, which is between Napoleonic France and Germany as the centre of a non-Napoleonic Europe.

These thoughts bring us back to Vico who as we saw in Chap. 2, sees modern wars as the prolongation of the duel. We see here how Clausewitz sees a possible return to savagery in the law-governed world of Vico's own time, which if Vico applied the principles of the

New Science fully he must have seen would end in a collapse into savagery at some point. Clausewitz, who served with the Tsar's army after the surrender of Prussia to Napoleon, is on object of Lev Nikolayevich Tolstoy's attacks in *War and Peace*, so does enter into the history of the novel. He is also mentioned by Proust in *In Search of Lost Time*, with regard to the discussions held by French army officers. These literary appearances suggest that there is more than coincidence in Girard discussing Clausewitz in one part of his career, even decades after his work on the novel. Clausewitzian focus on war as a dynamic complex system in which observation and general principles interact make him an appropriate object of interest for the novelist. Even if the mentions in Tolstoy and Proust are unconnected with any awareness of his thought, which is unlikely because some sense of Clausewitz as the theorist of war and as the examiner of passion in war is present, the mentions are deeply appropriate. War is at the limits of mimetic, in its experience of death, violence and terror. It is whole nations mobilised around collective non-mimetic experience of this kind, which results from the mimetic struggles of status, will and recognition. Ernst Jünger's *Storm of Steel* is one particularly manifest way in which this enters into the novel, though all novels which deal with war, battle and violence are integrating this. Since the possibility of death and the limits of experience condition all literature, along with duels, mimetic struggles and violence, at least of a symbolic kind and frequently of a more material kind, philosophy of war and violence enter into a complete philosophy of the novel. The place of these things in Homer and Vico suggests their fundamental role in any long narrative fiction form and any philosophy of such form. Clausewitz' book is itself a work on unity and integration of material diversity and the attempt at ideal arrangement of force. These are ways of thinking about the novel, particularly when we think about Clausewitz' concern with the commander as genius. War is about the unity and strength of state and nation in Clausewitz, a theme of the novel as a growing literary force, very tied to the idea and institutions of a nation, as discussed by Benedict Anderson in *Imagined Communities* (1991), a major work of nationalism theory. It also draws our attention to the pure violence underlying the legal state, where the possibility of death is more real than institutions that claim to represent the nation.

This underlies the anti-mimetic theories of Bataille, Blanchot and Girard. It also underlies the cultural pessimism and apocalyptic inclinations of Adorno and Benjamin, discussed in the last chapter.

Later French Anti-Mimeticism

The anti-memetic approach is continued by later French thinkers particularly Jacques Lacan, Michel Foucault and Jacques Derrida. Lacan's psychoanalytic approach to the novel can be found at its most influential in his seminars on Joyce, along with the essay 'Kant with Sade' (in Lacan 2006) and his commentary on Edgar Allen Poe, 'Seminar on "The Purloined Letter"' (in Lacan 2006). Neither deal with novels, but Sade's dialogue *Philosophy in the Boudoir* and Poe's story 'The Purloined Letter' connect closely enough to be discussed as context, and are more open to summary than the seminars on Joyce. The discussion of Sade suggests a dark sublime side of Kantian ethics, where duty to the law without reference to pleasure and personal interest is absolute. For Lacan, this is very open to the obsessive eroticism and role of pain in Sade. The Kantian respect for the law is an interest in exhaustive repetition of law, and submission to law at the price of life. Kant opens up, however inadvertently, to obsessive eroticism. The freedom at the basis of his idea of law must be the freedom to dispose of one's body. Law itself suggests a model of desire with no determinate object or hope of final satisfaction, expressed in Sade's fictions and essays of obsessive desire. Obsessive desire which sacrifices egotistical pleasure to a pursuit of something sublime and even sacral in desire, an extremism which reaches beyond the everyday and any kind of ethics devoted to satisfaction of individual needs. These themes are also explored in seminar papers related to James Joyce (in Lacan 2016).

Lacan's 'Seminar on the Purloined Letter' itself inspired a response from Derrida 'The Purveyor of Truth' (in Derrida also published in English with the original French title 'Le facteur de la vérité'). The approach of both Lacan and Derrida takes psychoanalysis away from literature as representation of Freudian dramas to a concern with the construction of narrative through desire. The plot of Poe's short story

'The Purloined Letter' revolves around possession of a letter, though the reader does not know what is in the letter. This is an indication that literary narrative may revolve more around circulation and concealment of meanings, the non-arrival of complete resolution, than around a narrative mimesis. Derrida's response is to suggest that Lacan still refers to a kind of mimesis, the revelation of truth when the letter is revealed in the Poe story. We do not know what is in the letter, so there is not truth revealed in that way, but the moment where the non-existence of the truth of message appears is another kind of revelation of truth.

Derrida also connects with Lacan in writing on Joyce. This comprises five essays (gathered in Mitchell and Slote 2013), along with scattered remarks elsewhere. The emphasis is on the divisibility of meaning, continuing Derrida's approach to Poe. That is *Ulysses* and *Finnegans Wake* are explored as novels in which there is constant resistance to a metaphysics of meaning including any mimetic essence. They are novels which undo the idea of representation, at least as the dominant unified part of the novel. Mimesis is challenged through the ways in which words are contextual in meaning, have a phonetic and a graphic materiality which is always part of the meaning, and have accidental connections which interact with the apparent literal meaning. That is where words appear in conjunction forms of alliance and repulsion emerge in the semantic, phonetic and graphic conjunction. *Finnegans Wake* can be taken as a perfect Derridean text in that it constantly enacts the ways in which words can be divided and joined, repeated and near repeated in different contexts, resemblances in sound and written form diverge and coincide, all interacting with the more structural and thematic issues of the text.

Foucault just wrote one essay on the novel, in a discussion of the novels of Raymond Roussel, *Death and the Labyrinth* (1986), emphasising the novel as broken down into word games and self-undermining writing strategies, playing on the separation of words from thing and using strict systems of verbal variation. He finds both formalisation of literature in Roussel and an engagement with death, both means of dealing with non-representation. If literature is a machine that produces, it is not essentially representational since it is driven by production not representation. Death is what resists representation since the moment of death is what cannot be experienced. This fits with the ways in which Foucault deals in other kinds of work with the limits of experience, e.g. *History of Madness* (2006) and the inherent possibilities of discourse shaping representation, e.g. *The Order of Things* (2002). Sade makes an appearance in *The Order of Things* as part of the last episteme Foucault discusses production. In Adam Smith, there is economic production without limit, in Sade there is production of desire without limit, both going beyond ideas of representability of mimesis of what can exist. This is a step beyond the 'representability' Foucault places at the centre of the previous episteme, according to which what can be represented exists. In the episteme, the way of ordering things, of production, and the possibilities of what can exist exceed representation. This is a way of reducing mimesis to one possibility in our ways of having knowledge and ordering our discourse. Even where mimesis of some kind, representability is put at the centre, the idea that representations mimic what exists is stretched so that any representation we can invent becomes the mimesis of some external entity. *Don Quixote* appears as the literary version of the scientific and philosophical assumptions of representability, with the Don marking a rather absurd belief that his representations must mimic something, compared with Descartes' commitment to the reality of whatever our clear and distinct ideas show us.

These ways in which Foucault's views of knowledge merge with his views of the novel, or examples of the novel, have a culmination of a kind in 'The Order of Discourse' (1981) where he opens his inaugural address at the Collège de France, by quoting the end of Samuel Beckett's *The Unnamable*, 'I can't go on…I'll go on'. This is partly Foucault's tribute to his predecessor Jean Hyppolite, on the grounds that Foucault is not competent to continue Hyppolite's discourse, but must nevertheless do so. It is also a way of setting up the issue that there is no correct discourse. There are various forms of discourse all of which contain silences, gaps and contradictions within their claims to some kind of clarification of reality. A discourse of knowledge is necessarily a struggle against these limitations of mimetic claims, in which the writer experiences some kind of struggle to create or release discourse as something other than pure mimesis.

Proust has already appeared, particularly in this chapter and the last chapter. *In Search of Lost Time* may seem to gather all previous novels, and novel related forms towards it, particularly but not only in the French tradition. Not everyone sees it as the culmination of the form of the novel, and there is no intention here of repeating Bakhtin's tendency to see the novel and its precursors building up to Dostoevsky, but many do see it as a culmination and it has certainly exercised an extreme fascination on writers on the philosophy of the novel. Any status given to *In Search of Lost Time* is in some degree arbitrary and open to debate, but it is clear enough that it is a work of great status and influence, for many, with regard to the form of the novel and literary achievement. The anti-mimetic and limits of mimesis themes of this chapter have been partly built up with reference to Proust and now is the time to examine this great work in the intersection of philosophy and the novel, without turning it into the all pervasive ideal and motivation of the novel and its forerunners.

References

Anderson, Benedict. 1991. *Imagined Communities*. London and New York, NY: Verso Books.

Auerbach, Erich. 1968. *Mimesis: The Representation of Reality in Western Literature*, trans. Willard R. Trask. Princeton, NJ: Princeton University Press.

Bataille, Georges. 2012. *Literature and Evil*, trans. Alasatair Hamilton. London: Penguin Books.

Beckett, Samuel, Marcel Brion, Frank Budgen, et al. 1929. *Our Exagmination Round His Factification for Incamination of Work in Progress*. London: Faber and Faber.

Blanchot, Maurice. 1982. *The Space of Literature*, trans. Anne Smock. Lincoln, NE and London: University of Nebraska Press.

Blanchot, Maurice. 2003. *The Book to Come*, trans. Charlotte Mandell. Stanford, CA: Stanford University Press.

Clausewitz, Carl von. 1984. *On War*, trans. and ed. Michael Howard and Peter Paret. Princeton, NJ and Chichester: Princeton University Press.

Derrida, Jacques. 1979. *Spurs: Nietzsche's Styles*, trans. Barbara Harlow. Chicago, IL: University of Chicago Press.

Derrida, Jacques. 1980. The Law of Genre, trans. Avital Ronell, *Critical Inquiry* VI (1): 55–81.

Derrida, Jacque. 1981. *Dissemination*, trans. Barbara Johnson. London: Athlone Press.

Derrida, Jacques. 1982. *Margins of Philosophy*, trans. Alan Bass. Chicago, IL: University of Chicago Press.

Derrida, Jacques. 1985. *Ear of the Other: Otobiography, Transference, Translation*, trans. Peggy Kamuf. New York, NY: Schocken Books.

Derrida, Jacque. 1987. *The Truth in Painting*, trans. Geoff Bennington and Ian McLeod. Chicago, IL and London: University of Chicago Press.

Derrida, Jacques. 1997. *Politics of Friendship*, trans. George Collins. London and New York, NY: Verso Books.

Derrida, Jacques. 2002. *Acts of Religion*, ed. Gil Anidjar. New York, NY and London: Routledge and Taylor & Francis.

Foucault, Michel. 1981. The Order of Discourse. In *Untying the Text: A Post-Structuralist Reader*, ed. Robert Young. London: Routledge & Kegan Paul.

Foucault, Michel. 1986. *Death and the Labyrinth: The World of Raymond Roussel*, trans. Charles Ruas. London and New York, NY: Continuum.

Foucault, Michel. 2002. *The Order of Things: An Archaeology of the Human Sciences*. London and New York, NY: Routledge/Taylor & Francis.

Foucault, Michel. 2006. *History of Madness*, ed. Jean Khalfa. trans. Jonathan Murphy and Jean Khalfa. Abingdon: Routledge and Francis & Taylor.

Frye, Northrop. 1957. *Anatomy of Criticism: Four Essays*. Princeton, NJ: Princeton University Press.

Gilbert, Stuart. 1955. *James Joyce's Ulysses: A Study by Stuart Gilbert*. New York, NY: Vintage Books and Random House.

Girard, René. 1965. *Deceit, Desire, and the Novel: Self and Other in Literary Structure*, trans. Yvonne Freccero. Baltimore, MD: Johns Hopkins University Press.

Girard, René. 1977. *Violence and the Sacred*, trans. Patrick Gregory. Baltimore, MD: Johns Hopkins University Press.

Girard, René. 2010. *Battling to the End: Conversations with Benoît Chantre*, trans. Mary Baker. East Lansing, MI: East Michigan University Press.

Goldman, Lucien. 2016. *The Hidden God: A Study of Tragic Vision in the Pensées of Pascal and the Tragedies of Racine*, trans. Philip Thody. London and New York, NY: Verso Books.

Kierkegaard, Søren A. 1981. *Concept of Anxiety: A Simple Psychologically Orienting Deliberation on the Dogmatic Issue of Hereditary Sin*. Kierkegaard's Writings, VIII, ed. Raidar Thomte with Albert B. Anderson. Princeton, NJ: Princeton University Press.

Kolakowski, Leszek. 1978. *Main Currents of Marxism, Volume 2: The Golden Age*, trans. P.S. Falla. Oxford and London: Clarendon Press and Oxford University Press.

Lacan, Jacques. 2006. *Écrits*, trans. Bruce Fink with Héloise Fink and Russell Grigg. New York, NY and London: W.W. Norton.

Lacan, Jacques. 2016. *The Sinthome: The Seminar of Jacques Lacan. Book XXIII*, ed. Jacques-Alain Miller. Cambridge and Malden, MA: Polity Press.

Mitchell, Andrew J., and Sam Slote (eds.). 2013. *Derrida and Joyce: Texts and Contexts*. Albany, NY: State University of New York Press.

Sorel, Georges. 2007. *Etudes sur Vico et autres textes*, ed. Ann-Sophie Menasseyre. Paris: Honoré Champion.

Stocker, Barry. 2006. *Derrida on Deconstruction*. London and New York, NY: Routledge and Taylor & Francis.

Stocker, Barry. 2000. Pascal and Derrida: Geometry, Origin and Discourse, *Symposium* IV (1): 117–141.

Watt, Ian. 1972. *The Rise of the Novel: Studies in Defoe, Richardson and Fielding*. London: Penguin Books.

9

The Absolute Novel Proust on Lost Time

Proust and Philosophy

Marcel Proust's lifework *In Search of Lost Time* is one of the major novels of the twentieth century, and in the whole history of the genre, on most accounts. Even this very high standing is exceeded by the philosophical, and philosophically related critical, attention it receives. The main alternatives candidates for philosophically significant novel of the century are *Ulysses* and *Finnegans Wake*, both by James Joyce, which have certainly received philosophical attention, but far less so than Proust's *roman-fleuve* (river novel), which is in a class of its own in this respect.

The last two chapters have already dealt with aspects of philosophical work on Proust, which is built on here, with the addition of some new perspectives, including: Samuel Beckett's essay on Proust, with distinctly philosophical elements; Proust as a source of philosophical investigation of consciousness in Maurice Merleau-Ponty and the discussion of discourse in Genette. There is no attempt here to cover all these points of views, or even create some allegedly representative overview. This chapter will simply develop of few of the lines of inquiry into Proust, which

© The Author(s) 2018
B. Stocker, *Philosophy of the Novel*,
https://doi.org/10.1007/978-3-319-65891-9_9

draw out what appears to be an inexhaustible interest from many kinds of commentator and reader, fitting Proust into the history of thought about the form of the novel.

One aspect of the significance of Proust in that knowledge of Proust's major fiction is in general a distinct advantage in understanding much French philosophy after Bergson. *In Search of Lost Time* is in particular full of a mixture of essayistic discussion and narrative of ideas about personal identity, consciousness, social distinction, aesthetics, love, memory and time of philosophical interest which continue and feed into philosophical discussion. Not philosophy in its most explicit and detailed argumentative forms, but the ideas which appear in philosophy, often written by philosophers who have read Proust.

Even Proust's family connections give rise to speculations on the interpretation of *In Search of Lost Time*. He was a cousin by marriage of the philosopher Henri Bergson (an influence himself on literary aesthetics, as has been mentioned with regard to Lukács in Chap. 6 and Adorno in Chap. 7) and while Bergson may not in reality have been a major influence on Proust there are some similar terms and related ideas, about time which have invited investigation. Beistegui suggests in *Proust as Philosopher* (2013) that the antecedents of Bergson's views on time and memory going back to Hyppolite Taine (who is mentioned briefly in Chap. 6 above with regard to Lukács), also a major figure in historical, social and political thought, are more important, but that still leaves Bergson's philosophical texts as a branch from the same trunk as *In Search of Lost Time*.

Philosophy, including that of Bergson, is a topic of discussion in Proust's novel; and as the narrator, Proust himself, or his invented self as implied narrator, makes significant comments on philosophy. The novel does not approach philosophy in the manner of a philosophical treatise, but not all philosophy is written as a philosophical treatise and large parts of *In Search of Lost Time* have philosophical interest. The discursive all encompassing nature of Proust's main novel, along with its philosophical elements suggest comparison with the *Essays* of Michel de Montaigne. The *Essays* loom over French literature and philosophy since, though they are not much read by 'professional' philosophers, or certainly not discussed if read, despite some strong impact on the development of philosophy. The category and name of 'essay' come from Montaigne as does a general approach to philosophy oriented towards the self and its self-exploration. The essay as a philosophical form carries on through Francis Bacon; self-exploration in the mind is a major theme in René Descartes. The self-consciousness of Proust's narrator and some of his characters carries on the Montaigne-Descartes line; the discursive nature of much of *In Search of Lost Time* carries on the Montaigne-Bacon line.

The presence of Descartes in the novel is even noted in the twentieth century as in this passage in Marcel Proust's *In Search of Lost Time* from Part VI *The Captive*

> and there was not even any need for analysis, for one understands at once this language of passion, even the most uneducated understands these remarks which can be explained only by vanity, rancour, jealousy, unexpressed as it happens, but detectable at once by the interlocutor through an intuitive faculty, which like the "good sense" of which Descartes speaks, is "the most evenly distributed thing in the world". (Proust 2000, 394)

Proust slightly misquotes from the opening to *The Discourse on Method*, where Descartes refers to the best distributed thing rather than the most distributed thing, though 'most distributed' anyway sometimes appears in English translations and there is not much of an issue here in terms of the Anglophone understanding of Descartes. The point is worth making though to remind ourselves that Proust while perhaps the most philosophically engaged and engaging of all novelists (as will be discussed in this chapter) was not a scholar of philosophy and quotes from memory, without even giving the title of the relevant text by Descartes. In addition, he perhaps thinking of *The Passions of the Soul*, as well as *The Discourse*, which is more engaged with the passions as they are explored by Proust, rather than the focus of the *Discourse* and the other 'standard' philosophical texts by Descartes (*Meditations* and *Principles of Philosophy*) on reason as sovereign.

These philosophical features are part of the reason for identify *In Search of Lost Time* as an absolute novel coming as close as any novel to the Romantic ambitions discussed in Chap. 3 of a philosophical poetry concerned with absolute communication. They are the most important reasons in the context of discussing philosophy in relation to the genre of the novel. Crossing over between philosophical and literary writing, Proust sets off a dynamic interaction between them. He leans in the literary direction, but it would be hard to claim a meaningful encounter with this novel without some thought on Proust's comments on time, memory, consciousness, the ethical aspects of human relationships and art in philosophically charged ways.

Proust and French Society

We should not just think of his river novel in aestheticised terms either. He does provide a picture of French society from the 1880s to the 1920s, to the world of the Third Republic after its stabilization following a traumatic birth from defeat in the Franco-Prussian War of 1870s and before the troubled 1920s and 1930s. This is the peak of the bourgeois republic in France, after the fall of the Second Empire and the adaption of France to republican institutions for longer than the First Republic of 1792 (effectively finished by Napoleon Bonaparte's seizure of absolute power in 1799) and the Second Republic of February 1848, formally finished by Bonaparte's nephew Louis Napoleon Bonaparte in 1852 when the Second Empire was instituted and effectively killed off when Louis Napoleon became Prince President in November 1848. The Bonapartist legacy leaves a mark in Proust's novel in the aristocracy who have titles awarded by Napoleon Bonaparte who are in tension with those aristocrats whose titles predate the 1789 French Revolution.

These social hierarchies and tensions in the French aristocracy are an aspect of *In Search of Lost Time* as the narrator moves through aristocratic circles. The snobbish social climbing has a romantic origin presented early in *Swann's Way* (the first part of Proust's novel) when the narrator remembers childhood magic lantern shows in which he sees an ancestor of the Duchesse de Guermantes, who is at the centre of the social world which the narrator rises into from his upper middle-class background, some way down socially from aristocrats with titles from the Middle Ages. This itself turns into a story of disillusion and awareness of the increasing irrelevance of the old families compared with the more bourgeois kind of upper class dominating Third Republic France. An apparently minute and absurd interest in old families has both an origin in childhood romanticism and is a way into an extraordinary saga of social observation over many hundreds of pages, which has a political aspect.

The Dreyfus case, the biggest political event of late nineteenth-century France plays a major part in the novel and interacts with the narrator's attitudes towards French society. The Dreyfus case refers to a Jewish army officer, Robert Dreyfus, falsely charged and convicted of treasonous passing of military secrets to Germany. The contrived conviction, which obscured the treason of an aristocrat, reflecting anti-semitic attitudes in the French army and large parts of broader French society, led to a ten years in a penal colony for Dreyfus and a campaign to acquit or at least pardon Dreyfus, which was a major source of political polarisation at the time. The narrator's friend, a friend of his whole family, is the upper-class Jew, Charles Swann, who has the most elevated social connections, but is still affected by antisemitism. The Guermantes family is itself split over the case. Swann serves in other ways as a disruptive presence in the categories of French society of the time.

The idea that a man of Swann's non-aristocratic if wealthy status could have social relations with the Guermantes family is too much for the Narrator's family. They live in a world, portrayed as charming even fairy tale like, which is distinctly upper middle class and highly privileged within the locality, but very distinct from the aristocracy. The family is portrayed as morally conservative almost to the point of innocence in cutting off relations with any family member known to have irregular amorous relations. This is certainly part of the celebrated fairy-tale atmosphere of the early parts of *In Search of Lost Time* a family life apparently insulated from actions not in accord with a simple ideal of marital and family life. Swann is their charming friend so cannot be imagined to connect with the class above. In fact, Swann is even referred to as a friend of King Edward VII of Britain, who is perhaps less socially grand in some ways than the Guermantes family. They are able to look down on the Bourbon family (which was deposed for the second and last time as France's royal family in 1830, though carrying on in the cadet Orléanist line of Louis Philippe until 1848) as less pure in aristocratic blood. Swann is not only more distinguished in his social connections than the Narrator's family can imagine, but also more dis-reputable in his infatuation with a woman who lives from rich admirers, Odette. Another social boundary is disrupted when Swann marries her.

The consciousness of the Narrator is one which experiences transfor-mation and uncertainty about identity over time and at any one time. The opening passage of *Swann's Way*, and therefore of the whole river novel, deals with the changes in sense of identity during insomnia and waking up from sleep. These two experiences merge when the Narrator's insomnia takes the form of waking up after going to sleep in the evening hours before his time to rise. The confused insomniac thoughts he has after waking in this way refer to Charles V and Francis I, two great monarchs of Renaissance Europe, in the early sixteenth century. Charles V was the German Emperor (Holy Roman Emperor) who was also King of Spain, so dominating the Europe of his time. Francis I was the French king of the time who was not as powerful as Charles V, but was a great Renaissance prince, providing a model of grandeur, kingly manners and patronage of culture. Proust does not concern himself with the history of the period in *The Search for Lost Time*, but it would be hard to grasp the full scope of the passage, or the novel as a whole, without some idea of who these people were, what they did and why they matter. The rivalry of the King and the Emperor is one moment in the frequent rivalry of France and Germany going back to the ninth century break up, Charlemagne's Frankish empire covering France, Germany and neighbouring territories. This is significant in relation to Auerbach's regret for the loss of a unified medieval Europe, as discussed in Chap. 7 above, and the associated sense that the novel belongs to a world of geographical, moral, cultural and social fragmentation.

The more recent moments of the split between France and Germany weigh on Proust's novel in the role of the Dreyfus case, which is important because of intense French-German rivalry heightened in France by the loss of Alsace-Lorraine in the Franco-Prussian war of 1870, the siege of Paris during that war, and the subsequent financial repara-tions imposed on France. The Narrator has a close connection with the French officer core through his friend Robert Saint-Loup and is aware of their interest in military theory, including that of the Prussian-German officer of the Napoleonic Wars, Carl von Clausewitz (who is discussed in relation to philosophy of the novel in the last chapter), who was the dominant influence on military thinking in the French army after 1870. This ambiguity is about the relations between France and Germany, just as much full of imitation and mutual influence as conflict. Maybe this an example of how imitation and conflict may reinforce each other, as René Girard suggests. This is a thought he developed in his early work on the novel and then towards the end of his life in work on Clausewitz' *On War*, where Girard plays on the theme of French-German rivalry (2010). The Narrator's world is transformed by World War I, by this greatest so far expression of violent rivalry between France and Germany. It is the great punctuating historical moment which forms the background to his revelations in *Time Regained* about how time transforms our visions of people and the world.

The mention of Francis I and Charles V sets up an unworldly dreamlike approach to history, as historical fragments go round in his consciousness in which dreams and semi-wakefulness merge. This becomes fairy tale and romance when his thoughts turn to Geneviève of Brabant and Golo, a fourteenth-century tale of false accusation of adultery against a virtuous wife in the French nobility. The story comes from a childhood magic lantern show, for the Narrator, and brings us into the world of romance parodied in *Don Quixote*. Proust does not make the link, but Cervantes's novel is mentioned a number of times across the river novel. Beyond unanswerable questions about Proust's intentions, the conjunction of these elements in *The Search for Lost Time* is powerful and suggestive. The power is increased by the liaison in the Narrator's consciousness between Geneviève and the Duchesse de Guermantes, the real life descendent of medieval French aristocracy, who is the centre of the Narrator's social ambitions for a long time, and his unattainable love object for a briefer period. History, legends, art, real people all intersect in his memories and inner consciousness. The Narrator's consciousness is not directed by political and historical interests, which are never more than one element of life for him, but they suffuse the novel just as much as the themes most readily associated with Proust: love for the mother, friendship, snobbery and social climbing, unrequited romantic love, jealousy, aestheticism, the power of memory and anticipation.

There is more to Proust's political and historical interests than the forebodings of social collapse Benjamin and Adorno attribute to him, discussed in Chap. 7 above. As Sprinker suggests in his Marxist reading, *History and Ideology in Proust* (1994), it is more a novel of the decline of the aristocracy in a liberal bourgeois republic. The Benjamin and Adorno reading of imminent apocalypse of capitalism (though in Adorno maybe more an endless immanent apocalypse) in Proust tends to conflate the declining aristocracy with the end of capitalism. Since the aristocracy has not completely vanished in France, maybe there is still time for a simultaneous bourgeois and aristocratic end of days, but this is perhaps not quite what Benjamin and Adorno mean when they refer to the catastrophic nature of Proust's world. Their analyses anyway are not so far from a bourgeois liberal Weberianism which is disturbed by the loss of meaning and tradition in modernity. A spirit which informed the Lukács of *The Theory of the Novel* and is therefore present in Benjamin and Adorno from there as well as more direct forms of acquaintance with Weber's thought. Sprinker is more precise in his reading of the economic, social and political history of the Third Republic and the place of Proust's literature in it, while still gesturing towards a looming Communist Party threat to the French bourgeoisie, a political threat that has yet to eliminate the French bourgeoise and has almost vanished itself, though perhaps living on in a constellation of Marxist and let-socialist forces in French politics.

The sense in the Narrator's consciousness of a disaggregated but unified inner consciousness is matched by a consciousness of a disaggregated but unified history of France as a cultural and political entity. His attitude towards France and its history is interwoven with his attitude towards his identity and its history in the movements of his consciousness. The mass destruction of World War I marks a point at which the aristocratic and royalist history of France, even its Bonapartist history seems very remote. The Narrator's friend Robert de Saint-Loup upholds aristocratic tradition by participating as an officer, but also marries the daughter of the Jewish bourgeois Swann and the 'demi-mondaine' Odette. Marrying into money has precedents for the old ruling classes, but Saint-Loup is a Guermantes and they have prided themselves on the 'purity' of their genealogy and regarded themselves as above the

Bourbon dynasty. It is in this period that the Narrator becomes sceptical of the attractions of the Guermantes, coinciding with his reassessment of his past, particularly his romantic desires. These now seem like the expression of his passions so that the objects (Gilberte Swann, the Duchesse de Guermantes and Albertine) are not important. This is part of the process in which time seems more a process of fixing individuals than dissolving them, in which the Narrator can equally be in connection with his self at an earlier stage.

Proust and Literary History

He refers to the two works of literature which he had most wanted to imitate and with which he had been obsessed with since childhood: *The Thousand and One Nights* and the *Memoirs* of Louis de Rouroy, duc de Saint-Simon. Letting go of them is necessary to emulate them in his own writing, just as letting go of particular love objects and social ambitions has enabled a new phase of his self-understanding and understanding of literature. What he is struggling to emulate by turning away from is significant for his posture towards literature and towards French culture. *The Thousand and One Nights* is a foreign text which is still part of French literature, and not just because of the power of the translation. The French translation of the early eighteenth century, by Antoine Galland, which was the first western translation, included material not in the Arabic manuscript and of debatable origin. It has an enormous impact on translations into other languages, and the way the text was understood in the Arabic world. The stories gathered there go beyond references to the Arab world, to Persia and India, and elsewhere. These places are where many stories originated though this is smoothed over by adopting a Near Eastern Arabic perspective in the translated text. Proust does not deal in explicit scholarship and interpretation of the *Thousand and One Nights*, but this is the most obvious information about the work and we can take it to be present in Proust's awareness. The essential point is that from the centre of classical Islamic civilisation in the Near East, stories spill out over a huge variety of territories in a profusion of eroticism, religion, war, trade, thieves, caliphs, back streets, palaces, animals, ascetic wisemen, princes, djinn, soldiers, Muslims, Christians, Jews and so on. This profusion has a perfect formal equivalent in the device of stories within stories. The tales are attributed to the Persian royal wife Scheherazade who protects herself from execution on the orders of her morbidly misogynistic husband by telling a story a night. So that sets up stories within the story of Scheherazade and these stories frequently generate stories within stories spread over many nights, creating the sense of a labyrinth of stories. Scheherazade delays death with stories of desire and death, which enable her in the end to avoid death and become the permanent object of desire of the king.

Saint-Simon also entered French literature in the eighteenth century, though from a very different place. He has never found the English language audience equivalent to that in France, so represents something particularly French, the element of any literature, however, international in its reach as French literature has been, which never finds an appeal in audiences for translation like that to be found in the country of origin. It is difficult to think of an English language equivalent though. Adam Smith noted there was more court-based literature in France than in Britain (*Lectures on Rhetoric and Belle Lettres* Lecture 20/Smith 1983, 112), because in his opinion, the British system gave less importance to royalty and the lives of courtiers. Smith refers to the plays and novels of Pierre de Marivaux and the novels of Claude Prosper Jolyot de Crébillon. These novels are now little read in the English speaking world. These are novelists rather than memoirists, but the point about courtly focus on inner character is apposite, particularly in comparison with the English historians Smith mentions in this lecture Clarendon (Edward Hyde, Earl of Clarendon) and Burnet (Bishop Gilbert Burnet), though both of whom are less read now. Proust takes aspects of French literature Smith refers to absolute monarchy, which is also his view of the histories of Tacitus in their relation to the power of Roman Emperors, into an age in which France could claim to be more republican, since it had ended all monarchical and imperial forms and more democratic, since there was universal male suffrage from the beginning of the Third Republic, something not attained in Britain until 1918. If Smith's judgements were appropriate to his time and antiquity, they appear to have lost their force by the early part of the last century. The

aristocratic and general social obsessions of the Narrator, always quali-
fied though by other inclinations, have a distant apex in Edward VII of
Britain, who has graced Swann with his friendship.

What can be seen here is the difficulty in creating a unitary study
of the novel, including its philosophy, since national literature are not
transparent to each other. Major texts in one literary tradition are hardly
known or translated into another tradition. Translations from another
tradition themselves make the transmission between traditions uncertain, because one tradition which has been translated into another tradition is looking at the relevant texts in the other tradition through the
mediation of translation into its own tradition, of texts which rely on
translations from the other tradition. Quite apart from the linguistic
impossibility of pure translation, or perfect transparency between languages, the linked questions of national context and how the national
literary tradition is seen by those for whom it is the tradition of the language they have spoken since earliest childhood always intrudes. The
importance of the Galland translation of the *Arabian Nights* within
French literature itself shows the difference to a literary tradition made
by translation in general and some translations in particular. The most
important literary translations into English include the *St James Bible*
of the early seventeenth century, which is the most widely read; but
also the translations of Homer which have had a major bearing on
English literature and are part of the history of English literature, particularly those of George Chapman in the early seventeenth century and
Alexander Pope in the early eighteenth century. Some similar remarks
apply to the C.K. Scott Moncrieff translation of *In Search of Lost Time*,
with the less literally translated title, *Remembrance of Things Past*, which
can is still read, has been revised and completely new translations exist.
Another old translation which has had a lasting force in English literature is Charles Jervas' 1742 translation of *Don Quixote*, itself in print
with minor facsimile republication imprints, but maybe living on for
a wider audience in the Tobias Smollett translation of 1755, available
through various editions and held to be dependent on the Jervas (Jarvis)
translation. Smollett (a Scotsman) is well known to those with any
interest in the history of English literature as a 'minor classic' author of
comic novels, which had an influence on later 'major' novels. So we see

again the complex ways classics in translation transmit between traditions in ways which hold traditions open to each other, but never make them completely transparent, and may even intensify the opacity.

Proust brings in the history of French literature in various ways, something René Girard brings out when he puts Proust at the end of a broad literary French tradition in *Deceit, Desire and the Novel* (discussed in the last chapter). Beyond this Proust sometimes connects with the historical aspects of the novel particularly with regard to the history of aristocratic families, and the ways famous novelists may have been part of Paris society and connected then in some way with characters from *In Search of Lost Time.* In this way, Proust's novel of inner consciousness and intimate relationships is also a historical novel and a work of sociopolitical investigation. It is a monument of the France of the Third Republic, as much as it is a work of self-consciousness and personal memory. The Dreyfus case and the differences between parts of the upper class interact with childhood, love, jealousy and attitudes towards art.

Authors from the history of French literature are just personally important through they ways their writings might be models for characters in *In Search of Lost Time*, interacting with the way that Proust writes, so that the narrator's understanding of the relationship between his grandmother and mother is shaped by the letters of Marie de Rabutin-Chantal, Marquise de Sévigné, usually known as Madame de Sévigné, to her daughter. Sévigné's letters themselves are part of the development of prose in French so are part of the general history of the novel. Proust's novel then brings up the issue of status of the novel incorporating other forms which is discussed by Schlegel (Chap. 3 above), Nietzsche (Chap. 5 above) and Bakthin (Chap. 6 above) and, with precedents in Aristotle's account of epic (Chap. 2 above).

Proust's river novel has a particular tendency to break down the distinction between literature and philosophy, just as in a connected way it tends to break down the distinction between novel and forms such as the essay and the aphorism, which are clearly important in the history of French novel, in its connections with the other kinds of prose written by Michel de Montaigne, Blaise Pascal, Jean de La Bruyère, François de La Rochefoucauld, François Fénelon and others.

The issue of what is at the limits of the genre of the novel is important for *In Search of Lost Time*, beyond literature as it explores other arts. There is broader issue of what is at the limits of literature as a whole, including visual art in the form of paintings and the magic lantern of the narrator's childhood, or as music as in the motif from Vinteuil's sonata that fascinates Swann. There is a synaesthetic aspect to this, which foreshadows the importance of synaesthesia in Merleau-Ponty's, *Phenomenology of Perception* (2011). In Proust, the novel has reached the status Aristotle gave to tragedy and Richard Wagner gave to opera, beyond their core aesthetic aspects of poetic writing and musical composition. For Aristotle, tragedy incorporates staging and musics; for Wagner, opera is a *Gesamtkunstwerk* incorporating poetry and staging as well as musical composition. Proust persistently explores the points at which novelistic writing is shaped by and drawn to the structure of other arts such as the flickering pictures of the magic lantern or role of the motif in a violin sonata.

Proust, France and Europe

While Proust is very largely concerned with the French tradition in the novel, and related prose writing, and philosophical engagement has most significantly come from French thinkers, he does draw on other national literature and even make suggestions about the vital aesthetic aspects of foreign novels, famously with regard to Thomas Hardy and Fyodor Mikhailovich Dostoevsky. His approach brings perspectives that can be used in the discussion of other national literatures, particularly as he can be taken as one of the major figures of European literature drawing it together around a classic recognised across the continent, and across the world, in the manner of Cervantes or even Virgil and Homer. Looking at the impact Proust has had on philosophy and literary aesthetics as well as the development of the novel, this is a very proportional distinction. There is a sense in Girard's analysis of Proust of an apocalyptic culmination of a French literary tradition in which characters struggle for closeness to an authentic moral centre distinct from the strong pull of the centre of the class and state orientated status systems. In Alexandre Dumas, the centre is the King's Musketeers of *The Three Musketeers* who are paradoxically an authentic moral alternative to the soldiers of Cardinal Richelieu, because the Cardinal is the real centre of the state system with the royal family as the romantic centre of more authentic sentiment. In Proust, the authentic centre is his grandmother, as opposed to the grand aristocratic families of France and their Paris salons which absorb the narrator's attention for a large part of *In Search of Lost Time*. The apocalyptic analysis of mimesis and the escape from mimesis is something discussed with regard to Girard in the last chapter as is the strange relationship between his Catholic Humanism and the expectation of absolute violence at the end of history. What is also remarkable is the parallel with the apocalyptic interpretation Benjamin has of *In Search of Lost Time*. A sense of apocalypse is contained in the novel itself, or so we might think given the tendency of a German Marxist and a French Catholic to find an apocalypse in there.

As the culmination of the European novelistic tradition, Proust is both very French and very European. *In Search of Lost Time* brings about a sense of immersion in various ways including an immersion in France whether Paris or the provinces, social manners or high politics. There is not much sense of nationalism in Proust, but his novel is a culmination, amongst other things, of the novel as a portrait of a nation, as a confirmation that there is a nation with a people who have a language from which great literature can be created. The nineteenth-century novel, particularly if we think of the 'historical novel' emphasised by Georg Lukács, or the ways Benedict Anderson brings Erich Auerbach into *Imagined Communities* (1991) is very tied up with the sense of nation so that even when not written to promote nationalism, it forms a sense of collective memory, shared literary references, distinctions between capital city and provinces, 'common sense' perceptions of different regions and character types in the nation. In Proust's novel, there is a sense of split between the old aristocracy which gives some sense of continuity between modern France and the romanticised medieval France of the narrator's childhood, a relation materialised as the Duchesse de Guermantes, on one side and the political world of the Third Republic on the other side. While some sense of historical national community has not died in France, or anywhere else since and nationalist politics is still with us, the sense of a self-contained nation over time with a unified elite, that has a clearly structured set of relations with the less aristocratic classes has disappeared. It continues in a popularised nostalgia for grand country residences and costume dramas, not as a way in which anyone can structure their experience of a social world. Whatever one might think of Marxist revolutionary apocalypse or the Christian religious version, there is something apocalyptic in Proust in bringing the French nation to an end, in some understandings of nation, in the exhaustive appreciation of what might seem like a familiar national world, itself of course a construct of nineteenth-century economic transformation and social change.

The idea of France has been very tied up with the idea of Europe, even in negative ways as when J.G. Fichte defined an opposition between Germanic and Latin Europe in his *Addresses to the German Nation*. The sense of absorption into the consciousness of what it is to be French in Proust's novel coincides with various references to European culture including Venice and John Ruskin's view of Venice, Delft and Vermeer's view of Vermeer, and the cult of Wagner which appears in the Salon of Mme Verdurin. The sense of a structured French nation and culture belongs in a sense of a structured European space with France at is centre and apex. *In Search of Lost Time* is maybe the nearest thing to a perfect culmination of the sense of the reflective and the universal in the novel, as discussed by Søren Kierkegaard and before him, the Idealists and the Romantics, who themselves had a sense of European identity and diversity in its background. In this context, we should think of Novalis' 'Christendom or Europe' (in Novalis 1997), which of course comes down on the side of 'Christendom', but is nevertheless an essay in the cross-national reality of Europe as 'cultural' as well as 'religious'. Thinking about the novel has been caught up with the issue of Europe, including precursors of Europe like the Greek polities and Rome. Post-colonial thinking and comparative literary studies on a global level challenge this, but do not eliminate this. As we have seen in Chap. 7, a major figure in the post-colonial constellation like Edward Said is a product of the Europeanist version of the history of literature, via Erich Auerbach.

Proust himself does not reflect on the history of France or Europe as primary concerns, but we can get the best sense of what the power of the novel is if we think about these issues which are part of the Proustian concern with memory. The famous passages on memory in *Swann's Way* refer to Celtic ideas of souls caught in natural objects and memories of the Combray of the narrator's childhood. The idea of memory is then expressed through the seemingly primordial France of the Celtic Gauls and the idea of idyllic provincial France. This is an instance of how Proust's integration of a diversity of material in the theme of the search for memory and lost time is what it is that allows the exploration of the aesthetic to lead to a form of integration of the self. The search for an integration of the self is also a search for the match between aesthetic expectation and reality, significant experience, real essences of things, revelatory memory, the real nature of love and the fusion of these quests in writing. The sense of memory of a nation, the parts of a nation and the broader context of the nation, largely meaning Europe in this context is an extension of this process and shapes it. Proust is the most intimate, subjective and aestheticised of novelists. He is also the most national, political and European, displaying how these elements coexist.

Philosophers on Proust

Gilles Deleuze wrote an early book *Proust and Signs* (2000) which examines *In Search of Lost Time* as a text of signs, so that it is something like an encyclopaedia of signs arising from the narrator's search for the essence of things. The search for essence can only be for the signs which convey most significance, since there is no concern with reality behind the signs. For Deleuze, this provides the opportunity for an investigation of the different kinds of signs, the nature of literature and the nature of style. Proustian signs multiply in the different spheres of experience. The search for truth or love in Proust's novel becomes a quest for signs, since there is no reality behind the signs of things. Material things are occasions for spiritual signs; we cannot get any closer to the reality of things.

The search for signs is the question of interpretation, since the sign is what is interpreted, but more broadly Deleuze refers to a world of constant interpretation rather than a world of very fixed signs in a single order of signs. There are different orders of truth revealed in Proust's novel and therefore interpretation is necessary to deal with the different kinds of truth that could be at stake. The interpreter in Proust, on this account, is not a unified self-conscious hero, but a narrator as function who lacks the capacity for self-consciousness. In Deleuze's language, the narrator is a body without organs, aware of what impinges on the body, but not aware of its own awareness. In Deleuze's view, Proust takes the role of the hero to a point where it vanishes into awareness of a complex world with no truth at its centre.

Deleuze puts signs at the centre of questions of aesthetics and literary interpretation, but for Miguel Beistegui (2013) metaphor is at the centre though in a philosophical perspective influenced by Deleuze. He develops his view of metaphor in Proust as part of work in aesthetics which aims to shift the centre of aesthetics from mimesis to metaphor. From this point of view, *In Search of Lost Time* is at the centre of a break with the role of mimesis in aesthetics since Plato, so is something of an apocalyptic text in aesthetic terms. It is the place where mimesis has to succumb to metaphor, where the idea of art as imitation is shown to be inadequate.

The idea of Proust standing at some aesthetic turning point, apocalyptic in some sense, can be taken back to Theodor Adorno for whom Proust stands at the end of novelistic tradition and a whole aesthetics of beauty. Proust's commentator, Samuel Beckett, stands at Adorno's alternative for the future, who is fully engaged with the emptiness of the world of the culture industry and of identity logic, a catastrophe that has been growing since Homer.

> And yet it is tempting to look for sense, not in life at large, but in the fulfilled moments—in the moments of present existence that make up for its refusal to tolerate anything outside it.
>
> Incomparable power flows from Proust the metaphysicist because he surrendered to this temptation with the unbridled urge to happiness of

no other man, with no wish to hold back his ego. Yet in the course of his novel the incorruptible Proust confirmed that even this fullness, the instant saved by remembrance, is not it. For all his proximity to the realm of experience of Bergson, who built a theory on the conception of life as meaningful in its concretion, Proust was an heir to the French novel of disillusionment and as such a critic of Bergsonianism. The talk of the fullness of life—a *lucus a non lucendo* even where it radiates— is rendered idle by its immeasurable discrepancy with death. Since death is irrevocable, it is ideological to assert that a meaning might rise in the light of fragmentary, albeit genuine, experience. This is why one of the central points of his work, the death of Bergotte, finds Proust helping, gropingly, to express hope for a resurrection— against all the philosophy of life, yet without seeking cover from the positive religions.

Negative Dialectics (Adorno 1973, 378)

In the darkness of the bourgeois world, as Adorno conceives it, the assertion of the possibility of happiness is itself ideological that is a justification of the bourgeois capitalist world view. Proust's own subordination to the goal of happiness might be seen as this kind of ideological act, but the unhappiness of the narrator of *In Search of Lost Time* at the death of his friend, the writer Bergotte, apparently rescues him from this classification as does the absence of religion from his hope for resurrection. Adorno rather sweepingly assumes an affinity with Henri Bergson, though balanced with critique. Both the affinity and the critique in Adorno's interpretation assume a centrality of Bergson's philosophy for Proust, which is not widely accepted amongst commentators. Anyway, Adorno agues at a level of generalisation where the issue is not the specifics of Proust's attitude towards Bergson but what Bergson stands for in the world of the time and in the world of *In Search of Lost Time*. Proust is presented as neither favouring philosophies of life (for which Bergson is the marker) nor religion. In this case, he represents a search for an aesthetics in which there is beauty in hopelessness. Beauty though may find it difficult to survive hopelessness. Implicitly for Adorno, beauty is linked to hope though as *Aesthetic Theory* (2002) suggests through a '*tour de force*' that is through the integration of diverse material in the artwork which seems impossible to integrate. Adorno considers that the 'ugly' should be part of the integration, which otherwise lacks completeness. In this case, Proust's achievement is limited if admirable within constraints, but less than that of Samuel Beckett in literature and Arnold Schönberg in musical composition.

Adorno's attention for Beckett is very largely directed towards the drama rather than the novels, Beckett's play *Endgame* is the subject of Adorno's principle essay on Beckett 'Understanding *Endgame*' (in Adorno 1991). Proust reaches a peak, and Adorno is not the only philosopher or critic, to think that Proust represents a peak of some kind, of something which has died or is dying: the possibility of hope in a bourgeois world. Proust is then a utopian of some kind, though also an indication of the thin possibilities for utopia in a bourgeois civilisation, that accumulates barbarism according to Adorno. Since Beckett then is a kind of heir of Proust, Beckett's essay on Proust (1965) might be germane here. It offers an interpretation in terms of the pessimism of Arthur Schopenhauer, and his claim that a world of pure will underlies the world of illusory representations, which has some value as a perspective on Proust, but is maybe more a manifesto for Beckett's own literary work. Adorno does not mention it, and while this may be mere accident, it seems appropriate that Adorno effectively makes Beckett the negative prophet of utopia, while Proust is more the poet of the dying bourgeois world. In Adorno's view, Beckett has made the step from faded beauty of hope in a bourgeois civilisation to a negative utopia in which the revelation of horror, in the sense of hopelessness more than manifest horror, creates the possibility of something opposite. The greater the horror represented, the greater the utopia which is its utopia. This still leaves Proust as the last hope of bourgeois civilisation, so marking *In Search of Lost Time* as maybe the aesthetic hope of the liberal bourgeoisie which survives the Beckettian world of complete horror. Proust stands for one pole of bourgeois world, a belief in individual self-perfection through memory and writing and the abundance of the world in his novel. Perhaps Adorno and Benjamin make Proust the new Dante or the new Balzac as in the creation of a comedy which is divine or human, so maybe implicitly elevating him in a way that does not completely fit with their other interests. Given the transcendental hopes contained within the Proustian search with regard to aesthetic creation and memory, it is both idealised Balzac and secularised Dante. As Auerbach points out Dante's epic is marked by the failure of the world, or the European Catholic part of it, to create the imperial-papal utopia, just as Balzac's work is situated in the failures of the utopian revolutionary ideas of 1789 and the conservative utopia of restored monarchy. In this framework, Proust keeps alive a kind of individualised and aestheticised connection with locality, nation and Europe. In 'Short Commentaries on Proust' (in Adorno 1991), Adorno's view is that he shows the end of liberal society. A world which claims to be harmonious but is disharmonious in deterministic ways. Proust's mythology creates physical-natural metaphor for human relations showing their alienated nature at the end of liberalism. He shows love despite himself confirming a catastrophic situation. Adorno seems to find Proust as displaying a world more alienated than it is, or some of his comments go in that direction. So in some ways, *In Search of Lost Time* shows the liberal bourgeois world to be worse than Proust directly acknowledges as if the catastrophe is bursting through its literary constraints. Adorno's diagnosis relies on seeing the absence of the ideal as catastrophic, as well as what is discussed in Chap. 7 above, confusing the end of the aristocratic world with the end of the bourgeois world.

The liberal bourgeois world has not encountered a literal version of the catastrophe Adorno sees within it. The apparent decay of the stronger kind individualism mourned by both Alexis de Tocqueville within liberal thought and Nietzsche as a double or obverse of liberal thought (see Stocker 2014) is still an issue for liberal thinkers without despair at the liberal world overwhelming it. In many cases, commentators on the 'catastrophe' of an administered society want to move from there into a more authentic liberal capitalism, or at least do not make a clear rejection of the liberal bourgeois world rather than the socialism signalled in utopian terms by Adorno. Joshua Landy (2004) provides an account of how *In Search of Lost Time* explores illusion, evasion and the idea of a true self, rather than an account of social catastrophe. There is no sense of impending apocalypse, Christian or Marxist, an issue Landy does not even acknowledge, though he does deal with what he regards as unduly reductive approaches to Proust as philosopher in Deleuze, along with Jonathan Dancy, Vincent Descombes and others. There are two main issues here, Proust as Schopenhauer and Proust as Bergson. As Landy points out, Proust did not consider himself to be Bergson's disciple in the field of literature even it they were related and Proust attended some of his lectures; and the novel cannot be read as a literary exposition of Bergsonism. Schopenhauer's influence was certainly very widespread in Proust's time and Proust had read him. As Landy points out though, what might look like Schopenhauerian moments in Proust's novel are not enough to sustain a Schopenhauerian reading, particularly when we consider his criticisms in the novel of 'subjective idealism'. The novel as a whole just is not on the model of Schopenhauer's philosophy which would entail a drive towards willlessness and loss of self. Proust does examine the self as lacking the strongest forms of continuity, but he does not deny the reality of the self, even in a Humean way. That is David Hume's view of the self in *A Treatise of Human Nature* (2000), according to which there is no substantial self so that identity is a matter of memories rather than underlying personhood over time. It is Hume that Jonathan Dancy (1995) refers to in comparison to Proust and to the disadvantage of Proust. Landy responds with an argument that Proust has a view of the self which is philosophically superior to that of Hume, as well as being a part of a remarkable aesthetic work of literature. Hume failed to notice that his own scepticism about the substantial 'I', as more than a fiction about a self enduring over moments of experience, rests on the assumption of an 'I' that inquiries into its own identity. Proust demonstrates a self beneath the level of this kind of conscious speculation, so offers something superior to Hume's philosophical arguments. Landy does not note how some of what he finds in Proust has precedents in Fichte and Kierkegaard, but he does establish *In Search of Lost Time* as a novel of philosophical significance, and not as something that can be reduced to an illustration of arguments in Hume, Schopenhauer, Bergson, or as Deleuze suggests, Plato. One way of taking Proust in literary and philosophical discussion has been as the culmination of the 'Romantic' aesthetic tradition in Schelling and Schopenhauer, which assumes some metaphysical significance art, as transmitted to Proust by his teachers at the Lycée Condorcet. The French education system has a class of lycée teachers who have passed the exam necessary to be a university teacher and very distinguished scholars tended to spend at least the early part of their career in a lycée with examples that go up to at least as recently as Michel Foucault. The idea of a transmission from Schelling through the French assimilation of German Metaphysical Romanticism as the core of *In Search of Lost Time* appears in Paul Ricouer's *Time and Narrative* Volume II (1985), Chap. 4, 'The Fictive Experience of Time' in the section 'From Time Regained to Time Lost'. This precedes the conclusion and so can be taken as the culminating point of the volume. The argument that Proust gives some literary form to Romantic Metaphysics of Art is taken from Anne Henry's work (1983) rather than through direct argument. What Ricoeur adds to is the mythos of art which has joined memory with time, through art in which metaphor unifies our limited perceptions with the thing, but particularly the person perceived. This also provides something beyond Genette's structural analysis of Proust which emphasises the difference between narrative and real time, along with the spatialisation of time on the pages of the narrative, and which disintegrates as discussed above. As we have seen the centrality of metaphor in Proust is followed up more recently by Miguel de Beistegui (2013) though in the context of an alternative to Platonic aesthetic forms (2012). Here, we can see another contribution to anti-mimetic literary aesthetics, as Beistegui argues for displacing mimesis with metaphor as the central category. The shifting work of language itself is put at the centre rather than the task of language to represent in a version of metaphysical constancy. This perhaps suggests the difficulty of harmonising the reading of Proust with metaphysical theories of form. Ricouer argues that metaphor and mythos need to be added to Romantic Metaphysics, but still sees the metaphysics as confirmed by Proust. Deleuze follows his own ambiguity in which Proust is a Platonist but also in *A Thousand Plateaus* (Deleuze and Guattari 1987) a Deleuzian adventurer across metaphysical, or apparently metaphysical forms. In all cases, like Ricoeur he argues for a Proust unified by the claim of the final volume, *Time Regained*, for the priority of memory transfigured by art. Deleuze and Ricoeur both situate themselves as sceptics of aesthetic salvationism in Proust, but offer different variations of this. Even metaphor puts an aesthetic ideal at the centre of Proust's writing, when the most distinctive aspect is an informal phenomenology of experience in which metaphor cannot fully match experience, which goes outside writing and the interior experience of time into the historical and social world, the familial and friendship communities which are never just aestheticised or made occasions of metaphor.

The extent of *In Search of Lost Time* in types of writing rhythm, and references to types of literature, is what makes it central to Gérard Genette when he was at the height of his structuralist phase. The relation between the narrative and discursive essayistic elements of Proust is key for Genette in *Narrative Discourse* and in essays on Proust. This also makes Proust's novel a very convenient context for discussing the limits of Structuralism as Genette himself found limits to what can be achieved in the analysis of narrative, even though, perhaps because he was one of the best, maybe the best of practitioners. In Proust, discourse swallows narrative so a structuralist type ensemble or sequence of narrative elements is difficult to make adequate. Proust provided an unstable destabilising object of analysis for structuralism, before it emerged, except in the very loose sense of writing on literature which discusses elements and relations between them. Any thorough reduction to schematic ideal forms is very difficult to apply to Proust. The swallowing of narrative by discourse is just one issue for Genette, who ends *Narrative Discourse* (1980) pondering the need to use concepts drawn from Proust to analyse Proust which will be abandoned by later readers, and finds that the Narrator swallows everything in a 'disguised' autobiography. Inferring a person behind the narrative and taking all the concepts of narrative analysis to be provisional and specific to a text, looks like the end of structuralism, indirectly conceded through a struggle with *In Search of Lost Time* and coming close to the Schlegelian idea of a novel so expansive it resists reductive analysis.

Merleau-Ponty has a less destructive encounter with Proust in his two definitive works: *Phenomenology of Perception* (2011) and *The Visible and The Invisible* (1968). There is evolution in Merleau-Ponty's thought but not the kind of disintegration that took place in Genette's commitment to structuralism, partly through his encounter with Proust. He does not offer a philosophical aesthetic account of *In Search of Lost Time*, but he does as much to illuminate it from that point of view as Genette. He takes examples from Proust to support a view of retention in memory

(2011, 83), memory of ideas from the past as connected with the lived past (88), the intelligible place of an artwork (410), our existence in our past (413) and the continuity of experience (449). This is the total number of references in *Phenomenology of Perception*, but is deeply suggestive about the importance of Proust, particularly if we put them in the context of the book as a whole, which is full of Proustian aspects. This continues in *The Visible and The Invisible* which is more 'transcendental' and less 'scientifically' oriented than *Phenomenology of Perception*. Merleau-Ponty takes Proust as explaining the importance of the invisible that is of hidden ideas in art (149), the sensibility of pure ideality (152), the unity of experience before its 'objective' analysis (153), the role of spontaneous creativity in relation to total Being in art (170), the relation between discourse and its history in writing (177), the past time which is not just a series of moment in the relationship between embodiment and the past (243). Again this is a complete list of references, but highly suggestive for reading Proust and in estimating his philosophical importance. Proust's writing gives us a sense of experience before we try to verbalise, articulate and analyse it, which amongst other things gives us a deep sense of language as a form of experience, not just a way of representing it.

Conclusion

In Search of Lost Time explores many kinds of writing, including as Genette notes discursive writing. The tension between narrative and discourse is fundamental, but so is the tension between metaphor and materiality, anticipation and reality, the power of tradition and historical memory in relation to change and growth, aesthetic hierarchies and the aestheticisation of the world, the writerliness of the world and its resistance to writing, continued imaginative production and created forms, memory and lived time, dispersed experience and shaping patterns of repetition and association. It is not just a work illustrating an aesthetic or philosophical attitude, but a work also engaging with aesthetic and philosophical attitudes in an immersive way. It is neither the pure exploration of aesthetic invention nor the portrait of Third

Republic France. There is a central exploring consciousness which develops without disappearing or becoming disguised autobiography. It explores what it is to be an individual living in a time and place that is absorbed in inner reflections, but finds them interwoven with cultural memory, place, national history and European culture. The multiple contexts are not sorted into a transparent hierarchy of universal references. Proust draws attention to the specificity of national tradition, the impossibility of complete transparent translatability while also showing how novelistic writing is embedded in a deep history and a European context which becomes a global context. It suggests how the aesthetic experience is a worldly experience so that it is a novel that retains epic type aspects, including the issues around the epic form built up in Chap. 2 above, while deepening the poetic subjective aspect of the novel.

Proust's river novel and the philosophical attention it has generated suggest some success in matching Schlegel's ambitions for the novel as a fusion of poetry and philosophy. It can be considered as a very long prose poem and as one of the most philosophically significant books of the twentieth century, which is not written primarily as a work of philosophy, and maybe of any century. Though it belongs to the story of philosophy and the novel, it is just outside the core of works which explicitly fuse philosophy and the novel. The next chapter will explore such works, in some part in relation to Proust's main rival as the novelist of the twentieth century, James Joyce.

References

Adorno, Theodor. 1973. *Negative Dialectics*, trans. E.B. Ashton. London: Routledge and Kegan Paul.

Adorno, Theodor. 1991. *Notes to Literature, Volume One*, trans. Shierry Weber Nicholsen and ed. Rolf Tiedeman. New York, NY and Chichester: Columbia University Press.

Adorno, Theodor. 2002. *Aesthetic Theory*, trans. and ed. Robert Hullot-Kentor. London and New York, NY: Continuum.

Anderson, Benedict. 1991. *Imagined Communities*. London and New York, NY: Verso Books.

Beckett, Samuel. 1965. *Proust and Three Dialogues*. London: John Calder.

Beistegui, Miguel de. 2013. *Proust as Philosopher: The Art of Metaphor*, trans. Dorothée Bonnigal Katz with Simon Sparks and Miguel de Beistegui. London and New York, NY: Routledge.

Dancy, Jonathan. 1995. New Truths in Proust? *The Modern Language Review* 90 (1): 18–28.

de Beistegui, Miguel. 2012. *Aesthetics after Metaphysics: From Mimesis to Metaphor*. New York, NY and Abingdon: Routledge.

Deleuze, Gilles. 2000. *Proust and Signs*, trans. Richard Howard. Minneapolis, MN: University of Minnesota Press.

Deleuze, Gilles, and Félix Guattari. 1987. *A Thousand Plateaus: Capitalism and Schizophrenia*, trans. Brian Massumi. Minneapolis, MN and London: University of Minnesota Press.

Genette, Gérard. 1980. *Narrative Discourse: An Essay in Method*, trans. Jane E. Lewin. Ithaca, NY: Cornell University Press.

Girard, René. 2010. *Battling to the End: Conversations with Benoît Chantre*, trans. Mary Baker. East Lansing, MI: East Michigan University Press.

Henry, Anne. 1983. *Proust romancier: le tombeau égyptien*. Paris: Flammarion.

Hume, David. 2000. *A Treatise of Human Nature*, ed. David Fate Norton and Mary J. Norton. Oxford and New York, NY: Oxford University Press.

Landy, Joshua. 2004. *Philosophy as Fiction: Self, Deception, and Knowledge in Proust*. Oxford and New York, NY: Oxford University Press.

Merleau-Ponty, Maurice. 2011. *Phenomenology of Perception*, trans. Donald A. Landes. Abingdon and New York, NY: Routledge and Taylor & Francis.

Novalis. 1997. *Philosophical Writings*, trans. and ed. Margaret Mahony Stoljar. Albany, NY: SUNY Press.

Proust, Marcel. 2000. *In Search of Lost Time V The Captive. The Fugitive*, trans. C.K. Scott Moncrieff and Terence Kilmartin. Revised by D.J. Enright. London: Vintage Books.

Ricoeur, Paul. 1985. *Time and Narrative, Volume 2*, trans. Kathleen McLaughlin and David Pellauer. Chicago, IL and London: University of Chicago Press.

Smith, Adam. 1983. *Lectures on Rhetoric and Belles Lettres*, ed. J.C. Bryce. Oxford and New York, NY: Oxford University Press.

Sprinker, Michael. 1994. *History and Ideology in Proust: A la recherche du temps perdu and the Third French Republic*. Cambridge and New York, NY: Cambridge University Press.

Stocker, Barry. 2014. A Comparison of Friedrich Nietzsche and Wilhelm von Humboldt as Products of Classical Liberalism. In *Nietzsche as Political Philosopher*, ed. Manuel Knoll and Barry Stocker. Berlin and New York, NY: De Gruyter.

10

The Philosophical Novel

Introduction

There is no history of philosophy without the novel and no history of the novel without philosophy. The form of philosophy is not intelligible without the form of the novel, and the form of philosophy is not intelligible without the form of the novel. There are two aspects to both these expressions of mutual dependency between philosophy and the novel. The first is that the histories of the novel and of philosophy overlap; the second is that any account of what philosophy and the novel can include as forms of writing must overlap. The second claim provides an argument from necessity which supports and is justified by the empirical reality of the first claim. At the very least, it would be strange to deny as a matter of fact that Kierkegaard and Nietzsche wrote texts which are novelistic and philosophical. *Repetition* and *Thus Spoke Zarathustra* in particular fit this pattern. For Kierkegaard, there are maybe more plausible candidates, certainly including *Either/Or* and its sequel *Stages on Life's Way*. Kierkegaard can maybe said to have done better as a novelist in *Repetition* and even more 'Diary of a Seducer' which can be regarded as a novella within *Either/*

© The Author(s) 2018
B. Stocker, *Philosophy of the Novel*,
https://doi.org/10.1007/978-3-319-65891-9_10

Or. These writings of Kierkegaard stand up better as novelistic works than *Thus Spoke Zarathustra* by most standards. The widespread availability of 'Diary of a Seducer' as a freestanding text is perhaps the best evidence of this, since, while it is of considerable philosophical interest, its more literary qualities as novel in the form of a diary are the obvious reason for its separate availability. In Nietzsche's case *Thus Spoke Zarathustra* stands more alone, though maybe a case can be made for saying that *Ecce Homo* is a kind of novel, or anti-novel, about a bombastic philosopher-prophet with some resemblance to its author Friedrich Nietzsche, claiming to be the author of the essays and books attributed to Nietzsche. Beyond Kierkegaard and Nietzsche, it is maybe difficult to think of works which are so clearly both novel and philosophy, but there are significant other kinds of overlap between the two histories.

Ancient writing is inherently less open to strict division between genres than more recent equivalents, though we can see separations begin to crystallise. No one will claim that Aristotle's surviving texts are at all novelistic or invite much literary attention. The complication is that Aristotle wrote dialogues which are all lost, so there is an Aristotle unknown to us who might be much more of a literary figure. The other side of this is that the ancients who had access to these dialogues do not appear to have placed them on a level with Plato's productions, so it is possible we might see Aristotle as a rather minor practitioner. In any case, he was a literary practitioner at some level of a form that feeds into the novel. Jumping a few centuries into Roman antiquity, during the dying years of the Republic, Cicero wrote dialogues which are of great quality in the development of Latin prose, but it would be difficult to make a case that they have novelistic qualities of character, conflict, tensions, storytelling, resolution and the like, except at the margins. Lucretius' philosophical poem, *On Nature*, has considerable literary qualities, but is no novel. Similar remarks apply to Seneca's letters.

Given the tendency of the novel to incorporate other genres, these texts can be said to contribute to the history of the novel, but not in a way is useful except for a philosophy of the novel of a kind likely to collapse in on itself by giving substantial coverage to all forms of literary writing. Augustine's *Confessions* are the first really plausible candidate after the most novelistic Platonic dialogues for a major contribution to the overlap of novel and philosophical writing. It is an autobiography rather than a novel, but it is nevertheless a novel of a spiritual self-discovery which can be grouped with the *Metamorphoses* of Apuleius, even if the latter lack matching philosophical sophistication. Autobiography itself has overlapped with the novel. Clearly, the *Confessions* of both Augustine and Rousseau contributed to the development of the novel, and a lot of novel writing contains thinly disguised autobiography, of which there is a strong element *In Search of Lost Time.*

The first texts that can be called philosophical novels might be Plato's Socratic dialogues. There is some precedent for this suggestion in Schlegel and Nietzsche, as discussed in Chaps. 3 and 5. The dialogues are in prose and have narrative of a kind in the development of arguments through personal interaction, which evolves over time. They are pure speech, so could be regarded as dramatic more than novelistic, and it has been suggested that they were staged, most famously by Gilbert Ryle in *Plato's Progress* (1975). Some of the dialogues are impersonal and less literary but many feature revelation of personal character through the approach to disagreement as well as some personal development in the dialogue.

Thrasymachus in *Republic I* is a portrait of an angry character lacking in self-control, an Achilles of philosophical argument. The *Symposium* has a strong element of character portrait of Socrates, which has particularly intense moments around his interactions with Alcibiades, themselves interacting with the discussion of love in the dialogue and building Plato's eristics, the dialogue of conflict, into its most intense moments. Ethics and philosophical capacity are both questions of character for Plato, and the dialogues build on this as we see what kind of characters speakers have, with the dialogues taken together creating an extensive portrait of Socrates, a little bit as if he was a character in the novelistic cycles of Balzac and Zola. Along with the *Symposium, Phaedrus* has the most literary quality and sets itself up as an escape from the rhetorical life of the city, set at noon outside the city as Socrates persuades Phaedrus of the limits of written texts and the importance of living speech. Like the *Symposium*, there is an erotic element to the central encounter which relates to the topic under discussion, though as with the *Symposium* the erotic is given a subsidiary role in the search for truth. Both end with something like death, the story of Toth in *Phaedrus* and Socrates' catatonia in the *Symposium*. The *Republic* is not so constantly literary in comparison with the erotics and story-telling of the other two dialogues, but it does feature at least two memorable characters, Socrates and Thrasymachus, along with a number of fictions internal to the dialogue and some storytelling in the set-up of the dialogue. The expulsion of the poet from the ideal polity is itself a memorable example of philosophical fiction as is the climatic myth of Er. *Phaedo* shows Socrates encountering death, *Crito* shows him in debate with the personified laws of Athens and the *Apology* shows him on trial.

As Bakhtin points out, the trial and the associated criminal investigation are important in novels as a way of connecting inner life with the public sphere: a connection which is always an issue in the novel (1981, 123). Following Bakhtin, we might see the antique novel as itself trying to replace the Greek agora Roman forum as a way in which individuals are gathered into a common space (132). In this sense, Plato's dialogues precede the novel and provide a paradigm which they try to match, of a public world in which inner ideas about truth, love and justice are revealed along with character.

An investigation of the philosophy of the novel should include an account of the ways in which philosophical writing may appear as a novel, or a novel may have substantial philosophical content, and the general ways in which there are overlaps. These situations of combination, or in-betweenness, are ways in which philosophy says something about what a novel is and what it can do. Chapter 9 above on Proust is partly concerned with how a novel can be philosophical, which is one of the major concerns of the philosophers and critics who have written on Proust, so demonstrating that the philosophy of the novel must to some degree include the novel as philosophy. Chapter 4 above refers to the novelistic aspect of Kierkegaard's production suggesting the importance of philosophical writing as novel though is a less widespread phenomenon than that of a novel containing philosophical themes. Chapter 2 had already pointed in that direction with its emphasis on Aristotle's comments on the closeness of philosophy and literature, along with Vico's comments on the philosophical importance of Homeric epic.

The connections between *In Search of Lost Time* and the way philosophy become novelistic in Kierkegaard, as well as concerned with discussion of the novel as a form, lead into a discussion of Joyce's *Finnegans Wake*. A work that contains references to one of Kierkegaard's novelistic philosophical works, *Either/Or* along with frequent references to Don Juan, who is a major object of discussion in *Either/Or*, largely but not entirely with reference to Mozart's opera *Don Giovanni* and the topic of the music-word relationship. Since Joyce refers to Vico in both *Ulysses* and *Finnegans Wake*, there is an opening here into discussing Vico as having an analysis of epic very relevant to the rise of the novel, and how it has been taken up in the novels of Joyce. Joyce's associate and follower, Samuel Beckett, contributed to the philosophically oriented literature on both Joyce and Proust, also writing novels full of philosophical issues and references. Thomas Mann also stands out as a writer whose novels engage with philosophical ideas and material, particularly from Nietzsche, but also Plato, Arthur Schopehauer, Adorno and others. In the nineteenth century, Herman Melville's *Moby-Dick* provides an example of novel in direct engagement with philosophy as well as the more implicit kind of engagement shared with many other novelists.

However, this chapter will move from the discussion of Joyce and Kierkegaard into the consideration of Jane Austen's novels, which have been discussed in philosophical terms (Knox-Shaw 2004; Elmsley 2005), but have never been placed amongst the most 'philosophical' novels. After the discussion of Joyce, Vico and Kierkegaard, Austen novels will be taken as an object of philosophical investigation and will be placed in relation to Kierkegaard.

Joyce

Finnegans Wake includes play on the Scottish equivalent of Kierkegaard, Kirk-yard (church yard), referring to the Norse influence on the Celtic and Anglo-Saxon worlds of Scotland, as well as Ireland and England, also suggesting that the reading of Kierkegaard should accompany the reading of Joyce, particularly the text which appears in the play with the Danish title in *Finnegans Wake*. That is *Enten-Eller*, known as *Either/*

Or in English, a long text with a fictional frame containing essays, a diary, long letters and a sermon, much of which has narrative aspects, particularly the 'Diary of a Seducer' that ends *Either/Of I*. *Either/Or* is deserving of the title novel, if in a marginal way, due to the strong elements of storytelling and an overall structure, which in *Either/Or I* builds up a story of a aesthetic individual who appears to be the author of a series of essays, some of which have a narrative 'I' point of view character, and who may be the author of the 'Diary of a Seducer', or if not at least has it in his papers and considers it an important story, which could be taken as a short novel, to share. Two very long letters from Judge William to a young man, who may be the implied author of *Either/Or* after the Preface which is narrated from the point of view of someone who accidentally discovers the papers in a hidden place, make up most of *Either/Or II* and contain narrative elements. Parts one and two compare an aesthetic view of life and an ethical view. The religious view of life appears as a sermon appended to the second letter, by an obscure country pastor, with the title 'Ultimatum'. It presents the idea of an unconditional love for God in which we prefer to be in the wrong rather than for God to be in the wrong, even when he commands an individual to go against ethics.

There is some tension between *Finnegans Wake* and *Either/Or* in that Joyce's novel seems like *Either/Or I*, taken to the extreme in the sense that it is something like a pure flow of aesthetic discourse at the limits of intelligibility and form. One way of taking *Finnegans Wake* is the continuation of the pure monologue of Molly Bloom at the end of *Ulysses*, which otherwise could be considered a novel of aesthetic and ethical viewpoints related to Stephen Daedalus and Leopold Bloom. The relation of Molly Bloom's monologue to 'Ultimatum' in *Either/Or* is clearly not at all direct. The monologue maybe replaces Christian love with a kind of worldly but absolute passion, which overflows the moral formal rule following kind of ethics that Kierkegaard criticises. In that case, *Finnegans Wake* is the discourse of that love which is more than aesthetic or ethical. The relationship between Kierkegaard and Joyce is here both tenuous and meaningful. Maybe *Finnegans Wake* is the closest that novelistic writing and form can come to a religious stage in a world with no transcendent faith, where the world, not God, is the absolute.

On the other hand, from Kierkegaard's point of view, *Finnegans Wake* might be the best possible exploration of the ethical universal and the religious absolute once the reality of anything outside the aesthetic moment is questioned. There is no harmonisation of Joyce and Kierkegaard, but their interaction is telling.

Another significant aspect of Joyce's use of philosophy though, certainly in the context of the present book and its emphasis on Vico, is the use Joyce makes of the *New Science*, rather passingly, in *Ulysses* and more centrally in *Finnegans Wake*, as emphasised by Samuel Beckett in 'Dante...Bruno. Vico...Joyce' (in Beckett et al. 1929).

Kierkegaard and Joyce

Kierkegaard makes perhaps the most important contribution to fusing philosophy and the novel or showing the novel as the place where philosophy and literature meet. A paradoxical element of Kierkegaard's contribution is that as we have seen he gives music the higher status, or at least his pseudonym in *Either/Or I* does. Kierkegaard argues that Don Juan can only be expressed musically. The whole of the opera cannot be dominated by reflection as in non-musical drama. Its unity comes from mood, which brings together a plurality of voices. Drama creates a sense of the contemporaneous nature of events through reflection; opera does through the harmony of forces. The impact of the musical situation is the unity produced by hearing together that which sounds together. The Don is the hero of Mozart's opera, and the main interest is concentrated upon him. He also gives the other characters interest. This is not an external giving, since in *Don Giovanni* the hero is the force in the other characters. His life is the life principle in them. His passion sets in motion the passion of the others and is echoed everywhere. It is music that can bring that into artistic form. The characters in the opera are not characters strictly speaking, but essential forces of life, dominated and unified by the force of the Don. Kierkegaard attributes a maximum force to music, and a capacity for one part of a composition to connect with, and focus the force of the entire composition, as 'one can enjoy a single fragment of it and yet be carried away instantly; one arrives at the middle of the performance and instantly one is in the heart of it, for this heart, which is the Don's life is everywhere' (EO I, Kierkegaard 1987, 119).

At this point, Kierkegaard emphasises that vision acts against such a unity, 'As soon as the eyes are involved, the impression is disrupted, for the dramatic unity that presents itself to the eye is altogether subordinate and deficient in comparison with the musical unity that is heard simultaneously' (EO I, Kierkegaard 1987, 120). So, an opera should be heard but not seen, though some of Kierkegaard's earlier comments about the relation between language and music, and his general dialectical approach might suggest such that a firm distinction cannot be made. Kierkegaard himself seems to be at least some of the time caught between reductively abstract categories of experience and the ways in which experiences consist of flows, emergence and interpenetration of forces.

> [I]f we hold fast to Don Giovanni as immediate life, then it is easy to understand that he can exercise a decisive influence on Loporello, that he assimilates him so that he can become almost an organ for Don Giovanni. In a certain sense Loporello is closer to being a personal consciousness than Don Giovanni. (Kierkegaard 1987 (Part I), 125)

The unity of the opera through desire is explained as harmony of voices. It strongly corresponds with Kierkegaard's account of irony going back to *The Concept of Irony* drawing on Socratic and Romantic versions of irony, which he implicitly brings into the apparently unreflective form of opera, through the power of death which ends the sensuousness. The death is maybe also necessary to sensuousness since the pure sensuousness of the Don is itself a form of self-dissolution in the sense of identity. The text of *Either/Or*, itself, has many of these aspects within itself. We can understand *Either/Or* as the ironic harmony of voices. The tension and harmony of voice and writing in language, and in communication, are present in the letters, the reports of conversations and so on, which make up the text.

Music is alluring to writers of pure writing, as it seems to be what is most pure writing, to be the essence of writing in its lack of meaning essence. The discussion of *Don Giovanni* is an indirect commentary on the form of the novel. It is an extended essay within a book which is itself a strong example of the fusion of novel and philosophy. The essay deals with an extended narrative, in the form of Mozart's opera, while engaging with other forms of aesthetic expression, including the novel in the form of *Don Quixote*. The essay offers a perspective on the whole of *Either/Or I* and therefore a perspective on how to take *Either/Or I* and *Either/Or II* together. Kierkegaard, speaking through a pseudonym, suggests that Christianity tends to promote the polarisation evident in the dual characters of the Don and Sancho Panza in Cervantes' novel or the Don and Loporello in Mozart's opera. The duality is that between spirituality and flesh.

The novel after Cervantes might be taken as offering a reconciliation of spirituality and flesh at least in the many occasions romantic love or marriage comes at the end of the novel. The idea of the novel as a form of reconciliation is well established, particularly as when the *Bildungsroman* is taken as the model, but, the reconciliatory force of even the most reconciliatory form of the novel suffers over time, as in Flaubert's *Sentimental Education* or Joyce's *Stephen Hero*, when possibility of disillusionment along with the changeable nature of individuality turns reconciliation into regret or even loss of self.

Writing *Either/Or* in 1842 and then *Stages on Life's Way* in 1844 and 1845, Kierkegaard already questions the idea of a reconciled world. In doing so, he more builds on what the novel already suggests, and his own literary analyses [*From the Papers of One Still Living* and *Literary Review*] suggest that the novel is concerned with dissatisfied subjectivity and restlessness. *Concept of Irony* shows Kierkegaard more concerned with the tendency of the novel towards shifting subjective dissatisfaction than confirmation of existing order. Kierkegaard's alter ego in the "'Guilty?'/'Not Guilty?'" section of *Stages on Life's Way* gives expression to the difficulty at the heart of the novelistic enterprise:

> My idea was to structure my life ethically in my innermost being and to conceal this inwardness in the form of deception. Now I am forced even further back into myself; my life is religiously structured and is so far back in inwardness that I have difficulty in making my way to actuality. (Kierkegaard 1988, 351)

In *Either/Or* and *Stages on Life's Way*, Kierkegaard follows up the ironic subjectivity, the aesthetic romantic attitude, in his own writing, maybe outdoing the German Romantic literature, he is concerned with and certainly matching previous novels. In doing so, he could be said to point the way to his systematic work on theological ethics and philosophy, most notably in *Works of Love*. However, he does not just abolish the aesthetic subjectivity in approaching the theological. *Works of Love* starts with a discussion of what it is to love the neighbour as yourself, in which we have to establish the self in order to discuss the relation with the neighbour. The understanding of the self in *Works of Love* does not directly refer to his work on subjectivity, but does belong to it. Something is lost if Kierkegaard's writing is separated into discrete non-communicating parts. The discourses of the country priest in *Either/Or* and of Father Taciturnus in *Stages on Life's Way* bring the theological point of view, the point of view of the absolute, into writing with a strong Romantic Ironic Subjectivist character.

Kierkegaard follows that idea to some degree in the unsettling implications of his account of the marriage of Judge [*Assessor*] William. William's letter to a young friend indicates an ideal marriage, at least on the surface. However, it is an absolute commitment to Christianity which is the real focus, and the attitude to William's marriage conveys some questioning. Is William's wife as apparently as happy as he is with the situation? What is her attitude to the Young Man writing to William who appears to be, or at least may be, the voice of *Either/Or I*, and how is a visitor to the marital home? How much does William understand of Christianity in his satisfaction in his married life, mixed with ethical language suggestive of Aristotle and Hegel? What does the joking about legal rights of a husband to beat his wife in *Stages on Life's Way* suggests about the fulfilment of a woman's life in marriage? Kierkegaard's novel writing is rather less certain about marriage than social ethical assumptions of the time tend to allow for. While the nineteenth-century novel may sometimes seem to advocate happy marriage as the inevitable end of the virtuous hero, of either gender, the reality is that it does just as much to show marriage, or at least individual marriages, as unsatisfactory forms of interaction between two personalities and the ethics of a bond that lasts over time. If marriage is not generally questioned as a goal, the certainty that it will satisfy all hopes certainly is.

Finnegans Wake alludes to *Either/Or* rather than making anything systematic of it. Nevertheless, awareness of it provides major insights into reading Joyce. Don Juan achieves an everyman presence in the *Wake*, which can be put in the context of Kierkegaard's view that he is part of the immediate sensuous. Music is a way of representing the immediate sensuous which becomes even more intensely representative when words combine with music. This is the limit of representation. It is a matter of debate whether music can represent or depict anything. If it does represent something then that could be our immediate sensuality. Though the immediate sensuous might be considered more as what music is in its performance, rather than as an object of representation. The interplay of representation and the performative aspect of words dominates *Finnegans Wake*. Its performative attitude to words makes it musical in nature. It is very closely related to the rhythms of spoken Irish English, but contains a multitude of word play across languages, which enhances the musicality. The word play and musicality inevitably go past Kierkegaard who is constrained by philosophical communication, or sometimes the limits of a kind of narrative continuity Joyce dispenses with. As we have seen, Kierkegaard was concerned with the relation between subjective poetry and myth in the novel, which Joyce takes to the extreme in his performative way. Constant references appear to mythical and story telling narratives in *Finnegans Wake*, including the place of Juan, but this always dissolves into the playful poetic-musical flow. For these reasons, taking the philosophical text *Either/Or* with the novelistic text *Finnegans Wake* multiplies the senses of play with limits already present in both of them, illuminating both. In the case of Joyce, we can at least suspect that Kierkegaard was part of what stimulated him to write the way he did, even if Kierkegaard is not put forward directly as a structuring inspiration.

Vico and Joyce

Going back to Joyce, *Either/Or* plays a role in *Finnegans Wake* through play on the Danish title '*Enten-Eller*' along with the resemblance between Kierkegaard's name and the Scots for churchyard, 'Kirkyard'. This itself reflects the relations between Old English and Norse, modern Scots (a variant of English) and Danish. There is a lot going on here with for *Finnegans Wake* in the allusions to alternation and choice in meaning along with a play across history and language involving sacred space and the place where the dead are buried. This last point brings us onto the major point of discussion here, which is the use of Vico in Joyce. The burial of the dead is something Vico places at the beginning of human history, in the escape from the primeval forest, alongside agriculture, marriage and the first cities. It would be difficult to adequately discuss Joyce's relations with both Kierkegaard and Vico, so this chapter and the book end with an account of how key modern novelist, uses Vico, with the intention of confirming Vico as a philosopher essential to analysing the novel and as significant for the inspirations ideas of history give to the novel.

Joyce's *Ulysses* makes one explicit reference to Vico, and even that has a disguise. Stephen Dedalus is giving a history lesson and addresses a boy called Armstrong, who lives in 'Vico Road, Dalkey' (Joyce, 30). Dedalus' thoughts give this some context with reference to Romantic aesthetics: 'Fabled by the daughters of memory. And yet it was in some way if not as memory fabled it. A phrase then of impatience, thud of Blake's wings of excess. I hear the ruin of all space, shattered glass and toppling masonry, and time one livid final flame. What's left us then' (Joyce, 30). And then in the context of history: 'Another victory like that and we are done for. That phrase the world had remembered. A dull ease of the mind. From a hill above a corpsestrewn plain a general speaking to his officers, leaned upon his spear. Any general to any officers. They lend ear' (Joyce, 30). The reference is Pyrrhus and his victory of Tarentum which was so costly it was a defeat and is the origin of the phrase 'Pyrrhic victory'. These excerpts establish certain aspects of Ulysses: the eternal aspect of literature; the melancholic aspect of the rejection of lived time in favour of eternity; the futility of historical struggles; and the repetition of historical events which establish their eternal aspect. The repetition and the sense of established eternal order suggest that the mention of Vico Road cannot be accidental or trivial.

The very name of the novel gives us the sense of historical repetition: Ulysses gestures back to the conventional beginning of Western literature in Homer's Odyssey. Ulysses is the Latinised form of Homer's hero Odysseus. The use of the Latinised form itself raises other issues of repetition, since this form is referred to by Dante in the *Divine Comedy*, Shakespeare in *Troilus and Cressida*, Tennyson in *Ulysses* etc. Joyce's novel both refers us to the supposed beginning of literature and the life of that beginning in its repetition.

For Vico, Homer has a special status because the Homeric epics reveal the origins of society. They are the poetic expressions of early heroic society, of the adventures of the original patricians (gentes/giants) and plebeians. Joyce brought this into Ulysses, and we can make some sense of the novel with reference to language and literature in Vico. The Joycean appropriation of Homer has strong traces of Vico and also of the Romantic aesthetics that takes one form in Schlegel's approach to irony. The Romantic aesthetics which emerged with idealist philosophy take irony and reflection in unlimited forms as the essence of literature. Literature merges with philosophy, not as historical narrative but in the constitution of self-consciousness. Cervantes and Shakespeare appear as ideal representatives of this irony. *Ulysses* contains passages which suggest that it is a deliberate attempt to create a national epic for Ireland of equal status with the British and Spanish works.

Ulysses should certainly be regarded as a work of Viconian history–literature but as mediated by Romantic and Idealist aesthetics, probably known by Joyce through Samuel Taylor Coleridge's popularisation of German philosophy, including his lectures on Shakespeare. *Ulysses* unifies the purity of imagination and playfulness of words with an emphasis on gross physical reality in sexuality, birth, death, eating, digestion, excretion and bodily effusions in general, which has distinctly Renaissance aspects in relation to Rabelais, who was definitely a major reference for Joyce. From the Viconian point of view, this is a literary language taken to a democratic human extreme; he does not appear to have entertained. If Vico can be seen as identifying democratic, heroic and divine aspects of language so does Joyce in way which mingles them, so transforming Vico in the use of his thought rather than remaining literally true to. Elevated and vulgar forms of language from all historical periods play with the Viconian differentiation across *Ulysses*. This is reflected in the many references to Irish nationalism divided itself between more vulgar and more aestheticised, more Celtic nostalgic and more modernist republican elements, against a kind of non-democratic-human power exercised over Ireland by the British Empire. There is certainly scope for many Viconian readings of the various aspects of *Ulysses*, though with no certainty about what is a reading of Joyce and what refers to the way he understood Vico himself at that time.

As Beckett indicated in the essay cited above, which appeared in a volume of 'approved' *Finnegans Wake* commentary published in Joyce's own lifetime, Vico's *New Science* is very definitely central to *Finnegans Wake* and overtly so. *Finnegans Wake* ends with a journey by sea into death and the father and then reorientates towards memory and flows back into the beginning, which brings us back to Dublin by happy coincidence: 'riverrun past Eve and Adam's from swerve of shore to bend of bay, brings us by a commodius vicus of recirculation back to Howth Castle and Environs' (p. 3). The male archetype, HCE (Here Comes Everybody/Humphrey Carpenter Earwicker), is the son of the female archetype (Anna Livia Plurabelle). The sea brings us back to him and to Adam and Eve, and therefore the Fall, by way of sea and river. The riverrun recalls memory in German '*Erinnerung*', so that the way of the river is back to the original beginning and memory itself. The way of the sea brings back the town of Dublin, and the family of ALP, through the vicus which amongst many things alludes to Vico: philosopher of historical cycles and eternal ideas patterning the contingencies of history. The Viconian forms of history are removed from the clear stages and cycle of Vico's own conception in a mingling of meanings, references and levels. This could be seen as either a disintegration of Vico's structure in which released energy disperse amongst the arranging of fragments, or of the moment Vico expects at the end of each cycle in history, when the force has disappeared from laws and institutions to contain violence and disorder in an apocalyptic collapse. The recirculation and Viconian cycles of history are present in the circular form of *Finnegans Wake*, as it's the last sentence 'A way a lone a last a loved a long the' is an incomplete sentence serving as the beginning of the incomplete sentence above, which opens the novel. The first page itself contains a 'thunder word', one of the ten hundred letter words that appear in *Finnegans Wake* (Verene 1997, 396) referring to the thunder which frights the giants in the wilderness, the paleo-humans of the *New*

Science so that they make sound which is the word for god. There are seven appearances of the word Vico in *Finnegans Wake* including one lightly disguised as 'vicous', which emphasise circularity and roads. As with *Ulysses*, it is all part of a Rabelaisian euphoria of words, bodies, knowledge and associations, though taken further with regard to fragmentation. While it is possible to reconstruction *Finnegans Wake* as an exemplification of Viconian science (Verene 2003) through picking the many references, many of which have to be teased out. The need to tease confirms that there is something arbitrary about the reconstruction and that what is most important is the kind of Viconian energy present. The most plausible answer to that is an excess of linguistic play containing within it the different possibilities of language explored by Vico, in which the singular poetic imaginative forms of Homer and other theological poets are present in literary language of all contexts. The other side of this is that the sacralised language of divine heroes in Homer is compromised by extreme linguistic interplay and the common contexts of usage.

Austen

However, it is not just in self-conscious and explicit mergers of philosophy and the novel that we find the relationship. The strength of the relationship is demonstrated by examining texts in which the underlying relationship is there but requires work for it to be explicit. The first chapter has included some exploration of how this might be the case for some work in Analytic philosophy. The second chapter has covered Vico's work on the relationship between the imaginative universals of Homer and the abstract universals of Athenian philosophy. The last chapter has looked at philosophical issues in Proust, which is known as a philosophically leaning literary text and is explicit its philosophical interests. Similar comments apply to the work of Joyce and Beckett, discussed more briefly above.

It is time to examine novelistic work where the philosophical interests are not made so obvious. Jane Austen's novels have attracted attention for their philosophical aspects particularly with regard to ethical significance, along with engagement with romantic aesthetics and feminist political thought. The intersection of these issues comes from the time at which the novel is debated with regard to its significance as a form. Austen published her first novel, *Pride and Prejudice* in 1811, but her literary work began in the 1790s so coinciding with the writings of Friedrich Schlegel, and other Jena Romantics, which elevated the condition of the novel. As Chap. 3 of this book suggests, this elevation was to some degree undercut by Hegel and Schelling, but we can at least say that Austen began writing, and then publishing, as Idealist and Romantic thinkers considered the status of the novel. It seems particularly appropriate to examine how Enlightenment and Romantic concerns in her novels overlap with the concerns of the German Idealists and Romantics. Austen's novels are part of the story of how the novel incorporates what Hegel doubts it can incorporate and become recognised as a major literary genre over the nineteenth century.

Austen makes as good an example as any of how ethical awareness is part of the philosophical nature of the novel. The incorporation of philosophy into the novel, as suggested by Schlegel, has many equivalents in Austen. She does not match the ostentatious playfulness with points of view preferred by Schlegel, but uses the novel to explore perspectives. The relation between the transcendental and relative, the awareness of the infinite, are also present in Austen amongst the relatively unappreciated aspects of her work. The limits of representation, the work of desire in narrative and the playfulness with fictionality are at work in Austen along with an ethical awareness which all challenge Hegel's assumptions about philosophy and religion superseding the novel. We will start with the ways in which Austen advocates religiously grounded community, a position itself deeply held but limited by the secularisation of society which is part of the novel, part of its breakdown of the hierarchy between secular and sacred registers.

(*Emma*, Vol. III, Chap. XI.)

Was it new for any thing in this world to be unequal, inconsistent, incongruous—or for chance and circumstance (as second causes) to direct the human fate? (Austen 2012, 285)

(*Mansfield Park*, Vol I, Chap. IX)

It is a pity, cried Fanny -, "that the custom should have been discontinued. It was a valuable part of former times. There is something in a chapel and chaplain so much in character with a great house, with one's ideas of what such a household should be! A whole family assembling regularly for the purpose of prayer, is fine!" (Austen 1998, 62)

We do not look in great cities for our best morality. It is not there, that respectable people of any denomination can do most good; and it certainly is not there, that the influence of the clergy can be most felt. A fine preacher can be followed and admired; but it is not in fine preaching only that a good clergyman will be useful in his parish and neighbourhood, where the parish and neighbourhood are of a size capable of knowing his private character, and observing his general conduct, which in London can rarely be the case. (Austen 1998, 66)

While Austen's central characters find some reconciling end, we should not ignore the extent to which they have good fortune in an uncertain world, or assume that in Austen's ethical fictional world, good character always protect against misfortune, when as is often suggested she offers a more readable version of Aristotle. *Nicomachean Ethics*, which is sometimes compared with Austen's novels (Ruderman 1995; Emsley 2005). As the quotations from *Mansfield Park* suggest, Austen sometimes refers to a community of religious guidance and communal belonging, which is lacking in the city and even in the domains of the old gentry.

As the quotations above suggest, there is a guiding fear of chance, including absurdities of chance, overwhelming individual judgement and the rationality of the social world. Individual judgement and a regular social order in which individual judgement can flourish. The first quotation shows the danger as it overwhelms Emma Woodhouse.

The difficulties of putting the ideals of Christian ethical community into practice themselves indicate the seriousness with which Austen takes these ideas, as implementing them is a challenge with which we must struggle if we are to see them implemented. This suggests that Austen is not putting forward an easy harmony of everyday ethics and

religion, in which religion disappears into an occasional social obliga-
tion. The strength of a community, its capacity to resist disturbing circumstances and cultivate individuals able to do so, rests on a strong
sense of the ethical as more than is what is convenient for everyday life,
which itself rests on a sense of religion as a living force imposing more
than minimal ethical obligations to follow useful social conventions.
Social conventions are important, but can achieve their deepest importance where strong ethics and strong religion are influences.

What Austen's novels present is part of the concerns articulated by
the novel in modern literature with an ethical shift that is a shift away
from the metaphysical form of theological Christian ethics along with
the Stoic version of the philosophical virtue ethics of Pagan antiquity,
which had a dominant influence on the understanding of ethics in the
early modern period. Ancient philosophy was very influential on the
educated in Austen times, who often learnt Latin in childhood and
might also learn Greek. This applied rather more to men than women,
but it does provide the cultural background for some one like Jane
Austen who did not have an education based on the classics. School
teaching of ethics often included a very large influence on the part of
Stoics, particularly Epictetus (Phillipson 2011, 19), so that non-Stoics
like Plato and Aristotle were seen with a Stoic emphasis.

Epictetus' Stoicism, as found in his *Discourses*, emphasises subordination of will and desire, of all ideas of pleasure including social prestige as well as physical comforts, to reason. There are strong echoes of
this approach in the early Christian thought of Augustine's ethical and
theological texts, which have conditioned Christian thinking ever since,
certainly in the Catholic tradition and the Protestant tradition which
stems from it, covering Austen's own Anglican Protestantism. However,
by the time of Austen, Anglicanism (the English state church) had itself
become strongly conditioned by Enlightenment ethics of a kind which
are not obviously Augustinian. A kind of militant Augustinianism is
central to the Reformation Protestantism of Martin Luther and John
Calvin, carrying on through the literary works of John Milton and
John Bunynan. However, even by this time, the Calvinist moment
in Anglicanism had given way to Arminianism, which is less strict in
its sense of an Augustinian fall of humanity. By the time of Austen,

Anglicanism had very much come under the influence of rationalised and the Enlightenment forms of ethics, which displaced stern Stoicism as much as stern Reformation Protestantism.

Augustine emphasised that sin means loss of control of desire, while salvation is an experience of capacity to command, and rise above, desires, which suggests strong Stoic influences on Augustine. These ideas are not absent from Christian Enlightenment ethics, but are placed in the context of moral sentiments of benevolence and sympathy together with a psychology of emotions and passions that can never be subordinated to reason, but are rather necessary to any exercise of reason.

The growth of the novel as a major literary form in the eighteenth and early nineteenth centuries was a major part of the waning of Stoicism, interacting with the philosophical developments. We can see the philosophical side of that progress through Scottish and Anglo-Irish Enlightenment work on ethics. Adam Smith's *The Theory of Moral Sentiments* (1984) and the latter parts of David Hume's *A Treatise of Human Nature* (2000, Parts II & III) have had the most influence and provide very valuable context for the ethical aspects of Austen's novel as does the slightly earlier work of Francis Hutcheson (Know-Shaw 2004), which is closer to her than Smith and Hume at least in its Christian orientation. That is not to say that Austen's view is that of these Scottish Enlightenment moralists. Her writing is best understood in relation to German Idealism and Kierkegaard's reactions to it.

There is a way of thinking that can be centred around the idea of 'ethical life' which is expounded by Hegel in *Phenomenology of Spirit* (1977) and *Philosophy of Right* (1991) and is discussed by Kierkegaard in ways which can be found in just about all his texts, but which are discussed in a particularly literary way in *Fear and Trembling* (1983), *Either/Or* (1987), and *Stages on Life's Way* (1988). In these books, Kierkegaard explains the limits of both self-absorbed aestheticism and community-oriented ethics from the point of view of Christianity subjectivity, what Kierkegaard refers to as the Single Individual [*Entkelde*].

Before getting onto Hegel and Kierkegaard though, it is necessary to go more into some of the issues around antique and Enlightenment ethics. The Enlightenment ethics at issue here differed from the Stoic heritage that was still influential at the time in that it allowed for a non-rational aspect to ethics arising from the structure of our mind, the ways in which we are socialised and the 'normal' standards of ethics with which we are confronted in life experience. That is the Scottish Enlightenment thinkers incorporated innate capacities for moral awareness, or to develop such an awareness, into their theories of human mind and action. The basic terms here were virtue and sentiment, along with benevolence and sympathy. The fundamental point was that to some degree moral goodness is its own reward when we see its impact on others, and it is this which enables us to develop the more austere ideas of virtue, duty and law.

There is a general heritage from Aristotle of restricting the role of theory in ethics, which is an aspect that acquires greater significance once the extreme Stoic emphasis on the sovereignty of reason is in decline. Aristotle relies on prudential judgement and habit in Book VI of the *Nicomachean Ethics*, as opposed to the pure theory to be found in metaphysics, rules of reasoning and the knowledge of nature. The idea that ethics arises from habits rather than reflection, even if reflection has its uses, can be found in the Scottish Enlightenment work on moral sentiments, sympathy and evolution of social morality.

Hegel continues the idea that ethics arises from the ways we live together in stages of society, rather than from pure reflection, and this continues further in Kierkegaard, though Kierkegaard thinks more of stages of existence the stages of history emphasised by Hegel. For Hegel and Kierkegaard, there is more of a sense of ethics as existing in relation to an absolute perspective which Hegel thinks of as emerging in history, and Kierkegaard relates the absolute more to individualised experience. Kierkegaard's ethical view gives the best insight into Austen, and Kierkegaard's view is best understood in relation to virtue ethics, Scottish Enlightenment and Hegel.

The anti-theoretical element in ethics from ancient virtue theory to Kierkegaard is enacted in Austen's writing as it leans in a direction that is distinct from, even opposed to, the superiority of theoretical reflection. What is given the most value is the life lived according to prudence rather than the theoretical use of prudential reason and certainly not the underlying commitments in metaphysics and intellectual rationalism. Prudence requires prudential reason, as is apparent in Austen, but it can only appear in ways in which it is marginalised and even ridiculed.

Mary Bennett, the youngest sister of Elizabeth Bennett in *Pride and Prejudice*, is perhaps the clearest example of a negative attitude to a personality dominated by the theoretical at the expense of living ethically. She is not just a negative character though as she expresses something that the Austen ethical view needs, a capacity to be a spectator of life and reflect on the rules of living, as well as more pure forms of knowledge. Mary Bennett is maybe the most bookish character in that novel, in even all of the Austen novels, and is apparently there for comic relief. Not only does she read excessively and talk too much in the language of the books she reads, she insists on singing too long on a public occasion (*Pride and Prejudice*, Volume I, Chap. XVIII).

Elizabeth Bennett is shown to be less tutored in musical accomplishments, but to be more pleasant to listen to than her sister. There is an important analogy between the ways that though she appears to have read less than Mary, she is better at putting moral reflections into her way of living. Mary Bennett is given a role (Austen 2001, Volume V, Chap. V) in articulating discussion of pride and vanity (Molar 1967) which can be found in Hume (2000, Book II, Part 3) and Smith (1984, Part VI, Section III), and which are important for the preoccupations of *Pride and Prejudice* as the title itself strongly hints, but is ridiculed in the book for such pedantry. There is some way in which Mary must be important to the world of *Pride and Prejudice*, in which good reading habits are taken as an important sign of merit. Nevertheless, Mary Bennett is not the main centre of sympathy. Elizabeth Bennett dominates the novel and that fits with her portrayal as someone, whose life and conversation show an implicit engagement with Enlightenment sensibility in conduct, morals and aesthetics, more than a bookish knowledge of such things, though she has certainly read widely.

Austen's novels show a persistent ambiguity about the value of learning and novels themselves. Catherine Moreland is mocked in *Northanger Abbey* (Austen 2004) for seeing the world through her reading of Gothic literature, but the fantastic world of Gothic literature is shown to have real world equivalents. General Tilney did not abuse or murder his wife at Catherine Moreland fears, but he is an overbearing father threatening the destruction of her hope of marriage to Henry Tilney (Austen 2004, Volume II, Chap. 9). Much of Enlightenment and Romantic culture is present in Austen's novels through attribution of thoughts to characters and parody of texts, at least partly because that is the easiest way to accommodate them in novels with a strong narrative drive, that is not full of discursive digression. This formal requirement reinforces the ethical tradition in which writing about ethics directs us to ethics as something that arises in pre-theoretical or non-theoretical ways.

In *Pride and Prejudice* (Austen 2001), bookishness is even a fault of Mr Bennett, who is presented as likeable, humorous and intelligent, but also as detached from family life and responsibilities, displayed in his wish to retreat into the peace and solitude of his library. Mr Bennett's library bound life stands in for the inevitability of a library in the home of the property owning classes who predominate in Austen's novels. The possession of a room called a library full of books does not itself mean that the inhabitants will read, but does suggest that book collecting and reading were meaningful parts of the lives of many at least in Austen's world, so Mr Bennett's bookishness stands on the boundary between a kind of average socially required interest in books and a more asocial absorption in books. Austen's fiction revolves round this kind of tension between the value of social requirements and the value of characters who take intellectual, aesthetic and moral virtues more seriously than the average, enough to appear at least for a moment as a challenge.

Fitzwilliam Darcy is shown to have accumulated a large library (Austen 2001, Volume I, Chap. 8), though significantly the preservation of old books in the family collection is as important as the addition of new books. Darcy is shown to read frequently, as are members of his family. We do not know what the titles of the books that absorb them are and only Mary Bennett is so gauche as to refer directly to what she has read. Reading is presented as important to the life of the better class of people, but not matched an obvious enthusiasm for what has been read. Elizabeth Bennett and the other heroes, the female ones observed from within and the male ones who generally exist more through their external presentation, are shown to live according to Enlightenment civility, which can itself uncomfortable about bringing intense preoccupation with ideas and reflection into spoken discourse or even into serious fiction as this is embarrassing enthusiasm. A discomfort in tension with the Enlightenment thinkers who evidently had an exceptional absorption in the intellectual virtues.

For Hegel, ethical life that as an aspect of civil society, which he understands in large part through the Scottish Enlightenment (Herzog 2013), civility as a way of life, can be taken as a form of social cohesion that rests on and implies a greater isolation of families from an integrating social order of the type known in earlier periods. The communities with the most developed society lack the most simple and immediate forms of community. Literature in which the choice of marriage partner is a lengthy and often confused process suggests a society in which expectations that marriage is a form of family alliance separate from individual preferences and so are part of a society in which communal bonds are more conditioned by individual autonomy.

What we also find in Austen is the strong brother–sister relation as in Fitzwilliam Darcy and his sister Georgina Darcy or the related theme of love between cousins brought up together as in *Mansfield Park* (Austen 1998). The brother–sister relation does not have the fundamental role in Austen it has in Hegel. Hegel discusses it briefly and indirectly but influentially in *Phenomenology of Spirit* § 437 (1977, 261) with regard to Antigone in Sophocles' play of that name and what she represents as ethics against state power in struggling for her brother. The discussion returns in *Philosophy of Right* § 166 (Hegel 1991, 206–207) as part of an argument which moves onto the ethical importance of the incest prohibition in *Philosophy of Right* § 168 (Hegel 1991, 207–208), since it is what puts ethical duty above natural desire. The love between sisters is maybe a bigger and certainly more obvious issue in Austen's fictional world. The idea of a family life in which sisters can maintain their love for each other after marriage, through marriage to men connected in some way is a very much desired situation. It both that connects with the role Hegel gives to the family in ethical life, while pushing at the limits of the incest prohibition, most obviously in the love between the cousins Fanny Price and Edmund Bertram in *Mansfield Park*, raised in a surrogate brother–sister relation. The relation between erotic love and family love is an issue that divides love but can also become a way in which different forms of love are combined, where marriage brings two families together or two distinct parts of a family and unified, intensifying the ethical role of the family in Hegel by pushing at the limits he established to it.

Issues of love, family bonds and marital choice are shown in Austen to be conditioned by the importance of remaining within the sphere of the property owning classes and so generally staying within some related areas of propriety. This is the desire for recognition, for consciousness that others give one prestige in their consciousness. Hegel provides a full account of that in the *Phenomenology of Spirit* (1977), particularly in the 'Lordship and Bondage' section of *Phenomenology* B, though it pervades large parts of the book. *Philosophy of Right* (1991) can be considered to be in large part a work on forms of recognition of individuality and social relations, but § 86 (Hegel 1991, 117–118) on the recognition of right in property and contract is where the issue becomes most explicit. There is not much direct drama of the struggle to the death and the relationship of master and slave, as described by Hegel in the *Phenomenology of Spirit* in Austen, or the other moments in Hegel where the extremes of violence against others and oneself are described, but there are hints as we will see. The need to be recognised as a master of some kind is very strong in Austen as is the trauma of losing such a status.

A number of female characters hover at the limits of respectability defined by private income at a level sufficient to avoid paid employment, and maintain membership of the property owning classes. This is a strong theme from the beginning of the first two novels, *Sense and Sensibility* and *Pride and Prejudice* and can be found very strongly present in *Mansfield Park* and *Persuasion*. The female characters are in a particularly awkward place with regard to this issue because they are not in a strong position to act in the economic sphere to improve their economic fortunes and are subject to extreme discrimination in inheritance laws, a big issue in *Pride and Prejudice*. *Persuasion* does show Anne Elliott pushing at the limits of these kinds of limitations on 'respectable' women in the economic sphere though, as in the help she arranges for Mrs Smith in obtaining her rightful inheritance.

The fear of an economic fall destroying the kind of social recognition and life style that includes the leisure to read and enjoy nature is an anxiety running through Austen's novels. The fear of loss of high-class status is accompanied by a horror of joining the labouring and serving classes, who are suitable objects of charity and kindly concern, but are never equals. There is a limited kind of egalitarian impulse in Austen in that the novels suggests the desirability of the recognition of the lower end of the property owning classes as equals by the upper end. That is recognition by the aristocracy in its strongest sense, of those families with national influence, possessing grand titles and very large land holdings, of the equal status of the lower end aristocracy, the gentry which dominates the locality in which it is located, but is not influential beyond this locality. It is a theme particularly associated with Elizabeth Bennett's marriage to Fitzwilliam Darcy against the misgivings of his aunt and social circle. In Viconian terms, Austen wishes for a more human world than that which places the great aristocracy on a higher level of rights and recognition than the rest of society, but hesitates to extend more than minimal recognition of common humanity to those lacking in sufficient property to be excused the need to work for a living.

This equal recognition of local gentry and national aristocracy involves a joint disdain for creating commercial wealth as opposed to enjoying its proceeds. Austen deals with the transition from the former to the latter in *Pride and Prejudice* in a humorous way, which nevertheless does not reject the distinction being made, in the history of the Lucas family who abandon 'trade' after award of a knighthood (Austen 2001, Volume I, Chap. 5) and through the aversion of Caroline Bingley to live near a place of trade (Volume I, Chap. 8). Though Austen makes a satirical character of Caroline Bingley with regard to her snobbery, the preference of the life of the gentry over that of trade, however close they often are in practice, is an assumption present throughout Austen's novels so that the character of Caroline Bingley is way of trying to protect that preference by mocking the most insensitive kind of overt snobbery. Though what we also see here is Austen's grasp of the ambiguities around valuing property while elevating the enjoyment of property over the acquisition of property.

War is a frequent reference in Austen or at least the possibility of war associated with members of the military. Soldiers are dangerously attractive to imprudent young women in *Pride and Prejudice* while a naval officer is the just object of considered love in *Persuasion*. Colonel Brandon has a similar role for Marianne Dashwood in *Sense and Sensibility*. The army can bring out a tendency noted by Adam Smith for irresponsible short-term behaviour due to the more risky behaviour indulged in by those for whom death is imminent. *Wealth of Nations* V.I.f 'the irregular, uncertain and adventurous life of a soldier' (Smith 1981, 782), but also as Smith suggests in *The Theory of Moral Sentiments* VI.iii.6 the solider can be se seen or was seen in Austen's historical era as more bound by duty and honour in an exemplary character: 'It is this habitual contempt of danger and death which ennobles the profession of a soldier, and bestows upon it, in the natural apprehensions of mankind, a rank and dignity superior to that of any other profession' (Smith 1984, 239).

Colonel Brandom sets up a more romantic association with death, but has a less romantic association with death when first introduced as he seems very old to Marianne Dashwood, something emphasised by his rheumatic tendencies. He later evolves, at least for the reader, into a sensitive and sympathetic character worthy of mature love, though we never see this through the perceptions of Marianne Dashwood, a gap of a kind Austen does not leave in later novels. His rival for her affections, John Willoughby, is a devoted huntsman while Brandom has a professional concern with inflicting death on humans and enduring the possibility of violent death.

In *Persuasion*, Captain Wentworth's naval profession links him with the sea, with death at sea and the associations between death and the sea which are evident to the Romantic imagination. This is part of the character portrait of him as a worthy of the love of a woman who is prudent and sensitive, Anne Elliott. She is built up across the whole novel as someone who is sensitive to her friends and relatives, even when they are not very sensitive to others, such as her sister Mary, as well as someone willing to help a friend in great need, most notably Mrs Smith, even where this requires considerable inconvenience. Wentworth also demonstrates this in his status as clearly a kind of superior male authority replacement for Anne Elliott's foolish and selfish father, bringing us to the issue of inadequate, missing or non-existent father figures in Austen, for which romantic love seeks a substitute. This can be seen at work in Fitzwilliam Darcy's superiority to Mr Bennett.

Austen and Kierkegaard

There is some implicit critique of the Church of England, in Austen's novels which accord more with Kierkegaard's view of Enlightenment societies which are in some sense Christian, than with Scottish Enlightenment or Hegelian ethics in which the ethical characteristics of community are deemed to contain what is worthy of preservation within Christian tradition. This has some connection with her emphasis on inadequate father figures, which is also a rather Kierkegaardian theme as can be seen in the figure of Judge William in *Either/Or II* (Kierkegaard 1987). William is a source of paternal 'ethical' advice' to a younger friend in letters which make up *Either/Or II*. William evidently considers himself to be communicating a Christian message, but Kierkegaard indicates that he is missing the deepest Christian message of the transformation of subjectivity based on a radical sense of individuality.

The limitation of the father figure, particularly in relation to God is a major theme in Kierkegaard, partly based around the troubling need to accept that a father's love should be subordinate to God's commands. Fatherhood is always limited by the possibility that the father might follow some higher command than ethics towards his children. Murderous or potentially murderous fathers appear in *Fear and Trembling* (Kierkegaard 1983). The Biblical Abraham is the central reference with regard to the near sacrifice of Isaac, when God apparently commands such a thing. Agamemnon appears as a major contrast with Abraham as the figure in Greek tragedies of Aeschylus and Euripides (Kierkegaard 1983, 57–58, 113–116), who is willing to sacrifice his daughter Iphigenia. Even if Abraham has faith that his sacrifice of his son will not be necessary in the end, his willingness to carry out the sacrifice, if commanded, puts him in the category of disturbing fathers, who have an uncertain relation with both ethics and religion. He represents a superior approach to that of Agamemnon, since the Christian God could never really require the sacrifice of this kind. However, awareness of the traumatic possibility that God might command child sacrifice, and the father would be bound to obey is important to Kierkegaard's account in which Christianity can never just be the following of ethical rules. Christianity refers to the absolute which is the necessary support for universal ethics, but only in having the power to supersede them. In *Either/Or*, William clearly represents the Hegelian understanding of ethical life. In *Fear and Trembling*, the idea of ethics, Hegelian or otherwise, existing independently of the religious sphere of single individuality, God as absolute and an absolute relation between individual and God is questioned in a way that William cannot grasp.

Austen's novels are not concerned with Abraham's crisis in relation to Isaac or anything else so extreme. Nevertheless, various father figures have William's self-deceiving complacency about their own ethical superiority. In *Northanger Abbey*, General Tilney is in Catherine Morland's imagination a monster out of the series of destructive male figures Kierkegaard investigates in *Fear and Trembling*. The William-like inadequacy of some father figures is accompanied by the frightening figure of Tilney who is not as monstrous as Catherine Morland fears but is driven by an ego which is close to the daemonic at times.

Fathers and father figures in various ways sacrifice the interests and desires of their children to their own priorities This applies to Mr Bennett's self-absorbed if non-malicious neglect of his daughters in *Pride and Prejudice*, Sir Walter Elliot's indifference to Ann Elliott in *Persuasion*, as well as General Tilney's interference in his son's marital choice. Given the place of Christianity in Austen's novels, we can see that the ethical failings of fathers are not just ethical failures but failures to overcome a self-satisfied attitude that can be can thought of through Kierkegaard's understanding where we believe that in following some general ethical rules exhausts our self-challenging responsibility for, and love, of others. English society often seems to lack authority from fathers and the church in Austen. Christianity provides a structure for dealing with the inadequate and terrifying aspects of paternal authority, as Kierkegaard emphasises, and we can better grasp the significance of male authority figures in Austen if we grasp Kierkegaard's approach which is to look at the ways that authority is a shadow of divine authority, both inadequate in relation to that authority and terrifying in resembling that authority.

Awareness in Austen's novels of ethical inadequacy includes a strong disdain for London, as a centre of immorality, and a preference for small rural communities, partly because the church minister can then live amongst his parishioners and gives them constant moral guidance. There is no question here of giving the church legal and state backed authority over private lives, but there is a belief that mere civility is not enough to hold a society together, which is one reason why Austen does not completely fit with Enlightenment ethics. Church ministers of exceptional moral and intellectual quality are essential to flourishing communities, which must in general preserve a moral order. Edward Ferrars in *Sense and Sensibility* and Henry Tilney in *Northanger Abbey* are not the most striking examples of intense preachers of the Christian message, but they are exemplary men who can influence a community in the right way. The humour with which Austen mocks inadequate churchmen on various occasions including William Collins in *Pride and Prejudice* and Philip Elton in *Emma* should not distract from the serious disdain with she regards them, and the role she assigns to the clergy. Kierkegaard remarks in *Stages on Life's Way* on the merits of a small city like Copenhagen (Kierkegaard 1998b, 452–453) where people are known to each other. The Copenhagen population at that time was about one hundred thousand, which is still large by Austen's standards but is taken by Kierkegaard as small enough to have something of the village sense of community.

The emptiness of a marriage without deep sympathy between both partners or of a life of seduction appears in texts by Austen and Kierkegaard. Kierkegaard presents the former situation, though in a very indirect way, in the unconsciously revealing letters of Judge William in *Either/Or II* (Kierkegaard 1998a). He presents the latter situation in *Either/Or I* (Kierkegaard 1998a) in the sections on 'The Immediate Erotic Stages or the Musical Erotic', a discussion of the Don Juan/Don Giovanni figure, and 'The Seducer's Diary'. For both, a successful marriage is a high-moral enterprise and should ideally take place in a morally committed community with strong leadership from the local churchman. Kierkegaard argues for a life oriented towards the Christian command to love your neighbour as yourself, which should be clearly placed above friendship and erotic love. One of his longer books, *Works of Love* (1998) is devoted to exactly those concerns. The most important thing in life was to experience yourself as a single individual, in a relation with the absolute that is God. Kierkegaard was also committed to the view that the individuation and personal responsibility demanded by Christianity must isolate the individual from the community so that the individual faces God and death in a state of loneliness. The Christian must separate Christianity from 'Christendom', which is how Kierkegaard referred to state churches, and any idea of being a Christian by virtue of living in a particular nation. Christianity must include a faith which accepted some sacrifice of social life, enjoyment and economic welfare. That is the Christian must attend Church regardless of other available diversions, must affirm faith regardless of social reception and must give to the poor with real generosity.

Taken seriously, and as seriously as Kierkegaard intends, this certainly looks like a very intense and committed Christian life, beyond that suggested in Austen even just looking at her more admirable church ministers. It is still the case that much of this can be found in Austen and thinking about this is a valuable exercise in which we can see that she writes with an ethical point of view that contains the sort of absolutism advocated by Kierkegaard. In Austen's world, those who fail to show charity to their fellows beyond minimal gestures and appearances are failures as moral agents. In *Pride and Prejudice*, Fitzwilliam Darcy is worthy of a marriage that combines attraction with moral development when he makes considerable efforts to anonymously assist the Bennett family by bribing George Wickham into marrying Lydia Bennett after their elopement. This requires not just financial sacrifice but a considerable sacrifice of Darcy's time and energy along with his much-prized dignity. His marriage to Elizabeth Bennett is only possible when he is ready to show charity in sociability with those inferior to him or status or irritating in personal qualities.

We know that Anne Elliott in *Persuasion* is worthy of a marriage of love and moral richness with Captain Wentworth, because of the efforts she makes on behalf of Mrs Smith with sacrifice of time, energy and dignity. Wentworth's assistance in the same case also shows his readiness. Austen heroes endure situations which show a capacity to learn and grow during marriage. Despite Darcy's many admirable qualities as a meritorious member of the aristocracy, he still needs Elizabeth Bennett to humble him before and after marriage to exist as a truly ethical individual in the community.

The plots of *Sense and Sentiment*, *Pride and Prejudice* and *Persuasion* are all stimulated by stories of failures to act to support relatives beyond the bare demands of the law and most unavoidable customary restraints. Obedience to law and custom is never enough, there must always be a genuine work to support those who need support, and most particularly where family members are involved.

There is not much of the kind of turn towards matters of theology and the immortal soul in Austen, which can be found in Kierkegaard. The difference is not so great though still real, when we are suitably conscious of how far Kierkegaard approaches these matters through our attitudes towards community, love and family, asking not that the genuine Christian go to a Christ-like extreme in behaviour, but that the Christian accept genuine challenging demands. Austen's characters encounter death, emptiness and despair; the issues Kierkegaard thinks drive us towards God. In *Sense and Sensibility*, Marianne Dashwood nearly dies and experiences weeks in bed debilitated. There is an element of descent into hell in Darcy's search for George Wickham in the less desirable parts of London in *Pride and Prejudice*. Fanny Price experiences something hell like in the descent from Mansfield Park into a form of pandemonium in Portsmouth, as she also does when insisting to Thomas Bertram that she will not marry Henry Crawford and is sent back to Portsmouth, in *Mansfield Park*. Catherine Morland experiences deep fears in *Northanger Abbey* which are absurd but no less real to her and do acquire a kind of reality in the difficulty personality of General Tilney. As has already been mentioned, the military and naval characters are innately close to death whether through the constant possibility of war or the dangers of the sea.

Austen's ideal characters and ideal communities look a lot like they would for Kierkegaard, if we exclude most of the overt religiosity, and he sometimes wrote in that way himself. As the quotations at the head of this chapter suggest, overt religiosity is not absent from Austen

novel's either and the occasions on which it appears are of great significance for the reading of Austen. There is significant difference between
Austen as social ethicist and Kierkegaard as religious philosopher, but
for Kierkegaard Christianity shows itself when we treat others as our
neighbour in the Christian ethics of *Works of Love* (1998), when our
erotic love and friendship relations, as described in particularly literary, even fictional style in *Either/Or* (1987), *Fear and Trembling* (1983),
Repetition (1983) and *Stages on Life's Way* (1988), take that as the guiding point for their own ethical richness, so converging with the world
of Austen's novels. While it would never be appropriate to see Austen
as writing novels that simply exemplify Kierkegaard's ethics, there is a
great deal that can be appreciated about the ethical world of her novels
if Kierkegaard's writing is brought into play.

Conclusion

Through Kierkegaard, Joyce and Vico, it is possible to see the ways that
philosophy and novelistic form can animate each other. What is possibly more revealing is to show how some kind of dialogue between philosophy and literature animates the reading of Jane Austen. It is not just
the strange and exceptional moments in literature where the encounter
between philosophy and the novel takes place. We cannot understand
the novel outside the philosophical context of its time, or at least not
the novels most distinguished as part of literary history. They engage in
philosophical exploration consciously or otherwise.

There is no clear line that can be drawn between a calculated incorporation of philosophical ideas and openness to continued philosophical discussion. All philosophy which is not pure logical symbolism and
all literary writing which is not completely formulaic has this energy.
While not all philosophy has much in the way of literary style and not
all literature incorporates much philosophical dialogue, the interaction
is always there at some level, and the two sides cannot be fully understood without some regard for it. What distinguishes the novel its historical status. It is the form of literature which is close to philosophy

through its historical nature and not distinguished from history by its philosophical nature, as Aristotle suggests is the defining situation. Kierkegaard and Joyce summon historical worlds and the main concerns of these worlds. Joyce begins in *Ulysses* with the historical setting of Dublin in the early years of the twentieth century, before moving on to the apparent abstraction of historical setting in *Finnegans Wake*. However, this a historical novel dealing with imaginative fragments of the history of the world, from the viewpoint of the 1930s, particularly the 1930 in Paris, with a strong Dublin influence. The history is not mournful or triumphal through it contains elements of both. It is what it is to be human, which means living outside the self and the more immediate community, in a linguistic cultural world full of historical resonances.

Going back to the opening of this chapter, the novel as a form establishes a union that was not possible or relevant for Plato and Lucretius, Cicero and Augustine, any more than it was possible for Homer or Virgil. That is it establishes an inclusive discourse where poetry and deductive reasoning are included and excluded. The novel includes poetry in its style and includes deductive reasoning in its judgements. The novel excludes poetry in the banal sense that it is prose not poetry and excludes deductive reasoning in that it is a narrative. The novel as a form is also distinct from rhetoric while absorbing it and absorbing the loose kind of deductive reasoning, the enthymeme, which goes back to Aristotle. Schlegel's conception of the novel was based on Idealist-Romantic assumptions about the resonance of nature and the creations of human consciousness. We can question this, while still exploring the ways in which the novel does absorb forms and establish dialogues of a kind not possible in antiquity, when the novel itself only existed in very limited forms. Plato and Boethius wrote in terms of hierarchies of style associated with ontology hierarchy, as did the epic authors. The novel can be illuminated by the antique precedents, but can never be reduced to them. Vico helps define this evolution, but did not grasp what was emerging in the novel as a form that does establish a poetic-philosophical fusion as Schlegel suggests.

B. Stocker

References

Austen, Jane. 1998. *Mansfield Park*, ed. Claudia L. Johnson. New York, NY: W.W. Norton & Company.

Austen, Jane. 2001. *Pride and Prejudice*, ed. Donald Gray. New York, NY: W.W. Norton & Company.

Austen, Jane. 2004. *Northanger Abbey*, ed. Susan Fraiman. New York, NY: W.W. Norton & Company.

Austen, Jane. 2012. *Emma*, ed. Claudia L. Johnson. New York, NY: W.W. Norton & Company.

Bakhtin, Mikhail. 1981. *The Dialogic Imagination: Four Essays*, trans. Caryl Emerson and Michael Holquist. Austin, TX: University of Texas Press.

Beckett, Samuel, Marcel Brion, Frank Budgen et al. 1929. *Our Exagmination Round His Factification for Incamination of Work in Progress*. London: Faber and Faber.

Emsley, Sarah. 2005. *Austen's Philosophy of the Virtues*. New York, NY: Palgrave Macmillan.

Hegel, G.W.F. 1977. *Phenomenology of Spirit*, trans. A.V. Miller. Oxford: Oxford University Press.

Hegel, G.W.F. 1991. *Elements of the Philosophy of Right*, trans. H.B. Nisbet. Cambridge: Cambridge University Press.

Herzog, Lisa. 2013. *Inventing the Market: Smith, Hegel, and Political Theory*. Oxford: Oxford University Press.

Hume, David. 2000. *A Treatise of Human Nature*, ed. David Fate Norton and Mary J. Norton. Oxford and New York, NY: Oxford University Press.

Kierkegaard, Søren A. 1983. *Fear and Trembling/Repetition*. Kierkegaard's Writings, VI, trans. and ed. Howard V. Hong and Edna H. Hong. Princeton, NJ: Princeton University Press.

Kierkegaard, Søren A. 1987. *Either/Or, Part I & Either/Or, Part II*, Kierkegaard's Writings, III & IV, trans. and ed. Howard V. Hong and Edna H. Hong. Princeton, NJ: Princeton University Press.

Kierkegaard, Søren A. 1988. *Stages on Life's Way*, trans. and ed. Howard V. Hong and Edna H. Hong. Princeton, NJ: Princeton University Press.

Know-Shaw, Peter. 2004. *Jane Austen and the Enlightenment*. Cambridge and New York, NY: Cambridge University Press.

Molar, Kennth L. 1967. The Bennett Girls and Adam Smith on Vanity and Pride. *Philological Quarterly* 46(4): 567–569.

Phillipson, Nicholas. 2011. *Adam Smith: An Enlightened Life*. London: Penguin Books.

Ruderman, Anne. 1995. *The Pleasures of Virtue: Political Thought in the Novels of Jane Austen*. Lanham ML: Rowman & Littlefield.

Ryle, Gilbert. 1975. *Plato's Progress*. Cambridge: Cambridge University Press.

Smith, Adam. 1981. *An Inquiry into the Nature and Causes of the Wealth of Nations*, ed. R.H. Campbell, A.S. Skinner and W.B. Todd. Indianapolis, IN: Liberty Fund.

Smith, Adam. 1984. *The Theory of Moral Sentiments*, ed. D.D. Raphael and A.L. Macfie. Indianapolis, IN: Liberty Fund.

Verene, Donald Phillip. 1997. Vico's *Scienza Nuova* and Joyce's *Finnegans Wake*. *Philosophy and Literature* 21(2): 392–402.

Verene, Donald Phillip. 2003. *Knowledge of Things Human and Divine: Vico's New Science and Finnegans Wake*. New Haven, CT and London: Yale University Press.

Bibliography

Adorno, Theodor. 1973. *Negative Dialectics*, trans. E.B. Ashton. London: Routledge and Kegan Paul.

Adorno, Theodor. 1989. *Kierkegaard: Construction of the Aesthetics*, trans. Robert Hullot-Kentor. Minneapolis, MN: University of Minnesota Press.

Adorno, Theodor. 1991. *Notes to Literature*, vol. 1, ed. Rolf Tiedeman, trans. Shierry Weber Nicholsen. New York and Chichester: Columbia University Press.

Adorno, Theodor. 2002. *Aesthetic Theory*, trans. and ed. Robert Hullot-Kentor. London and New York: Continuum.

Adorno, Theodor, and Max Horkheimer. 1986. *Dialectic of Enlightenment*, trans. John Cumming. London and New York: Verso.

Anderson, Benedict. 1991. *Imagined Communities*. London and New York, NY: Verso Books.

Aristotle. 1984a. *The Complete Works of Aristotle, Volume I*, ed. Jonathan Barnes. Princeton, NJ: Princeton University Press.

Aristotle. 1984b. *The Complete Works of Aristotle, Volume II*, ed. Jonathan Barnes. Princeton, NJ: Princeton University Press.

Arnold, Matthew. 2006. *Culture and Anarchy*, ed. Jane Garnett. Oxford and New York: Oxford University Press.

Auerbach, Erich. 1949. Vico and Aesthetic Historicism. *The Journal of Aesthetics and Art Criticism* VIII (2): 110–118.

© The Editor(s) (if applicable) and The Author(s) 2018
B. Stocker, *Philosophy of the Novel*,
https://doi.org/10.1007/978-3-319-65891-9

Auerbach, Erich. 1968. *Mimesis: The Representation of Reality in Western Literature*, trans. Willard R. Trask. Princeton, NJ: Princeton University Press.

Auerbach, Erich. 2007. *Dante, Poet of the Secular World*, trans. Ralph Manheim. New York: New York Review of Books.

Austen, Jane. 1998. *Mansfield Park*, ed. Claudia L. Johnson. New York, NY: W.W. Norton & Company.

Austen, Jane. 2001. *Pride and Prejudice*, ed. Donald Gray. New York, NY: W.W. Norton & Company.

Austen, Jane. 2002. *Sense and Sensibility*, ed. George Justice. New York, NY: W.W. Norton & Company.

Austen, Jane. 2004. *Northanger Abbey*, ed. Susan Fraiman. New York, NY: W.W. Norton & Company.

Austen, Jane. 2012. *Emma*, ed. Claudia L. Johnson. New York, NY: W.W. Norton & Company.

Austen, Jane. 2013. *Persuasion*, ed. Patricia Meyer Sacks. New York, NY: W.W. Norton & Company.

Bataille, Georges. 2012. *Literature and Evil*, trans. Alastair Hamilton. London: Penguin Books.

Bakhtin, Mikhail. 1981. *The Dialogic Imagination: Four Essays*, trans. Caryl Emerson and Michael Holquist. Austin, TX: University of Texas Press.

Bakhtin, Mikhail. 1984a. *Rabelais and His World*, trans. Hélène Iswolsky. Bloomington, IN and Indianapolis, IN: Indiana University Press.

Bakhtin, Mikhail. 1984b. *Problems of Dostoevsky's Poetics*, trans. and ed. Caryl Emerson and Wayne C. Booth. Manchester: Manchester University Press.

Barthes, Roland. 1968. *Writing Degree Zero*, trans. Annette Lavers and Colin Smith. New York, NY: Hill and Wang.

Barthes, Roland. 1974. *S/Z*, trans. Richard Miller. Malden, MA and Oxford: Farrar, Straus and Giroux.

Barthes, Roland. 1977a. *Image Music Text*, trans. and ed. Stephen Heath. London: Fontana Press/Harper Collins.

Barthes, Roland. 1977b. *Roland Barthes by Roland Barthes*, trans. Richard Howard. Malden, MA and Oxford: Farrar, Straus and Giroux.

Barthes, Roland. 1981. Textual Analysis of Poe's "Valdemar". In *Untying the Text: A Post-Structuralist Reader*, ed. Robert Young. London: Routledge and Kegan Paul.

Beckett, Samuel. 1965. *Proust and Three Dialogues*. London: John Calder.

Beckett, Samuel, Marcel Brion, Frank Budgen, et al. 1929. *Our Exagmination Round His Factification for Incamination of Work in Progress*. London: Faber and Faber.

Beiser, Frederick C. 2009. *Diotima's Children: German Aesthetic Rationalism from Leibniz to Lessing*. Oxford: Oxford University Press.

Beistegui, Miguel de. 2012. *Aesthetics after Metaphysics: From Mimesis to Metaphor*. New York, NY and Abingdon: Routledge.

Beistegui, Miguel de. 2013. *Proust as Philosopher: The Art of Metaphor*, trans. Dorothée Bonnigal Katz with Simon Sparks and Miguel de Beistegui. London and New York, NY: Routledge.

Benjamin, Walter. 1985. *The Origin of German Tragic Drama*, trans. John Osborne. London and New York: Verso Books.

Benjamin, Walter. 1996. *Selected Writings, Volume 1: 1913–1926*, ed. Marcus Bullock and Michael W. Jennings. Cambridge, MA and London: Harvard University Press.

Benjamin, Walter. 2005a. *Selected Writings, Volume 2. Part 1: 1927–1930*, ed. Michael W. Jennings, Howard Eiland, and Gary Smith. Cambridge, MA and London: Harvard University Press.

Benjamin, Walter. 2005b. *Selected Writings, Volume 2. Part 2: 1931–1934*, ed. Michael W. Jennings, Howard Eiland, and Gary Smith. Cambridge, MA and London: Harvard University Press.

Benjamin, Walter. 2006a. *Selected Writings, Volume 3: 1935–1938*, ed. Michael W. Jennings and Howard Eiland. Cambridge, MA and London: Harvard University Press.

Benjamin, Walter. 2006b. *Selected Writings, Volume 4: 1938–1940*, ed. Howard Eiland and Michael W. Jennings. Cambridge, MA and London: Harvard University Press.

Bennett, Jonathan. 1974. The Conscience of Huckleberry Finn. *Philosophy, XLIX*, 123–134.

Bergson, Henri. 1991. *Matter and Memory*, trans. N.M. Paul and W.S. Palmer. New York, NY: Zone Books.

Bernstein, J.M. 1984. *The Philosophy of the Novel: Lukács, Marxism and the Dialectics of Form*. Minneapolis, MN: University of Minnesota Press.

Blanchot, Maurice. 1982. *The Space of Literature*, trans. Anne Smock. Lincoln, NE and London: University of Nebraska Press.

Blanchot, Maurice. 2003. *The Book to Come*, trans. Charlotte Mandell. Stanford, CA: Stanford University Press.

Cavell, Stanley. 1979. *The Claim of Reason: Wittgenstein, Scepticism, Morality, and Tragedy*. Oxford and London: Oxford University Press.

Clausewitz, Carl von. 1984. *On War*, trans. and ed. Michael Howard and Peter Paret. Princeton, NJ and Chichester: Princeton University Press.

Deleuze, Gilles. 2000. *Proust and Signs*, trans. Richard Howard. Minneapolis, MN: University of Minnesota Press.

Deleuze, Gilles, and Félix Guattari. 1987. *A Thousand Plateaus: Capitalism and Schizophrenia*, trans. Brian Massumi. Minneapolis, MN and London: University of Minnesota Press.

Derrida, Jacques. 1978. *Writing and Difference*, trans. Alan Bass. Chicago, IL: University of Chicago Press.

Derrida, Jacques. 1979. *Spurs: Nietzsche's Styles*, trans. Barbara Harlow. Chicago, IL: University of Chicago Press.

Derrida, Jacques, and Avital Ronell. 1980. The Law of Genre. *Critical Inquiry* 7 (1): 55–81.

Derrida, Jacque. 1981. *Dissemination*, trans. Barbara Johnson. London: Athlone Press.

Derrida, Jacques. 1982. *Margins of Philosophy*, trans. Alan Bass. Chicago, IL: University of Chicago Press.

Derrida, Jacques. 1985. *Ear of the Other: Otobiography, Transference, Translation*, trans. Peggy Kamuf. New York, NY: Schocken Books.

Derrida, Jacques. 1987a. *The Postcard: From Socrates to Freud and Beyond*, trans. Alan Bass. Chicago, IL and London: University of Chicago Press.

Derrida, Jacque. 1987b. *The Truth in Painting*, trans. Geoff Bennington and Ian McLeod. Chicago, IL and London: University of Chicago Press.

Derrida, Jacques. 1997a. *Of Grammatology*, trans. Gayatri Chakravorty Spivak. Baltimore, MD: Johns Hopkins University Press.

Derrida, Jacques. 1997b. *Politics of Friendship*, trans. George Collins. London and New York, NY: Verso Books.

Derrida, Jacques. 2002. *Acts of Religion*, ed. Gil Anidjar. New York, NY and London: Routledge and Taylor & Francis.

Emsley, Sarah. 2005. *Austen's Philosophy of the Virtues*. New York, NY: Palgrave Macmillan.

Fichte, J.G. 1982. *The Science of Knowledge*, trans. and ed. Peter Heath and John Lachs. Cambridge and New York, NY: Cambridge University Press.

Foucault, Michel. 1981. The Order of Discourse. In *Untying the Text: A Post-Structuralist Reader*, ed. Robert Young. London: Routledge & Kegan Paul.

Foucault, Michel. 1986. *Death and the Labyrinth: The World of Raymond Roussel*, trans. Charles Ruas. London and New York, NY: Continuum.

Foucault, Michel. 2002. *The Order of Things: An Archaeology of the Human Sciences*. London and New York, NY: Routledge/Taylor & Francis.

Foucault, Michel. 2006. *History of Madness*, ed. Jean Khalfa, trans. Jonathan Murphy and Jean Khalfa. Abingdon: Routledge and Francis & Taylor.

Frye, Northrop. 1957. *Anatomy of Criticism: Four Essays*. Princeton, NJ: Princeton University Press.

Genette, Gérard. 1980. *Narrative Discourse: An Essay in Method*, trans. Jane E. Lewin. Ithaca, NY: Cornell University Press.

Gettier, Edmund. 1963. Is Justified True Belief Knowledge? *Analysis* XXIII (6): 121–123.

Gilbert, Stuart. 1955. *James Joyce's Ulysses: A Study by Stuart Gilbert*. New York, NY: Vintage Books and Random House.

Girard, René. 1965. *Deceit, Desire, and the Novel: Self and Other in Literary Structure*, trans. Yvonne Freccero. Baltimore, MD: Johns Hopkins University Press.

Girard, René. 1977. *Violence and the Sacred*, trans. Patrick Gregory. Baltimore, MD: Johns Hopkins University Press.

Girard, René. 2010. *Battling to the End: Conversations with Benoît Chantre*, trans. Mary Baker. East Lansing, MI: East Michigan University Press.

Goldman, Lucien. 2016. *The Hidden God: A Study of Tragic Vision in the Pensées of Pascal and the Tragedies of Racine*, trans. Philip Thody. London and New York, NY: Verso Books.

Granatella, Mariagrazia. 2015. Imaginative Universals and Human Cognition in the *New Science* of Giambattista Vico. *Culture and Psychology* XXI (2): 185–206.

Haddock, B.A. 1979. Vico's "Discovery of the True Homer": A Case-Study in Historical Reconstruction. *Journal of the History of Ideas* 40 (4): 583.

Hegel, G.W.F. 1975. *Aesthetics: Lectures on Fine Art [2 vols]*, trans. T.M. Knox. Oxford: Clarendon Press.

Hegel, G.W.F. 1977. *Phenomenology of Spirit*, trans. A.V. Miller. Oxford: Oxford University Press.

Hegel, G.W.F. 1991. *Elements of the Philosophy of Right*, trans. H.B. Nisbet. Cambridge: Cambridge University Press.

Hegel, G.W.F. 1999. *Hegel's Science of Logic*, trans. A.V. Miller. New York, NY: Humanity Books.

Heidegger, Martin. 2000. *Introduction to Metaphysics*, trans. Gregory Fried and Richard Polt. New Haven, CT and London: Nota Bena and Yale University Press.

Henry, Anne. 1983. *Proust romancier: le tombeau égyptien*. Paris: Flammarion.

Herzog, Lisa. 2013. *Inventing the Market: Smith, Hegel, and Political Theory*. Oxford: Oxford University Press.

Hume, David. 1975. *Enquiries Concerning Human Understanding and Concerning the Principles of Morals*, ed. P.H. Nidditch. Oxford and New York, NY: Oxford University Press.

Hume, David. 2000. *A Treatise of Human Nature*, ed. David Fate Norton and Mary J. Norton. Oxford and New York, NY: Oxford University Press.

Jameson, Fredric. 1981. *The Political Unconscious: Narrative as a Socially Symbolic Act*. Ithaca: Cornell University Press.

Jameson, Frederic. 2013. *The Antinomies of Realism*. London and New York: Verso.

Jonathan Dancy. 1995. New Truths in Proust? *The Modern Language Review* 90 (1): 18.

Kant, Immanuel. 1993. *Opus Postumum*, trans. Eckhart Förster and Michael Rosen. Cambridge: Cambridge University Press.

Kant, Immanuel. 2000. *Critique of the Power of Judgement*, ed. Paul Guyer, trans. Paul Guyer and Eric Matthews. Cambridge and New York, NY: Cambridge University Press.

Kierkegaard, Søren. 1978. *Two Ages. The Age of Revolution and the Present Age. A Literary Review*. Kierkegaard's Writings, XIV, trans. and ed. Howard V. Hong and Edna H. Hong. Princeton, NJ: Princeton University Press.

Kierkegaard, Søren A. 1980. *The Sickness unto Death: A Christian Psychological Exposition for Upbuilding and Awakening*. Kierkegaard's Writings, XIX, trans. Howard V. Hong and Edna H. Hong. Princeton, NJ: Princeton University Press.

Kierkegaard, Søren A. 1981. *Concept of Anxiety: A Simple Psychologically Orienting Deliberation on the Dogmatic Issue of Hereditary Sin*. Kierkegaard's Writings, VIII, ed. Raidar Thomte and Albert B. Anderson. Princeton, NJ: Princeton University Press.

Kierkegaard, Søren A. 1983. *Fear and Trembling/Repetition*. Kierkegaard's Writings, VI, trans. and ed. Howard V. Hong and Edna H. Hong. Princeton, NJ: Princeton University Press.

Kierkegaard, Søren A. 1985. *Philosophical Fragments/Johannes Climacus*. Kierkegaard's Writings, VII, trans. Howard V. Hong and Edna H. Hong. Princeton, NJ: Princeton University Press.

Kierkegaard, Søren A. 1987. *Either/Or, Part I & Either/Or, Part II*. Kierkegaard's Writings, III & IV, trans. Howard V. Hong and Edna H. Hong. Princeton, NJ: Princeton University Press.

Kierkegaard, Søren A. 1988. *Stages on Life's Way*, ed. and trans. Howard V. Hong and Edna H. Hong. Princeton, NJ: Princeton University Press.

Kierkegaard, Søren A. 1989. *The Concept of Irony With Continual Reference to Socrates/Notes of Schelling's Berlin Lectures*. Kierkegaard's Writings, II, trans. Howard V. Hong and Edna H. Hong. Princeton, NJ: Princeton University Press.

Kierkegaard, Søren A. 1990. *Early Polemical Writings*. Kierkegaard's Writings, I, trans. Julia Watkin. Princeton, NJ: Princeton University Press.

Kierkegaard, Søren A. 2009. *Upbuilding Discourses in Various Spirits*. Kierkegaard's Writings, XV, trans. and ed. Howard V. Hong and Edna H. Hong. Princeton, NJ: Princeton University Press.

Know-Shaw, Peter. 2004. *Jane Austen and the Enlightenment*. Cambridge and New York, NY: Cambridge University Press.

Kolakowski, Leszek. 1978. *Main Currents of Marxism, Volume 2: The Golden Age*, trans. P.S. Falla. Oxford and London: Clarendon Press and Oxford University Press.

Kripke, Saul A. 1972. *Naming and Necessity*. Cambridge, MA: Harvard University Press.

Lacan, Jacques. 2006. *Écrits*, trans. Bruce Fink with Héloise Fink and Russell Grigg. New York, NY and London: W.W. Norton.

Lacan, Jacques. 2016. The Sinthome: The Seminar of Jacques Lacan. *Book XXIII*, ed. Jacques-Alain Miller. Cambridge and Malden, MA: Polity Press.

Landy, Joshua. 2004. *Philosophy as Fiction: Self, Deception, and Knowledge in Proust*. Oxford and New York, NY: Oxford University Press.

Lukács, Georg. 1969. *The Historical Novel*, trans. Hannah and Stanley Mitchell. London: Penguin Books.

Lukács, Georg. 1971a. *History and Class Consciousness: Studies in Marxist Dialectic*, trans. Rodney Livingstone. London: Merlin Press.

Lukács, Georg. 1971b. *The Theory of the Novel: A Historico-Philosophical Essay on the Forms of Great Epic Literature*, trans. Anna Bostock. London: Merlin Press.

Lukács, Georg. 1974. *Soul and Form*, trans. Anna Bostock. London: Merlin Press.

Lukács, Georg. 1978. *Studies in European Realism*, trans. Edith Bone. London: Merlin Press.

Merleau-Ponty, Maurice. 2011. *Phenomenology of Perception*, trans. Donald A. Landes. Abingdon and New York, NY: Routledge and Taylor & Francis.

Mitchell, Andrew J., and Sam Slote (eds.). 2013. *Derrida and Joyce: Texts and Contexts*. Albany, NY: State University of New York Press.

Molar, Kennth L. 1967. The Bennett Girls and Adam Smith on Vanity and Pride. *Philological Quarterly* 46 (4): 567–569.

Moretti, Franco. 2000. *The Way of the World: The Bildungsroman in European Culture*, trans. Albert Sbragia. London and New York, NY: Verso.

Moretti, Franco. 2013. *The Bourgeois: Between History and Literature*. London and New York.

Morris, Pam (ed.). 1997. *The Bakhtin Reader: Selected Writings of Bakhtin, Medvedev, Voloshinov*. London and Oxford: Bloomsbury Academic.

Nietzsche, Friedrich. 1968. *Twilight of the Idols/The Anti-Christ*, trans. and ed. R.J. Hollingale. Harmondsworth: Penguin Books.

Nietzsche, Friedrich. 1997. *Untimely Mediations*, ed. Daniel Brezeale, trans. R.J. Hollingdale. Cambridge and New York, NY: Cambridge University Press.

Nietzsche, Friedrich. 2000. *Basic Writings*, trans. and ed. Walter Kaufmann. New York, NY: Modern Library and Random House.

Novalis. 1997. *Philosophical Writings*, trans. and ed. Margaret Mahony Stoljar. Albany NY: SUNY Press.

Nussbaum, Martha C. 1986. *The Fragility of Goodness: Luck and Ethics in Greek Tragedy and Philosophy*, 2nd ed. Cambridge and New York, NY: Cambridge University Press.

Nussbaum, Martha C. 1990. *Love's Knowledge: Essays on Philosophy and Literature*. New York, NY and Oxford: Oxford University Press.

Nussbaum, Martha C. 1994. *The Therapy of Desire: Theory and Practice in Hellenistic Ethics*. Princeton, NJ: Princeton University Press.

Phillipson, Nicholas, 2011. *Adam Smith: An Enlightened Life*. London: Penguin Books.

Proust, Marcel. 2000. *In Search of Lost Time V The Captive. The Fugitive*, trans. C.K. Scott Moncrieff and Terence Kilmartin. Revised by D.J. Enright. London: Vintage Books

Putnam, Hilary. 1975. The Meaning of "Meaning". *Minnesota Studies in the Philosophy of Science* VII: 131–193.

Quine, Willard Van Orman. 1960. *Word and Object*. Cambridge, MA: Harvard University Press.

Quine, Willard Van Orman. 1969. *Ontological Relativity and Other Essays*. New York, NY: Columbia University Press.

Quine, Willard Van Orman. 1980. *From a Logical Point of View: Nine Logico-Philosophical Essays*. Cambridge, MA and London: Harvard University Press.

Rawls, John. 1971. *A Theory of Justice*. Cambridge, MA: Harvard University Press.

Ricoeur, Paul. 1985. *Time and Narrative*, vol. 2, trans. Kathleen McLaughlin and David Pellauer. Chicago, IL and London: University of Chicago Press.

Ruderman, Anne, 1995. *The Pleasures of Virtue: Political Thought in the Novels of Jane Austen*. Lanham ML: Rowman & Littlefield.

Ryle, Gilbert. 1966. *Plato's Progress*. Cambridge: Cambridge University Press.

Ryle, Gilbert. 1975. *Plato's Progress*. Cambridge: Cambridge University Press.

Said, Edward W. 1985. *Beginnings: Intention and Method*. New York: Columbia University Press.

Said, Edward W. 1994. *Culture and Imperialism*. London: Vintage.

Schelling, F.W.J. 1989. *The Philosophy of Art*, trans. and ed. Douglas W. Stott. Minneapolis, MN: University of Minnesota Press.

Schelling, F.W.J. 1997. *System of Transcendental Idealism*, trans. Peter Heath. Charlottesville, VA: University Press of Virginia.

Schmitt, Carl. 1986. *Political Romanticism*, trans. Guy Oakes. Cambridge, MA: Massachusetts Institute of Technology Press.

Schmitt, Carl. 2005. *Political Theology: Four Chapters on the Concept of Sovereignty*, trans. George Schwab: Chicago IL: University of Chicago Press.

Schlegel, Friedrich. 1991. *Philosophical Fragments*, trans. Peter Firchow. Minneapolis: University of Minnesota Press.

Schopenhauer, Arthur. 1969. *The World as Will and Representation, volume I*, trans. E.F.J. Payne. New York, NY: Dover Publications.

Shaftesbury, Earl of, Anthony Ashley Cooper. 1999. *Characteristic of Men, Manners, Opinion, Time*, ed. Lawrence E. Klein. Cambridge and New York, NY: Cambridge University Press.

Shaftesbury, Earl of, Anthony Ashley Cooper. 2000. *Characteristics of Men, Manners, Opinions, Times*, ed. Lawrence E. Klein. Cambridge: Cambridge University Press.

Smith, Adam. 1981. *An Inquiry into the Nature and Causes of the Wealth of Nations*, ed. R.H. Campbell, A.S. Skinner, and W.B. Todd. Indianapolis, IN: Liberty Fund.

Smith, Adam. 1983. *Lectures on Rhetoric and Belles Lettres*, ed. J.C. Bryce. Oxford: Oxford University Press.

Smith, Adam. 1984. *The Theory of Moral Sentiments*, ed. D.D. Raphael and A.L. Macfie. Indianapolis, IN: Liberty Fund.

Sorel, Georges. 1999. *Reflections on Violence*, ed. Jeremy Jennings. Cambridge: Cambridge University Press.

Sorel, Georges. 2007. *Etudes sur Vico et autres textes*, ed. Ann-Sophie Menasseyre. Paris: Honoré Champion.

Sprinker, Michael. 1994. *History and Ideology in Proust: A la recherche du temps perdu and the Third French Republic*. Cambridge and New York, NY: Cambridge University Press.

Stewart, John (ed.). 2007a. *Kierkegaard and His German Contemporaries: Tome I: Philosophy*. Aldershot and Burlington, VT: Ashgate.

Stewart, John (ed.). 2007b. *Kierkegaard and His German Contemporaries: Tome II: Theology*. Aldershot and Burlington, VT: Ashgate.

Stewart, John (ed.). 2007c. *Kierkegaard and His German Contemporaries: Tome I: Philosophy*. Aldershot and Burlington, VT: Ashgate.

Stocker, Barry. 2000. Pascal and Derrida. *Symposium* 4 (1): 117–141.

Stocker, Barry. 2004. From Tragedy to Philosophical Novel. In *Nietzsche and Antiquity: His Reaction and Response to the Classical Tradition*, ed. Paul Bishop. New York, NY and Woodbridge: Camden House/Boydell & Brewer.

Stocker, Barry. 2006. *Derrida on Deconstruction*. London and New York, NY: Routledge and Taylor & Francis.

Stocker, Barry. 2014a. A Comparison of Friedrich Nietzsche and Wilhelm von Humboldt as Products of Classical Liberalism. In *Nietzsche as Political Philosopher*, ed. Manuel Knoll and Barry Stocker. Berlin and New York, NY: De Gruyter.

Stocker, Barry. 2014b. *Kierkegaard on Politics*. London: Palgrave Macmillan.

Sweet, Dennis. 1999. The Birth of The Birth of Tragedy. *Journal of the History of Ideas* 60 (2): 345–359.

Verene, Donald Phillip.1997. Vico's *Scienza Nuova* and Joyce's *Finnegans Wake*. *Philosophy and Literature* 21 (2): 392–404.

Verene, Donald Phillip. 2003. *Knowledge of Things Human and Divine: Vico's New Science and Finnegans Wake*. New Haven, CT and London: Yale University Press.

Vico, Giambattista. 1984. *The New Science*, trans. Thomas Goddard Bergin and Max Harold Fisch. Ithaca, NY and London: Cornell University Press.

Watt, Ian. 1972. *The Rise of the Novel: Studies in Defoe, Richardson and Fielding*. London: Penguin Books.

Weber, Max. 1994. The Profession and Vocation of Politics. In *Weber: Political Writings*, ed. Peter Lassman, trans. Ronald Speirs. Cambridge and New York: Cambridge University Press.

White, Hayden. 1978. *Tropics of Discourse: Essays in Cultural Criticism*. Baltimore, MD: Johns Hopkins University Press.

White, Hayden. 1999. *Figural Realism: Studies in the Mimesis Effect*. Baltimore, MD: Johns Hopkins University Press.

Wolf, Friedrich August. 1985. *Prolegomena to Homer, 1795*, trans. Anthony Grafton. Princeton, NJ: Princeton University Press.

Author Index

© The Editor(s) (if applicable) and The Author(s) 2018
B. Stocker, *Philosophy of the Novel*,
https://doi.org/10.1007/978-3-319-65891-9

Subject Index

Made in the USA
Middletown, DE
06 January 2022

57940057R00186